FAVORITE BRAND NAME

Bake Sale

COOKBOOK

PUBLICATIONS INTERNATIONAL, LTD.

Front cover photography: Peter Dean Ross Photographs, Chicago

Pictured on the front cover *(clockwise from top left):* Peanut Butter Crisscross Cookies *(page 48),* Crispy Oat Drops *(page 20),* Deep Dark Chocolate Cake *(page 234),* Rocky Road Brownies *(page 156),* Lemon Poppy Seed Cupcakes *(page 200),* Polka Dot Cupcakes *(page 190)* and Captivating Caterpillar Cupcake *(page 186).*

Pictured on the back cover *(clockwise from top left):* Apple Cranberry Pie *(page 344),* Naomi's Revel Bars *(page 122),* Mocha Walnut Crunch Coffeecake *(page 316)* and Kids' Favorite Jumbo Chippers *(page 40).*

ISBN: 0-7853-2643-X

Library of Congress Catalog Card Number: 97-67158

Manufactured in U.S.A.

8 7 6 5 4 3 2 1

Microwave Cooking: Microwave ovens vary in wattage. Use the cooking times as guidelines and check for doneness before adding more time.

Contents

Bake Sale Basics

*Everyone loves a bake sale. It's the perfect time to bake your favorite treats, share them with friends and neighbors and raise money for a good cause. The hard part is deciding what to bake—and that's where the **Bake Sale Cookbook** fits in. You'll find every kind of cookie, bar and brownie imaginable, plus dozens of irresistible pies, cakes, muffins and breads. Need a quick no-bake bar? The world's easiest peanut butter cookies? An old-fashioned apple pie? They're all here in one jam-packed book! We've also included lots of practical baking tips, storage information and great decorating and wrapping ideas to make all your baked goods extra special.*

General Baking Guidelines

- Read the entire recipe before you begin to be sure you have all the necessary ingredients.

- Adjust oven racks and preheat the oven. Check oven temperature for accuracy with an oven thermometer.

- Remove butter, margarine and cream cheese from the refrigerator to soften, if necessary.

- Toast and chop nuts, peel and slice fruit and melt chocolate before preparing the dough.

- Grease cookie sheets only when the recipe recommends it, otherwise the cookies may spread too much. When making bar cookies, use the pan size specified in the recipe.

- Measure the ingredients accurately and assemble them in the order they are listed in the recipe.

- When baking more than one sheet of cookies at a time, rotate them from top to bottom halfway through the baking time.

- Check for doneness at the minimum baking time given in each recipe.

Measuring, Melting & More

Measuring Dry Ingredients: Always use standard measuring spoons and cups. Fill the appropriate measuring spoon or cup to overflowing and level it off with a metal spatula or flat edge of a knife. When measuring flour, lightly spoon it into the measuring cup and then level it off. Do not tap or bang the measuring cup since this will pack the flour. If a recipe calls for "sifted flour," sift the flour before it is measured. If a recipe calls for "flour, sifted," measure the flour first and then sift.

Measuring Liquid Ingredients: Use a standard glass or plastic measuring cup with a pouring spout. Place the cup on a flat surface, fill to the desired mark and check the measurement at eye level. When measuring sticky liquids, such as honey and molasses, grease the measuring cup or spray it with nonstick cooking spray before filling; this ensures that the sticky liquid won't cling.

Melting Chocolate: Make sure the utensils used for melting chocolate are completely dry. Moisture causes chocolate to "seize," which means it becomes stiff and grainy. If this happens, add ½ teaspoon shortening (not butter) for each ounce of chocolate and stir until smooth. Avoid high heat as well as moisture when melting chocolate, as chocolate scorches easily and once scorched cannot be used. Follow one of these three methods for successful melting:

Double boiler: This is the safest method because it prevents scorching. Place the chocolate in the top of a double boiler or in a heatproof bowl over hot, not boiling, water; stir until smooth. (Make sure that the water remains just below a simmer and is one inch below the bottom of the top pan.) Be careful that no steam or water gets into the chocolate.

Direct heat: Place the chocolate in a heavy saucepan and melt over very low heat, stirring constantly. Remove the chocolate from the heat as soon as it is melted. Be sure to watch the chocolate carefully because it is easily scorched when using this method.

Microwave oven: Place an unwrapped 1-ounce square or 1 cup of chips in a small microwavable bowl. Microwave on HIGH 1 to 1½ minutes, stirring after 1 minute. Stir the chocolate at 30-second intervals until smooth. Be sure to stir microwaved chocolate since it may retain its original shape even when melted.

Folding Ingredients: Folding is a technique that combines two mixtures while retaining the air in the lighter mixture. Place about one-third of the lighter mixture (egg whites or whipped cream) on top of the heavier mixture. Using a rubber spatula, cut down through the center of the mixture, then sweep across the bottom of the bowl and up the side using a circular motion. Turn the bowl slightly and repeat until blended. Add the remaining airy mixture and continue folding until combined.

Toasting Nuts: Toasting nuts brings out their flavor and fragrance. Spread the nuts in a single layer on a baking sheet. Bake in a 325°F oven for 8 to 10 minutes or until golden, stirring occasionally to ensure even toasting. The nuts will darken and become crisper as they cool. To toast a small amount of nuts, place them in a dry skillet over low heat. Stir constantly for 2 to 4 minutes or until the nuts darken slightly and are fragrant.

Toasting Coconut: Spread the flaked coconut out in a thin layer on a baking sheet. Bake in a 325°F oven for 7 to 10 minutes. Shake the pan or stir the coconut occasionally during baking to promote even browning and prevent burning.

Whipping Cream: Chill the beaters, bowl and cream for the best results. Beat the cream slowly, increasing speed as it thickens to prevent spattering. To sweeten, add granulated or powdered sugar in small amounts while beating until you reach the desired sweetness. If possible, whip cream shortly before using to prevent separation.

Storing and Freezing

Unfortunately, bake sales don't always happen at the most convenient times. The simple solution? Plan ahead—many items can be baked and frozen; a variety of unbaked doughs can also be frozen to be baked up fresh in a few minutes. Not all baked goods are ideal for freezing, however, so choose carefully before you begin baking.

Cookies & Bars: Unbaked cookie dough can be refrigerated for up to one week or frozen for up to six weeks. Rolls of dough (for slice-and-bake-type cookies) should be sealed tightly in plastic wrap; other doughs should be stored in airtight containers. Label dough or container with baking information for convenience.

Store soft and crisp cookies separately at room temperature to prevent changes in texture and flavor. Keep soft cookies in airtight containers. If they begin to dry out, add a piece of apple or bread to the container to help them retain moisture. Store crisp cookies in containers with loose-fitting lids to prevent moisture buildup. If they become soggy, heat undecorated cookies in a 300°F oven for 3 to 5 minutes to restore crispness. Store cookies with sticky glazes, fragile decorations and icings in single layers between sheets of waxed paper.

As a rule, crisp cookies freeze better than soft, moist cookies. Rich, buttery bar cookies are an exception since they freeze extremely well. Freeze baked cookies in airtight containers or freezer bags for up to six months. Thaw cookies and brownies unwrapped at room temperature. Meringue-based cookies do not freeze well and chocolate-dipped cookies will discolor if frozen.

Cakes: Store one-layer cakes in their baking pans, tightly covered. Store two- or three-layer cakes in a cake-saver or under a large inverted bowl. Cakes with whipped cream frostings or cream fillings should be stored in the refrigerator. Unfrosted cakes can be frozen for up to four months if well-wrapped in plastic; thaw them, unwrapped, at room temperature. Frosted cakes should be frozen unwrapped until the frosting hardens, and then wrapped, sealed and frozen for up to two months. To thaw, remove the wrapping and thaw at room temperature or in the refrigerator. Cakes with fruit or custard fillings do not freeze well because they become soggy when thawed.

Pies: Unbaked pie dough can be frozen in bulk for later use. Simply flatten the dough into circles and stack them in a freezer bag with waxed paper separating each layer. Freeze prepared pastry shells in pie pans with waxed paper between the shells. Bulk pie dough must be thawed before using while pastry shells should be baked frozen.

Meringue-topped pies are best when served the day they are made; leftovers should be refrigerated. Custard or cream pies should be refrigerated immediately after cooling. Fruit pies should be covered and stored at room temperature overnight; refrigerate them for longer storage.

To freeze unbaked pies, do not cut steam vents in the top crust. Cover it with an inverted paper plate for extra protection and package in freezer bags or plastic wrap. To bake, do not thaw. Cut slits in the top crust and allow an additional 15 to 20 minutes of baking time. Baked pies can also be cooled and frozen. To serve, let the pie thaw at room temperature for two hours, then heat until warm.

Pies with cream or custard fillings and meringue toppings do not freeze well.

Breads & Muffins: Quick breads should be wrapped well in plastic wrap and stored at room temperature to stay fresh up to one week, or they may be frozen for up to three months wrapped in heavy-duty foil. Muffins should be stored in a sealed plastic food storage bag up to three days, or they may be frozen for up to one month wrapped in heavy-duty foil.

Special Touches: Decorating & Packaging

For a successful bake sale, the goodies have to look great. A few extra minutes spent on easy decorations can make all the difference. Try any of the following ideas to jazz up your baked goods.

Chocolate for Dipping: Nothing makes a cookie stand out more than being partially or completely covered in chocolate! Simply dip cookies in melted chocolate (milk, dark, white or some of each) and place on waxed paper until the chocolate is set.

Chocolate for Drizzling: Use a spoon or fork to drizzle melted chocolate over cookies, bars, cakes and breads. Or, melt chocolate in a small resealable plastic freezer bag, cut off a very tiny corner of the bag and squeeze out the chocolate in patterns or designs over your baked goods.

Powdered Sugar Glaze or Icing: The recipe on page 319 makes a simple glaze that looks and tastes great on a variety of cookies, cakes, breads and muffins.

Powdered Sugar: This is the quickest and easiest of toppings—just a dusting of powdered sugar adds a beautiful finishing touch to many cookies, bars, muffins and coffeecakes. If sprinkled far in advance, the powdered sugar may dissolve and disappear, so be sure to bring a container of powdered sugar to the bake sale to sprinkle on at the last minute.

Nuts: Whole, halved, chopped and sliced nuts can add extra flavor and texture to cookies, bars and muffins. Try using nuts in combination with a white or chocolate drizzle for a truly eye-catching, irresistible topping.

Prepared Toppings: Bottled ice cream toppings, such as fudge, caramel or butterscotch can be used for a quick and easy decorative drizzle over cookies, bars, cakes and breads.

Colored Sugar, Sprinkles and Candies: Used primarily for cookies, bars and cupcakes, these decorations are fun and simple to use. Best of all, they are bright and colorful enough to attract attention.

Once the decorating is done, it's time for the presentation. If your baked goods will be sold by the piece, then they can be presented in an attractive display. Stack rich, chocolatey brownies high on a colorful platter, or pile muffins into a big basket lined with a bright cloth napkin.

If your baked goods will be sold whole, then use colored plastic wrap, cellophane, ribbons and raffia to package cookies, breads and pies. Cookies can be stacked and tied together with cord or sold in decorative boxes, bags or tins. It is a good idea to include storage directions for any perishable items that should be held in the refrigerator. As a special touch, you might want to include the recipe on a decorative card tied to the package, or have it on hand for anyone who asks for it.

Weights and Measures

Dash = less than ⅛ teaspoon

½ tablespoon = 1½ teaspoons

1 tablespoon = 3 teaspoons

2 tablespoons = ⅛ cup

¼ cup = 4 tablespoons

⅓ cup = 5 tablespoons plus 1 teaspoon

½ cup = 8 tablespoons

⅔ cup = 10 tablespoons plus 2 teaspoons

¾ cup = 12 tablespoons

1 cup = 16 tablespoons

½ pint = 1 cup or 8 fluid ounces

1 pint = 2 cups or 16 fluid ounces

1 quart = 4 cups or 2 pints or 32 fluid ounces

1 gallon = 16 cups or 4 quarts

1 pound = 16 ounces

Substitution List

If you don't have:	Use:
1 teaspoon baking powder	¼ teaspoon baking soda + ½ teaspoon cream of tartar
½ cup firmly packed brown sugar	½ cup granulated sugar mixed with 2 tablespoons molasses
1 cup buttermilk	1 tablespoon lemon juice or vinegar plus milk to equal 1 cup (Stir; let mixture stand 5 minutes.)
1 ounce (1 square) unsweetened baking chocolate	3 tablespoons unsweetened cocoa + 1 tablespoon shortening
3 ounces (3 squares) semisweet baking chocolate	3 ounces (½ cup) semisweet chocolate morsels
½ cup corn syrup	½ cup granulated sugar + 2 tablespoons liquid
1 cup honey	1¼ cups granulated sugar + ¼ cup water
1 teaspoon freshly grated orange or lemon peel	½ teaspoon dried peel
1 teaspoon pumpkin pie spice	Combine: ½ teaspoon ground cinnamon, ¼ teaspoon ground nutmeg and ⅛ teaspoon *each* ground allspice and cardamom

Equivalents

Almonds, blanched, slivered	4 ounces = 1 cup
Apples	1 medium = 1 cup sliced
Bananas	1 medium, mashed = ⅓ cup
Butter or margarine	2 cups = 1 pound or 4 sticks 1 cup = ½ pound or 2 sticks ½ cup = 1 stick or 8 tablespoons ¼ cup = ½ stick or 4 tablespoons
Chocolate	6-ounce package chocolate chips = 1 cup chips or 6 (1-ounce) squares semisweet chocolate
Cocoa, unsweetened	8-ounce can = 2 cups
Coconut, flaked	3½ ounces = 1⅓ cups
Cream cheese	3-ounce package = 6 tablespoons 8-ounce package = 1 cup
Flour **White or all-purpose**	1 pound = 3½ to 4 cups
Whole wheat	1 pound = 3¾ to 4 cups
Honey, liquid	16 ounces = 1⅓ cups
Lemons	1 medium = 1 to 3 tablespoons juice and 2 to 3 teaspoons grated peel
Marshmallows	1 cup cut-up = 16 large
Milk **Evaporated**	5-ounce can = ⅝ cup 12-ounce can = 1½ cups
Sweetened, condensed	14-ounce can = 1¼ cups
Oranges	1 medium = 6 to 8 tablespoons juice and 2 to 3 teaspoons grated peel
Pecans, shelled	1 pound = 4 cups halves, 3½ to 4 cups chopped
Raisins, seedless, whole	1 pound = 2¾ to 3 cups
Shortening	1 pound = 2½ cups
Sugar **Granulated**	1 pound = 2½ cups
Brown, packed	1 pound = 2¼ cups
Powdered	1 pound = 3¾ to 4 cups, unsifted
Walnuts, chopped	4½ ounces = 1 cup

Chock-full of Chips

Canned Peanut Butter Candy Cookies

¾ cup chunky peanut butter
½ cup (1 stick) butter or margarine, softened
1 cup packed light brown sugar
½ teaspoon baking powder
½ teaspoon baking soda
1 egg
1½ teaspoons vanilla
1¼ cups all-purpose flour
2 cups quartered miniature peanut butter cups
⅓ cup milk chocolate chips or chopped milk
   chocolate bar
Decorative container

1. Beat peanut butter and butter in large bowl with electric mixer at medium speed until well blended. Beat in sugar, baking powder and baking soda until well blended. Beat in egg and vanilla. Beat in flour at low speed just until combined. Stir in peanut butter cups. Cover with plastic wrap; refrigerate 1 hour or until firm.

2. Preheat oven to 375°F. For test cookie, measure inside diameter of container. Form ⅓ cup dough into ¼-inch-thick disc, about 2 inches in diameter less than the diameter of container. One-third cup dough patted into 4-inch disc yields 5-inch cookie. (Measure amount of dough used and diameter of cookie before and after baking. Make adjustments before making remaining cookies.)

3. Place cookies on *ungreased* baking sheet. Bake 10 minutes or until lightly browned. Remove to wire racks; cool completely.

4. Place chocolate in small resealable plastic freezer bag; seal bag. Microwave at MEDIUM (50% power) 1 minute. Turn bag over; microwave at MEDIUM 1 minute or until melted. Knead bag until chocolate is smooth.

5. Cut off very tiny corner of bag; pipe chocolate decoratively onto cookies. Let stand until chocolate is set. Stack cookies between layers of waxed paper in container. Store at room temperature up to 1 week.   *Makes 9 (5-inch) cookies*

Canned Peanut Butter Candy Cookies

Chocolate Chip Sandwich Cookies

COOKIES
1 package DUNCAN HINES® Chocolate
  Chip Cookie Mix
1 egg
⅓ cup CRISCO® Oil or CRISCO®
  PURITAN® Canola Oil
3 tablespoons water

CREAM FILLING
1½ cups marshmallow creme
¾ cup butter or margarine, softened
2½ cups confectioners sugar
1½ teaspoons vanilla extract

1. Preheat oven to 375°F.

2. For cookies, combine cookie mix, egg, oil and water in large bowl. Stir until thoroughly blended. Drop by rounded teaspoons 2 inches apart onto ungreased baking sheets. Bake at 375°F for 8 to 10 minutes or until light golden brown. Cool 1 minute on baking sheets. Remove to cooling racks.

3. For cream filling, combine marshmallow creme and butter in large bowl. Add confectioners sugar and vanilla extract, beating until smooth.

4. To assemble, spread bottoms of half the cookies with 1 tablespoon cream filling; top with remaining cookies. Press together to make sandwich cookies. Refrigerate to quickly firm the filling, if desired. Store in airtight container.

Makes about 24 sandwich cookies

Tip: *After chilling the assembled cookies, wrap individually in plastic wrap. Store in the refrigerator until ready to serve.*

Chocolate Hazelnut Cookie Drops

1 cup (2 sticks) butter or margarine, softened
1 cup firmly packed light brown sugar
2 large eggs
1¾ cups all-purpose flour
1 package (4-serving size) chocolate-flavor
  instant pudding mix
½ teaspoon baking soda
1¾ cups "M&M's"® Semi-Sweet Chocolate
  Mini Baking Bits
1 cup coarsely chopped toasted hazelnuts or
  filberts*

*To toast hazelnuts, spread in single layer on baking sheet. Bake at 350°F for 7 to 10 minutes or until light golden, stirring occasionally. Remove hazelnuts from pan and cool completely before chopping.

Preheat oven to 350°F. In large bowl cream butter and sugar until light and fluffy; beat in eggs. In small bowl combine flour, pudding mix and baking soda; blend into creamed mixture. Stir in "M&M's"® Semi-Sweet Chocolate Mini Baking Bits and nuts. Drop by teaspoonfuls about 2 inches apart onto ungreased cookie sheets. Bake 8 to 10 minutes or until set. *Do not overbake.* Cool completely on wire racks. Store in tightly covered container. *Makes about 5 dozen cookies*

Chocolate Chip Sandwich Cookies

Chocolate Chip Almond Biscotti

1 cup sliced almonds
2¾ cups all-purpose flour
1½ teaspoons baking powder
¼ teaspoon salt
½ cup (1 stick) butter or margarine, softened
1 cup sugar
3 large eggs
3 tablespoons almond-flavored liqueur
1 tablespoon water
1 cup mini semisweet chocolate chips

1. Preheat oven to 350°F. To toast almonds, spread on baking sheet. Bake 8 to 10 minutes or until golden brown, stirring frequently. Remove almonds from baking sheet and cool. Coarsely chop almonds to measure ¾ cup.

2. Place flour, baking powder and salt in medium bowl; stir to combine. Beat butter and sugar in large bowl with electric mixer at medium speed until light and fluffy. Beat in eggs, 1 at a time. Beat in liqueur and water. Gradually add flour mixture. Beat at low speed, scraping down side of bowl occasionally. Stir in chips and almonds.

3. Divide dough into fourths. Spread each quarter evenly down center of waxed paper. Using waxed paper to hold dough, roll back and forth to form 15-inch log. Wrap logs in plastic wrap. Refrigerate until firm, about 2 hours.

4. Preheat oven to 375°F. Lightly grease cookie sheet. Unwrap and place each log on prepared cookie sheet. With floured hands, shape each log 2 inches wide and ½ inch thick.

5. Bake 15 minutes. Remove cookie sheet from oven. Cut each log with serrated knife into 1-inch-thick diagonal slices. Place slices, cut side up, on cookie sheet; bake 7 minutes. Turn cookies over; bake 7 minutes or until cut surfaces are golden brown and cookies are dry. Remove cookies to wire racks; cool completely. Store tightly covered at room temperature or freeze up to 3 months.

Makes about 4 dozen cookies

Chewy Chocolate Cookies

1 package (2-layer size) chocolate cake mix
2 eggs
1 cup MIRACLE WHIP® or MIRACLE WHIP® LIGHT Dressing
1 cup BAKER'S® Semi-Sweet Real Chocolate Chips
½ cup chopped walnuts

MIX cake mix, eggs and dressing in large bowl with electric mixer on medium speed until blended. Stir in remaining ingredients. Drop by rounded teaspoonfuls onto greased cookie sheets.

BAKE at 350°F for 10 to 12 minutes or until edges are lightly browned. *Makes 4 dozen cookies*

Prep time: 10 minutes
Baking time: 12 minutes

Chocolate Chip Almond Biscotti

Hershey's Soft & Chewy Cookies

1 cup (2 sticks) butter (no substitutes)
¾ cup packed light brown sugar
½ cup granulated sugar
¼ cup light corn syrup
1 egg
2 teaspoons vanilla extract
2½ cups all-purpose flour
1 teaspoon baking soda
¼ teaspoon salt
1 package (10 or 12 ounces) HERSHEY'S Chips or Baking Bits (any flavor)

1. Heat oven to 350°F.

2. In large bowl, beat butter, brown sugar and granulated sugar until light and fluffy. Add corn syrup, egg and vanilla; beat well. Stir together flour, baking soda and salt; gradually add to butter mixture, beating until well blended. Stir in chips or bits. Drop by rounded teaspoons onto ungreased cookie sheet.

3. Bake 8 to 10 minutes or until lightly browned and almost set. Cool slightly; remove from cookie sheet to wire rack. Cool completely. Cookies will be softer the second day.

Makes about 3½ dozen cookies

Chocolate Chocolate Cookies: *Decrease flour to 2¼ cups and add ¼ cup HERSHEY'S Cocoa or HERSHEY'S European Style Cocoa.*

Chocolate Chip Cinnamon Crinkles

½ cup (1 stick) butter or margarine, softened
½ cup packed brown sugar
¼ cup plus 2 tablespoons granulated sugar, divided
1 teaspoon vanilla
1 egg
1 teaspoon cream of tartar
½ teaspoon baking soda
⅛ teaspoon salt
1⅓ cups all-purpose flour
1 cup (6 ounces) semisweet chocolate chips
2 teaspoons unsweetened cocoa
1 teaspoon ground cinnamon

Preheat oven to 400°F. Line cookie sheets with parchment paper or leave ungreased. Cream butter with brown sugar, ¼ cup granulated sugar, vanilla and egg in large bowl until light and fluffy. Beat in cream of tartar, baking soda and salt. Add flour; mix until dough is blended and stiff. Stir in chocolate chips. Combine remaining 2 tablespoons granulated sugar, cocoa and cinnamon in small bowl. Shape rounded teaspoonfuls of dough into balls about 1¼ inches in diameter. Roll balls in cinnamon mixture until coated on all sides. Place 2 inches apart on cookie sheets. Bake 8 to 10 minutes or until firm. Do not overbake. Remove to wire racks to cool. *Makes about 3½ dozen cookies*

Hershey's Soft & Chewy Cookies

Chocolate-Pecan Angels

1 cup mini semisweet chocolate chips
1 cup chopped pecans, toasted
1 cup sifted powdered sugar
1 egg white

Preheat oven to 350°F. Grease cookie sheets. Combine chips, pecans and powdered sugar in medium bowl. Add egg white; mix well. Drop batter by teaspoonfuls 2 inches apart onto prepared cookie sheets.

Bake 11 to 12 minutes or until edges are light golden brown. Let cookies stand on cookie sheets 1 minute. Remove cookies to wire racks; cool completely. *Makes about 3 dozen cookies*

Double Chocolate Chunk Cookies

4 squares BAKER'S® Semi-Sweet Chocolate
½ cup (1 stick) margarine or butter, slightly softened
½ cup granulated sugar
¼ cup firmly packed brown sugar
1 egg
1 teaspoon vanilla
1 cup all-purpose flour
½ teaspoon CALUMET® Baking Powder
¼ teaspoon salt
¾ cup chopped walnuts (optional)
4 squares BAKER'S® Semi-Sweet Chocolate

MELT 1 square chocolate; set aside. Cut 3 squares chocolate into large (½-inch) chunks; set aside.

BEAT margarine, sugars, egg and vanilla until light and fluffy. Stir in 1 square melted chocolate. Mix in flour, baking powder and salt. Stir in chocolate chunks and walnuts. Refrigerate 30 minutes.

HEAT oven to 375°F. Drop dough by heaping tablespoonfuls, about 2 inches apart, onto greased cookie sheets. Bake for 8 minutes or until lightly browned. Cool 5 minutes on cookie sheets. Remove and finish cooling on wire racks.

MELT 4 squares chocolate. Dip ½ of each cookie into melted chocolate. Let stand on waxed paper until chocolate is firm.

Makes about 2 dozen cookies

Prep time: 30 minutes
Chill time: 30 minutes
Baking time: 8 minutes

Double Chocolate Chunk Mocha Cookies: *Prepare Double Chocolate Chunk Cookies as directed, adding 2 tablespoons instant coffee to the margarine mixture before beating.*

Chocolate-Pecan Angels

Crispy Oat Drops

1 cup (2 sticks) butter or margarine, softened
½ cup granulated sugar
½ cup firmly packed light brown sugar
1 large egg
2 cups all-purpose flour
½ cup quick-cooking or old-fashioned oats, uncooked
1 teaspoon cream of tartar
½ teaspoon baking soda
¼ teaspoon salt
1¾ cups "M&M's"® Semi-Sweet Chocolate Mini Baking Bits
1 cup toasted rice cereal
½ cup shredded coconut
½ cup coarsely chopped pecans

Preheat oven to 350°F. In large bowl cream butter and sugars until light and fluffy; beat in egg. In medium bowl combine flour, oats, cream of tartar, baking soda and salt; blend flour mixture into creamed mixture. Stir in "M&M's"® Semi-Sweet Chocolate Mini Baking Bits, cereal, coconut and pecans. Drop by heaping tablespoonfuls about 2 inches apart onto ungreased cookie sheets. Bake 10 to 13 minutes or until lightly browned. Cool completely on wire racks. Store in tightly covered container. *Makes about 4 dozen cookies*

Giant Raisin-Chip Frisbees

1 cup (2 sticks) butter or margarine, softened
1 cup packed brown sugar
½ cup granulated sugar
2 eggs
1 teaspoon vanilla
1½ cups all-purpose flour
¼ cup unsweetened cocoa powder
1 teaspoon baking soda
1 cup (6 ounces) semisweet chocolate chips
¾ cup raisins
¾ cup chopped walnuts

Preheat oven to 350°F. Line cookie sheets with parchment paper or lightly grease and dust with flour.

Beat butter and sugars in large bowl. Add eggs and vanilla; beat until light. Combine flour, cocoa and baking soda in small bowl. Add to butter mixture with chocolate chips, raisins and walnuts; stir until well blended.

Scoop out about ½ cup dough for each cookie. Place on prepared cookie sheets, spacing about 5 inches apart. Using knife dipped in water, smooth balls of dough out to about 3½ inches in diameter. Bake 10 to 12 minutes or until golden. Remove to wire racks to cool. *Makes about 16 cookies*

Crispy Oat Drops

Cowboy Cookies

½ cup (1 stick) butter or margarine, softened
½ cup packed light brown sugar
¼ cup granulated sugar
1 egg
1 teaspoon vanilla
1 cup all-purpose flour
2 tablespoons unsweetened cocoa
½ teaspoon baking powder
¼ teaspoon baking soda
1 cup uncooked rolled oats
1 cup (6 ounces) semisweet chocolate chips
½ cup raisins
½ cup chopped nuts

Preheat oven to 375°F. Lightly grease cookie sheets or line with parchment paper. Cream butter with sugars in large bowl until blended. Add egg and vanilla; beat until fluffy. Combine flour, cocoa, baking powder and baking soda in small bowl; stir into creamed mixture with oats, chocolate chips, raisins and nuts. Drop dough by teaspoonfuls 2 inches apart onto prepared cookie sheets. Bake 10 to 12 minutes or until lightly browned around edges. Remove to wire racks to cool.

Makes about 4 dozen cookies

Child's Choice

2⅓ cups all-purpose flour
1 BUTTER FLAVOR* CRISCO® Stick or
    1 cup BUTTER FLAVOR CRISCO
    all-vegetable shortening
1 teaspoon baking soda
½ teaspoon baking powder
1 cup granulated sugar
1 cup firmly packed brown sugar
2 eggs
1 teaspoon maple flavor
2 cups oats (quick or old fashioned), uncooked
¾ cup semi-sweet chocolate chips
¾ cup peanut butter chips
¾ cup miniature marshmallows

*Butter Flavor Crisco is artificially flavored.

1. Preheat oven to 350°F. Grease cookie sheet with shortening.

2. Combine flour, shortening, baking soda and baking powder in large bowl. Beat at low speed of electric mixer until blended. Increase speed to medium. Mix thoroughly. Beat in granulated sugar, brown sugar, eggs and maple flavor. Add oats. Stir in chocolate chips, peanut butter chips and marshmallows with spoon until well blended.

3. Shape dough into 1½-inch balls. Flatten slightly. Place 2 inches apart on greased cookie sheet.

4. Bake at 350°F for 9 to 10 minutes or until light golden brown. Cool 1 minute on cookie sheet before removing to cooling rack.

Makes about 3½ dozen cookies

Cowboy Cookies

Chocolate Chip Lollipops

1 package DUNCAN HINES® Chocolate Chip Cookie Mix
1 egg
⅓ cup CRISCO® Oil or CRISCO® PURITAN® Canola Oil
2 tablespoons water
Flat ice cream sticks
Assorted decors

1. Preheat oven to 375°F.

2. Combine cookie mix, egg, oil and water in large bowl. Stir until thoroughly blended. Shape dough into 32 (1-inch) balls. Place balls 3 inches apart on ungreased baking sheets. Push ice cream stick into center of each ball. Flatten dough ball with hand to form round lollipop. Decorate by pressing decors onto dough. Bake at 375°F for 8 to 9 minutes or until light golden brown. Cool 1 minute on baking sheets. Remove to cooling racks. Cool completely. Store in airtight container.

Makes 2½ to 3 dozen cookies

Tip: For best results, use shiny baking sheets for baking cookies. Dark baking sheets cause cookie bottoms to become too brown.

White Chocolate Biggies

1½ cups (3 sticks) butter or margarine, softened
1 cup granulated sugar
¾ cup packed light brown sugar
2 teaspoons vanilla
2 eggs
2½ cups all-purpose flour
⅔ cup unsweetened cocoa
1 teaspoon baking soda
½ teaspoon salt
1 package (10 ounces) large white chocolate chips
¾ cup pecan halves, coarsely chopped
½ cup golden raisins

Preheat oven to 350°F. Lightly grease cookie sheets or line with parchment paper. Cream butter, sugars, vanilla and eggs in large bowl until light. Combine flour, cocoa, baking soda and salt in medium bowl; blend into creamed mixture until smooth. Stir in white chocolate chips, pecans and raisins. Scoop out about ⅓ cupful of dough for each cookie. Place on prepared cookie sheets, spacing about 4 inches apart. Press each cookie to flatten slightly. Bake 12 to 14 minutes or until firm in center. Cool 5 minutes on cookie sheets, then remove to wire racks to cool completely.

Makes about 2 dozen cookies

Chocolate Chip Lollipops

Jumbo Corn Flake Cookies

1¾ cups all-purpose flour
1 teaspoon baking powder
½ teaspoon baking soda
¼ teaspoon salt
1 cup margarine, softened
1 cup sugar
2 eggs
½ teaspoon vanilla
6 cups KELLOGG'S CORN FLAKES®
   cereal, crushed to 4 cups, divided
½ cup milk chocolate morsels
½ cup peanut butter morsels
   Vegetable cooking spray

1. Stir together flour, baking powder, soda and salt. Set aside.

2. In large mixing bowl, beat together margarine and sugar until light and fluffy. Add eggs and vanilla. Beat well. Add flour mixture, mixing until combined.

3. Fold in 2 cups Kellogg's Corn Flakes® cereal and morsels. Drop batter from ¼-cup measure; roll in remaining cereal. Place on baking sheets coated with vegetable cooking spray. Flatten to 3-inch diameter.

4. Bake at 350°F about 15 minutes or until light golden brown. Remove immediately from baking sheets. Cool on wire racks.

Makes about 16 cookies

Chocolate Chip Macaroons

2½ cups flaked coconut
⅔ cup mini semisweet chocolate chips
⅔ cup sweetened condensed milk
1 teaspoon vanilla

Preheat oven to 350°F. Grease cookie sheets. Combine coconut, chocolate chips, milk and vanilla in medium bowl; mix until well blended. Drop dough by rounded teaspoonfuls 2 inches apart onto prepared cookie sheets. Press dough gently with back of spoon to flatten slightly.

Bake 10 to 12 minutes or until light golden brown. Let cookies stand on cookie sheets 1 minute. Remove cookies to wire racks; cool completely.

Makes about 3½ dozen cookies

To soften butter or margarine, remove wrapper and place on a microwavable plate. Microwave at MEDIUM-LOW (30% power) for 20 to 30 seconds for one stick.

Chocolate Chip Macaroons

Peanut Butter Chip Pineapple Drops

¼ cup (½ stick) butter or margarine, softened
¼ cup shortening
1 cup packed light brown sugar
1 egg
1 teaspoon vanilla extract
2 cups all-purpose flour
1 teaspoon baking powder
½ teaspoon baking soda
½ teaspoon salt
1 can (8 ounces) crushed pineapple, drained
1 cup REESE'S® Peanut Butter Chips
½ cup chopped nuts (optional)
   Red candied cherries, halved

1. Heat oven to 375°F.

2. In large bowl, beat butter and shortening until blended. Add sugar, egg and vanilla; beat until fluffy. Stir together flour, baking powder, baking soda and salt; add to butter mixture, beating until well blended. Stir in pineapple, peanut butter chips and nuts, if desired. Drop by teaspoons onto ungreased cookie sheet. Lightly press cherry half in center of each cookie.

3. Bake 10 to 12 minutes or until lightly browned. Remove from cookie sheet to wire rack. Cool completely. *Makes about 3½ dozen cookies*

Choc-Oat-Chip Cookies

1¾ cups all-purpose flour
1 teaspoon baking soda
½ teaspoon salt (optional)
1 cup (2 sticks) butter or margarine, softened
1¼ cups packed brown sugar
½ cup granulated sugar
2 eggs
2 tablespoons milk
2 teaspoons vanilla extract
2½ cups quick or old fashioned oats
2 cups (12-ounce package) NESTLÉ® TOLL HOUSE® Semi-Sweet Chocolate Morsels
1 cup coarsely chopped nuts (optional)

COMBINE flour, baking soda and salt in small bowl. Beat butter, brown sugar and granulated sugar in large mixer bowl. Beat in eggs, milk and vanilla. Gradually beat in flour mixture. Stir in oats, morsels and nuts; mix well. Drop by rounded tablespoon onto ungreased baking sheets.

BAKE in preheated 375°F. oven for 9 to 10 minutes for a chewy cookie; 12 to 13 minutes for a crispy cookie. Cool on baking sheets for 1 minute; remove to wire racks to cool completely.
Makes about 4 dozen cookies

Peanut Butter Chip Pineapple Drops

Cherry Chocolate Chip Walnut Cookies

1 cup sugar
¼ cup Prune Purée (page 198) or prepared prune butter *or* 1 jar (2½ ounces) first-stage baby food prunes
¼ cup water
2 tablespoons nonfat milk
1 teaspoon vanilla
½ teaspoon instant espresso coffee powder or 1 teaspoon instant coffee granules
1 cup all-purpose flour
½ cup unsweetened cocoa powder
¾ teaspoon baking soda
½ teaspoon salt
½ cup dried sour cherries
¼ cup chopped walnuts
¼ cup semisweet chocolate chips

Preheat oven to 350°F. Coat baking sheets with vegetable cooking spray. In large bowl, whisk together sugar, prune purée, water, milk, vanilla and espresso powder until mixture is well blended, about 1 minute. Combine flour, cocoa, baking soda and salt; mix into prune purée mixture until well blended. Stir in cherries, walnuts and chocolate chips. Spoon twelve equal mounds of dough onto prepared baking sheets, spacing at least 2 inches apart. Bake in center of oven 18 to 20 minutes or until set and tops of cookies feel dry to the touch. Cool on baking sheets 2 minutes; remove to wire rack to cool completely. *Makes 12 large cookies*

Peanut Butter Chip Oatmeal Cookies

1 cup (2 sticks) butter or margarine, softened
¼ cup shortening
2 cups packed light brown sugar
1 tablespoon milk
2 teaspoons vanilla extract
1 egg
2 cups all-purpose flour
1⅔ cups (10-ounce package) REESE'S® Peanut Butter Chips
1½ cups quick-cooking or regular rolled oats
½ cup chopped walnuts
½ teaspoon baking soda
½ teaspoon salt

Heat oven to 375°F. In large bowl, beat butter, shortening, brown sugar, milk, vanilla and egg until light and fluffy. Add remaining ingredients; mix until well blended. Drop dough by rounded teaspoons about 2 inches apart onto ungreased cookie sheet. Bake until light brown, 10 to 12 minutes for soft cookies or 12 to 14 minutes for crisp cookies. Remove from cookie sheet to wire rack. Cool completely. *Makes 6 dozen cookies*

Cherry Chocolate Chip Walnut Cookies

Chocolate Macadamia Chewies

¾ cup (1½ sticks) butter or margarine, softened
⅔ cup firmly packed light brown sugar
1 large egg
1 teaspoon vanilla extract
1¾ cups all-purpose flour
¾ teaspoon baking soda
¼ teaspoon salt
¾ cup (3½ ounces) coarsely chopped
    macadamia nuts
½ cup shredded coconut
1¾ cups "M&M's"® Chocolate Mini Baking Bits

Preheat oven to 350°F. In large bowl cream butter and sugar until light and fluffy; beat in egg and vanilla. In medium bowl combine flour, baking soda and salt; blend into creamed mixture. Blend in nuts and coconut. Stir in "M&M's"® Chocolate Mini Baking Bits. Drop by heaping teaspoonfuls about 2 inches apart onto ungreased cookie sheets; flatten slightly with back of spoon. Bake 8 to 10 minutes or until set. *Do not overbake.* Cool 1 minute on cookie sheets; cool completely on wire racks. Store in tightly covered container.

Makes about 4 dozen cookies

Tracy's Pizza-Pan Cookies

1 cup (2 sticks) butter or margarine, softened
¾ cup granulated sugar
¾ cup packed brown sugar
1 package (8 ounces) cream cheese, softened
1 teaspoon vanilla
2 eggs
2¼ cups all-purpose flour
1 teaspoon baking soda
¼ teaspoon salt
1 package (12 ounces) semisweet chocolate
    chips
1 cup chopped walnuts or pecans

Preheat oven to 375°F. Lightly grease two 12-inch pizza pans. Cream butter, sugars, cream cheese and vanilla in large bowl. Add eggs; beat until light. Combine flour, baking soda and salt in small bowl. Add to creamed mixture; blend well. Stir in chocolate chips and nuts. Divide dough in half; press each half evenly into a prepared pan. Bake 20 to 25 minutes or until lightly browned around edges. Cool completely in pans on wire racks. To serve, cut into slim wedges or break into pieces.

Makes two 12-inch cookies

Chocolate Macadamia Chewies

Hershey's Milk Chocolate Chip Giant Cookies

6 tablespoons butter or margarine, softened
½ cup granulated sugar
¼ cup packed light brown sugar
½ teaspoon vanilla extract
1 egg
1 cup all-purpose flour
½ teaspoon baking soda
2 cups (11.5-ounce package) HERSHEY'S Milk Chocolate Chips
Frosting (optional)
Ice cream (optional)

1. Heat oven to 350°F. Line two 9-inch round baking pans with foil, extending foil over edges of pans.

2. Beat butter, granulated sugar, brown sugar and vanilla until light and fluffy. Add egg; beat well. Stir together flour and baking soda; gradually add to butter mixture, beating until well blended. Stir in milk chocolate chips. Spread one-half of batter into each prepared pan, spreading to 1 inch from edge. (Cookies will spread to edge when baking.)

3. Bake 15 to 20 minutes or until lightly browned. Cool completely; carefully lift cookies from pan and remove foil. Frost, if desired. Cut each cookie into wedges; serve topped with scoop of ice cream, if desired.

Makes about 16 servings

Pineapple Oatmeal "Scotchies"

2 cans (8 ounces each) DOLE® Crushed Pineapple
1½ cups margarine
1½ cups brown sugar, packed
1 egg
3 cups rolled oats
2 cups all-purpose flour
1 teaspoon baking powder
1 teaspoon ground cinnamon
½ teaspoon salt
6 ounces butterscotch chips

• Drain pineapple well, save juice for a beverage.

• Beat margarine and sugar until light and fluffy. Beat in egg and pineapple.

• Combine dry ingredients; blend into pineapple mixture. Stir in chips.

• Drop by 2 tablespoonsful onto cookie sheets coated with cooking spray; flatten top with back of spoon. Bake in 375°F oven 20 minutes until browned.

Makes 3½ dozen cookies

Prep time: 20 minutes
Bake time: 20 minutes per batch

Hershey's Milk Chocolate Chip Giant Cookie

Choco-Scutterbotch

⅔ BUTTER FLAVOR* CRISCO® Stick or
  ⅔ cup BUTTER FLAVOR CRISCO
  all-vegetable shortening
½ cup firmly packed brown sugar
 2 eggs
 1 package DUNCAN HINES® Moist Deluxe
   Yellow Cake Mix
 1 cup toasted rice cereal
½ cup milk chocolate chunks
½ cup butterscotch chips
½ cup semi-sweet chocolate chips
½ cup coarsely chopped walnuts or pecans

*Butter Flavor Crisco is artificially flavored.

1. Preheat oven to 375°F.

2. Combine shortening and brown sugar in large bowl. Beat at medium speed with electric mixer until well blended. Beat in eggs.

3. Add cake mix gradually at low speed. Mix until well blended. Stir in cereal, chocolate chunks, butterscotch chips, chocolate chips and nuts with spoon. Stir until well blended. Shape dough into 1¼-inch balls. Place 2 inches apart on ungreased cookie sheet. Flatten slightly. Shape sides to form circle, if necessary.

4. Bake at 375°F for 7 to 9 minutes or until lightly browned around edges. Cool 2 minutes before removing to paper towels.

Makes about 3 dozen cookies

Walnut-Orange Chocolate Chippers

1½ cup all-purpose flour
1½ teaspoon baking powder
 ½ teaspoon salt
 ½ cup brown sugar
 ½ cup white sugar
 ⅓ cup butter, softened
 2 eggs, slightly beaten
 2 tablespoons grated orange peel
 1 cup coarsely chopped California walnuts
 2 cups (12 ounces) semisweet chocolate chips

Combine flour, baking powder, salt and sugars; mix in butter and eggs. Add remaining ingredients and mix thoroughly (batter will be stiff). Spread dough evenly in greased and floured 9-inch square pan (use wet hands to smooth). Bake at 350°F 25 minutes or until golden brown. Cool; cut into squares. *Makes 36 squares*

Favorite recipe from **Walnut Marketing Board**

Choco-Scutterbotch

Quick Chocolate Softies

1 package (18.25 ounces) devil's food cake mix
⅓ cup water
¼ cup (½ stick) butter or margarine, softened
1 large egg
1 cup white chocolate baking chips
½ cup coarsely chopped walnuts

Preheat oven to 350°F. Combine cake mix, water, butter and egg in large bowl. Beat with electric mixer at low speed until moistened. Increase speed to medium; beat 1 minute. (Dough will be thick.) Stir in chips and nuts; mix until well blended. Drop dough by heaping teaspoonfuls 2 inches apart onto greased cookie sheets. Bake 10 to 12 minutes or until set. Let cookies stand on cookie sheets 1 minute. Remove cookies to wire racks; cool completely. *Makes about 4 dozen cookies*

Store soft cookies in airtight containers. If they begin to dry out, add a piece of apple or bread to the container to help them retain moisture.

Peanut Chip Cookies

1½ cups packed dark brown sugar
1 cup PETER PAN® Crunchy Peanut Butter
¾ cup butter
¾ cup granulated sugar
¼ cup water
1 egg
1¼ teaspoons vanilla extract
2 cups rolled oats
1½ cups all-purpose flour
1½ teaspoons baking powder
¼ teaspoon salt
1 cup semi-sweet chocolate chips

In large mixer bowl, beat *first 4* ingredients until creamy and well blended. Beat in water, egg and vanilla. In medium bowl, mix *remaining* ingredients. Stir into peanut butter mixture until well blended. Drop by heaping teaspoonfuls onto greased baking sheets. Bake at 350°F 12 to 15 minutes or until lightly browned around edges. Cool on wire racks and store in an airtight container. *Makes 4 dozen cookies*

Quick Chocolate Softies

Kids' Favorite Jumbo Chippers

1 cup (2 sticks) butter or margarine, softened
¾ cup granulated sugar
¾ cup packed brown sugar
2 large eggs
1 teaspoon vanilla
2¼ cups all-purpose flour
1 teaspoon baking soda
¾ teaspoon salt
1 (12-ounce) package candy-coated semisweet chocolate mini baking pieces
1 cup peanut butter flavored chips

Preheat oven to 375°F. Beat butter, granulated sugar and brown sugar in large bowl until light and fluffy. Beat in eggs and vanilla. Add combined flour, baking soda and salt. Beat until well blended. Stir in baking pieces and chips. Drop dough by heaping tablespoonfuls 3 inches apart onto ungreased cookie sheets. Bake 10 to 12 minutes or until edges are golden brown. Let cookies stand on cookie sheets 2 minutes. Remove cookies to wire racks; cool completely.

Makes 3 dozen jumbo cookies

Double Nut Chocolate Chip Cookies

1 package DUNCAN HINES® Moist Deluxe Yellow Cake Mix
½ cup butter or margarine, melted
1 egg
1 cup semi-sweet chocolate chips
½ cup finely chopped pecans
1 cup sliced almonds, divided

1. Preheat oven to 375°F. Grease baking sheets.

2. Combine cake mix, butter and egg in large bowl. Mix at low speed with electric mixer until just blended. Stir in chocolate chips, pecans and ¼ cup almonds. Shape rounded tablespoonfuls of dough into balls. Place remaining ¾ cup almonds in shallow bowl. Press tops of cookies in almonds. Place 1 inch apart on greased baking sheets. Bake at 375°F for 9 to 11 minutes or until lightly browned. Cool 2 minutes on baking sheets. Remove to cooling racks. Cool completely. Store in airtight containers.   *Makes 3 to 3½ dozen cookies*

Oatmeal Butterscotch Cookies

¾ cup (1½ sticks) butter or margarine, softened
¾ cup granulated sugar
¾ cup packed light brown sugar
2 eggs
1 teaspoon vanilla extract
1¼ cups all-purpose flour
1 teaspoon baking soda
½ teaspoon ground cinnamon
½ teaspoon salt
3 cups quick-cooking or regular rolled oats
1⅔ cups (10-ounce package) HERSHEY'S Butterscotch Chips

1. Heat oven to 375°F.

2. In large bowl, beat butter, granulated sugar and brown sugar until well blended. Add eggs and vanilla; blend thoroughly. Stir together flour, baking soda, cinnamon and salt; gradually add to butter mixture, beating until well blended. Stir in oats and butterscotch chips; mix well. Drop by teaspoons onto ungreased cookie sheet.

3. Bake 8 to 10 minutes or until golden brown. Cool slightly; remove from cookie sheet to wire rack. Cool completely.

Makes about 4 dozen cookies

Peanut Butter Chocolate Chip Cookies

1 cup sugar
½ cup SKIPPY® Creamy or SUPER CHUNK® Peanut Butter
½ cup undiluted evaporated milk
1 package (6 ounces) semisweet chocolate chips
1 cup coarsely chopped nuts

1. Preheat oven to 325°F. Line large cookie sheets with foil.

2. In medium bowl, stir sugar and peanut butter until well blended. Stir in evaporated milk, chips and nuts until well mixed.

3. Drop batter by heaping teaspoonfuls 1½ inches apart onto prepared cookie sheets. Spread batter evenly into 2-inch rounds.

4. Bake 18 to 20 minutes or until golden. Cool completely on foil on wire racks. Peel foil from cookies. *Makes about 3½ dozen cookies*

Oatmeal Butterscotch Cookies

Chocolate Crackletops

2 cups all-purpose flour
2 teaspoons baking powder
2 cups granulated sugar
½ cup (1 stick) butter or margarine
4 squares (1 ounce each) unsweetened baking chocolate, chopped
4 large eggs, lightly beaten
2 teaspoons vanilla extract
1¾ cups "M&M's"® Chocolate Mini Baking Bits
Additional granulated sugar

Combine flour and baking powder; set aside. In 2-quart saucepan over medium heat combine 2 cups sugar, butter and chocolate, stirring until butter and chocolate are melted; remove from heat. Gradually stir in eggs and vanilla. Stir in flour mixture until well blended. Chill mixture 1 hour. Stir in "M&M's"® Chocolate Mini Baking Bits; chill mixture an additional 1 hour.

Preheat oven to 350°F. Line cookie sheets with foil. With sugar-dusted hands, roll dough into 1-inch balls; roll balls in additional granulated sugar. Place about 2 inches apart onto prepared cookie sheets. Bake 10 to 12 minutes. *Do not overbake.* Cool completely on wire racks. Store in tightly covered container. *Makes about 5 dozen cookies*

Whole Grain Chippers

1 cup (2 sticks) butter or margarine, softened
⅔ cup granulated sugar
1 cup packed light brown sugar
2 eggs
1 teaspoon vanilla
1 teaspoon baking soda
Pinch salt
1 cup whole wheat flour
1 cup all-purpose flour
2 cups uncooked rolled oats
1 package (12 ounces) semisweet chocolate chips
1 cup sunflower seeds

Preheat oven to 375°F. Lightly grease cookie sheets or line with parchment paper. Cream butter with sugars and eggs in large bowl until light and fluffy. Beat in vanilla, baking soda and salt. Blend in flours and oats to make a stiff dough. Stir in chocolate chips. Shape rounded teaspoonfuls of dough into balls; roll in sunflower seeds. Place 2 inches apart on prepared cookie sheets. Bake 8 to 10 minutes or until firm. Do not overbake. Cool a few minutes on cookie sheet, then remove to wire racks to cool completely. *Makes about 6 dozen cookies*

Chocolate Crackletops

Cookie Jar Favorites

Chewy Oatmeal Cookies

1¼ cups firmly packed light brown sugar
¾ BUTTER FLAVOR* CRISCO® Stick or
    ¾ cup BUTTER FLAVOR CRISCO
    all-vegetable shortening
1 egg
⅓ cup milk
1½ teaspoons vanilla
3 cups quick oats, uncooked
1 cup all-purpose flour
½ teaspoon baking soda
½ teaspoon salt
¼ teaspoon cinnamon
1 cup raisins
1 cup coarsely chopped walnuts

*Butter Flavor Crisco is artificially flavored.

1. Heat oven to 375°F. Grease baking sheets. Place sheets of foil on countertop for cooling cookies.

2. Place brown sugar, shortening, egg, milk and vanilla in large bowl. Beat at medium speed of electric mixer until well blended.

3. Combine oats, flour, baking soda, salt and cinnamon. Add to shortening mixture; beat at low speed just until blended. Stir in raisins and walnuts.

4. Drop dough by rounded measuring tablespoonfuls 2 inches apart onto prepared baking sheets.

5. Bake one baking sheet at a time at 375°F for 10 to 12 minutes or until cookies are lightly browned. *Do not overbake.* Cool 2 minutes on baking sheet. Remove cookies to foil to cool completely.   *Makes about 2½ dozen cookies*

Chewy Oatmeal Cookies

Peanut Butter Chocolate Stars

1 cup peanut butter
1 cup packed light brown sugar
1 egg
24 milk chocolate candy stars or other solid milk chocolate candy

Preheat oven to 350°F. Line cookie sheets with parchment paper or leave ungreased. Combine peanut butter, sugar and egg in medium bowl until blended and smooth.

Shape dough into 24 balls about 1½ inches in diameter. Place 2 inches apart on cookie sheets. Press one chocolate star on top of each cookie. Bake 10 to 12 minutes or until set. Transfer to wire racks to cool completely. *Makes 24 cookies*

Peanut Butter Crisscross Cookies: *Prepare dough and shape cookies as directed above, omitting chocolate stars. Dip fork into granulated sugar; press criss-cross pattern onto each cookie, flattening to ½-inch thickness. Bake as directed above.*

Allow cookie sheets to cool between batches because the dough will spread if placed on a hot cookie sheet.

Chocolate Cherry Cordial Drops

1 package DUNCAN HINES® Chocolate Chip Cookie Mix
1 egg
⅓ cup CRISCO® Oil or CRISCO® PURITAN® Canola Oil
3 tablespoons water
⅓ cup chopped maraschino cherries, well drained
⅓ cup flaked coconut
2 cups chopped pecans

1. Preheat oven to 375°F.

2. Combine cookie mix, egg, oil and water in large bowl. Stir until thoroughly blended. Stir in cherries and coconut. Shape dough into 48 (1-inch) balls. Roll in chopped pecans. Place 2 inches apart on ungreased baking sheets. Bake at 375°F for 11 to 12 minutes or until cookies are set and lightly browned. Cool 1 minute on baking sheets. Remove to cooling racks. Cool completely. Store in airtight container. *Makes 4 dozen cookies*

Tip: *You may substitute chopped walnuts or almond slices for the pecans.*

Peanut Butter Chocolate Stars

Watermelon Slices

**1 package DUNCAN HINES® Golden
    Sugar Cookie Mix
1 egg
¼ cup CRISCO® Oil or CRISCO®
    PURITAN® Canola Oil
1½ tablespoons water
12 drops red food coloring
 5 drops green food coloring
    Chocolate sprinkles**

1. Combine cookie mix, egg, oil and water in large bowl. Stir until thoroughly blended; reserve ⅓ cup dough.

2. For red cookie dough, combine remaining dough with red food coloring. Stir until evenly tinted. On waxed paper, shape dough into 12-inch-long roll with one side flattened. Cover; refrigerate with flat side down until firm.

3. For green cookie dough, combine reserved ⅓ cup dough with green food coloring in small bowl. Stir until evenly tinted. Place between 2 layers of waxed paper. Roll dough into 12×4-inch rectangle. Refrigerate 15 minutes. Preheat oven to 375°F.

4. To assemble, remove green dough rectangle from refrigerator. Remove top layer of waxed paper. Trim edges along both 12-inch sides. Remove red dough log from refrigerator. Place red dough log, flattened side up, along center of green dough. Mold green dough up to edge of flattened side of red dough. Remove bottom layer of waxed paper. Trim excess green dough, if necessary.

5. Cut chilled roll, flat side down, into ¼-inch-thick slices with sharp knife. Place 2 inches apart on ungreased baking sheets. Sprinkle chocolate sprinkles on red dough for seeds. Bake at 375°F for 7 minutes or until set. Cool 1 minute on baking sheets. Remove to cooling racks. Cool completely. Store between layers of waxed paper in airtight container. *Makes 3 to 4 dozen cookies*

Tip: *To make neat, clean slices, use unwaxed dental floss.*

Peanut Meringue Cookies

**4 egg whites
½ teaspoon cream of tartar
1 cup sugar
¼ cup ground peanuts**

Preheat oven to 250°F. Line cookie sheets with parchment paper. Set aside.

Beat egg whites in large bowl with electric mixer until foamy. Add cream of tartar; beat until soft peaks form. Gradually add sugar; beat until stiff peaks form. Stir in peanuts.

Drop by teaspoonfuls onto prepared cookie sheets. Bake 20 minutes or until lightly browned. Cool on wire racks. *Makes about 3 dozen cookies*

Watermelon Slices

Harvest Pumpkin Cookies

2 cups all-purpose flour
1 teaspoon baking powder
1 teaspoon ground cinnamon
½ teaspoon baking soda
½ teaspoon salt
½ teaspoon ground allspice
1 cup (2 sticks) butter, softened
1 cup sugar
1 cup canned pumpkin
1 large egg
1 teaspoon vanilla
1 cup chopped pecans
1 cup dried cranberries (optional)
Pecan halves (about 36)

1. Preheat oven to 375°F. Place flour, baking powder, cinnamon, baking soda, salt and allspice in medium bowl; stir to combine.

2. Beat butter and sugar in large bowl with electric mixer at medium speed until light and fluffy. Beat in pumpkin, egg and vanilla. Gradually add flour mixture; beat at low speed until well blended. Stir in chopped pecans and cranberries.

3. Drop heaping tablespoonfuls of dough 2 inches apart onto *ungreased* cookie sheets. Flatten mounds slightly with back of spoon. Press one pecan half into center of each mound. Bake 10 to 12 minutes or until golden brown.

4. Let cookies stand on cookie sheets 1 minute. Remove cookies to wire racks; cool completely. Store tightly covered at room temperature or freeze up to 3 months.   *Makes about 3 dozen cookies*

Fresh Orange Cookies

1½ cups all-purpose flour
½ teaspoon baking soda
¼ teaspoon salt
½ cup butter or margarine, softened
½ cup granulated sugar
½ cup packed light brown sugar
1 egg
1 unpeeled SUNKIST® Orange, finely chopped*
½ cup chopped walnuts
Orange Glaze (recipe follows)

*Chop orange in blender or food processor, or by hand, to equal ¾ cup chopped fruit.

Sift together flour, baking soda and salt. In large bowl, beat butter and sugars until light and fluffy. Add egg and chopped orange; beat well. Gradually blend in dry ingredients. Stir in walnuts. Cover and chill at least 1 hour. Drop dough by teaspoons onto lightly greased cookie sheets. Bake at 375°F for 10 to 12 minutes. Cool on wire racks. Spread cookies with Orange Glaze.

Makes about 4 dozen cookies

Orange Glaze

1 cup confectioners' sugar
1 to 2 tablespoons fresh orange juice
1 tablespoon butter or margarine, softened
1 teaspoon grated orange peel

In small bowl, combine all ingredients until smooth.   *Makes about ½ cup*

Harvest Pumpkin Cookies

Cherry Surprises

**1 package DUNCAN HINES® Golden
 Sugar Cookie Mix**
48 to 54 candied cherries
¾ cup semisweet chocolate chips
**1½ teaspoons CRISCO® all-vegetable
 shortening**

1. Preheat oven to 375°F. Grease baking sheets.

2. Prepare cookie mix following package directions for cut cookies. Shape thin layer of dough around each candied cherry. Place 2 inches apart on greased baking sheets. Bake at 375°F for 8 minutes or until set but not browned. Cool 1 minute on baking sheets. Remove to cooling racks. Cool completely.

3. Combine chocolate chips and shortening in small resealable plastic bag. Place bag in bowl of hot water for several minutes. Dry with paper towel. Knead until blended and chocolate is smooth. Cut pinpoint hole in corner of bag. Drizzle chocolate over cooled cookies. Allow drizzle to set before storing between layers of waxed paper in airtight container.

Makes 4 to 4½ dozen cookies

Pecan Florentines

¾ cup pecan halves, pulverized*
½ cup all-purpose flour
⅓ cup packed brown sugar
¼ cup light corn syrup
¼ cup (½ stick) butter or margarine
2 tablespoons milk
⅓ cup semisweet chocolate chips

*To pulverize pecans, place in food processor or blender. Process until thoroughly ground with a dry, not pasty texture.

Preheat oven to 350°F. Line cookie sheets with foil; lightly grease foil. Combine pecans and flour in small bowl. Combine sugar, syrup, butter and milk in medium saucepan. Stir over medium heat until mixture comes to a boil. Remove from heat; stir in pecan mixture.

Drop batter by teaspoonfuls about 3 inches apart onto prepared cookie sheets. Bake 10 to 12 minutes or until lacy and golden brown (cookies are soft when hot, but become crispy as they cool). Cool completely on foil.

Place chocolate chips in small resealable plastic bag; close securely. Set bag in bowl of hot water until chips are melted, being careful not to let any water into bag. Remove bag from water. Knead bag lightly to make sure chips are completely melted; pat bag dry. With scissors, cut pinpoint hole in corner from one side of bag. Squeeze melted chocolate over cookies to decorate. Let stand until chocolate is set. Peel cookies off foil.

Makes about 3 dozen cookies

Cherry Surprises

Peanut Butter Bears

1 cup SKIPPY® Creamy Peanut Butter
1 cup (2 sticks) MAZOLA® Margarine or
** butter, softened**
1 cup firmly packed brown sugar
⅔ cup KARO® Light or Dark Corn Syrup
2 eggs
4 cups flour, divided
1 tablespoon baking powder
1 teaspoon ground cinnamon (optional)
¼ teaspoon salt

1. In large bowl with mixer at medium speed, beat peanut butter, margarine, brown sugar, corn syrup and eggs until smooth. Reduce speed; beat in 2 cups flour, baking powder, cinnamon and salt. With spoon, stir in remaining 2 cups flour. Wrap dough in plastic wrap; refrigerate 2 hours.

2. Preheat oven to 325°F. Divide dough in half. On floured surface, roll out half the dough to ⅛-inch thickness. Cut with floured bear cookie cutter. Repeat with remaining dough.

3. Bake on ungreased cookie sheets 10 minutes or until lightly browned. Remove from cookie sheets; cool completely on wire racks. Decorate as desired.

Makes about 3 dozen bears

Prep time: 35 minutes, plus chilling
Bake time: 10 minutes, plus cooling

Note: Use scraps of dough to make bear faces. Make one small ball of dough for muzzle. Form 3 smaller balls of dough and press gently into unbaked cookies to create eyes and nose; bake as directed. If desired, use frosting to create paws, ears and bow ties.

Choco-Coco Pecan Crisps

1 cup packed light brown sugar
½ cup (1 stick) butter or margarine, softened
1 egg
1 teaspoon vanilla
1½ cups all-purpose flour
⅓ cup unsweetened cocoa powder
½ teaspoon baking soda
1 cup chopped pecans
1 cup flaked coconut

Beat sugar and butter in large bowl with electric mixer until blended. Beat in egg and vanilla.

Combine flour, cocoa, baking soda and pecans in small bowl. Add to butter mixture, stirring until stiff dough forms.

Sprinkle coconut on work surface. Divide dough into 4 pieces. Shape each piece into log about 1½ inches in diameter; roll in coconut until thickly coated. Wrap in plastic wrap; refrigerate until firm, at least 1 hour or up to 2 weeks. (Or freeze up to 6 weeks.)

Preheat oven to 350°F. Line cookie sheets with parchment paper or leave ungreased. Cut logs into ⅛-inch-thick slices; place 2 inches apart on prepared cookie sheets. Bake 10 to 13 minutes or until firm and lightly browned. Transfer to wire racks to cool.

Makes about 72 cookies

Peanut Butter Bears

Raspberry Pecan Thumbprints

2 cups all-purpose flour
1 cup pecan pieces, finely chopped, divided
½ teaspoon ground cinnamon
¼ teaspoon ground allspice
⅛ teaspoon salt
1 cup (2 sticks) butter, softened
½ cup packed light brown sugar
2 teaspoons vanilla
⅓ cup seedless raspberry jam

Preheat oven to 350°F. Combine flour, ½ cup pecans, cinnamon, allspice and salt in medium bowl. Beat butter in large bowl with electric mixer at medium speed until smooth. Gradually beat in sugar; increase speed to high and beat until light and fluffy. Beat in vanilla until blended. Beat in flour mixture at low speed just until blended.

Form dough into 1-inch balls; flatten slightly and place on *ungreased* cookie sheets. Press down with thumb in center of each ball to form indentation. Pinch together any cracks in dough. Fill each indentation with generous ¼ teaspoon jam. Sprinkle filled cookies with remaining ½ cup pecans.

Bake 14 minutes or until just set. Let cookies stand on cookie sheets 5 minutes; transfer to wire racks to cool completely. Store in airtight container at room temperature. Cookies are best day after baking.

Makes 36 cookies

Hollywood Walk of Fame Stars

1 (12-ounce) package milk chocolate chips
1 (12-ounce) package butterscotch chips
½ cup PETER PAN® Extra Crunchy Peanut Butter
1 bag popped ORVILLE REDENBACHER'S® REDENBUDDERS® MOVIE THEATER BUTTER POPPING CORN, unpopped kernels discarded
1 cup cornflakes cereal
1 cup honey graham cereal
WESSON® No Stick Cooking Spray
Large star-shaped cookie cutter

1. Melt chocolate and butterscotch chips in large saucepan over low heat.

2. Stir in peanut butter until smooth. Remove from heat. Stir in popcorn, cornflakes and graham cereal. Coat evenly.

3. Line 15½×10-inch jelly roll pan with foil. Lightly spray with cooking spray.

4. Spread popcorn mixture evenly in pan. Refrigerate 15 minutes.

5. Spray cookie cutter with cooking spray.

6. Carefully press out stars. Store in refrigerator.

Makes 12 medium or 6 to 8 large stars

Total preparation time: 50 minutes

Raspberry Pecan Thumbprints

Cocoa Crinkle Sandwiches

1¾ cups all-purpose flour
½ cup unsweetened cocoa
1 teaspoon baking soda
¼ teaspoon salt
½ cup (1 stick) butter
1¾ cups sugar, divided
2 eggs
2 teaspoons vanilla
1 can (16 ounces) chocolate or favorite flavor frosting
½ cup crushed candy canes* (optional)

*To crush candy canes, place candy in sealed heavy-duty plastic food storage bag. Break into pieces with heavy object (such as meat mallet or can of vegetables); crush pieces with rolling pin.

Combine flour, cocoa, baking soda and salt in medium bowl. Melt butter in large saucepan over medium heat; cool slightly. Add 1¼ cups sugar; whisk until smooth. Whisk in eggs, 1 at a time, until blended. Stir in vanilla until smooth. Stir in flour mixture just until combined. Wrap dough in plastic wrap; refrigerate 2 hours.

Preheat oven to 350°F. Grease cookie sheets. Shape dough into 1-inch balls. Place remaining ½ cup sugar in shallow bowl; roll balls in sugar. Place 1½ inches apart on cookie sheets.

Bake 12 minutes or until cookies feel set to the touch. Let cookies stand on cookie sheets 5 minutes; transfer to wire racks to cool completely.

Stir frosting until soft and smooth. Place crushed candy canes on piece of waxed paper. Spread about 2 teaspoons frosting over flat side of one cookie.

Place second cookie, flat side down, over frosting, pressing down to allow frosting to squeeze out slightly between cookies. Press exposed frosting into crushed candy canes. Repeat with remaining cookies. Store in airtight container.

Makes about 21 sandwich cookies
(about 42 unfilled cookies)

Fudgy Raisin Pixies

½ cup (1 stick) butter
2 cups granulated sugar
4 eggs
2 cups all-purpose flour, divided
¾ cup unsweetened cocoa powder
2 teaspoons baking powder
½ teaspoon salt
½ cup chocolate-covered raisins
Powdered sugar

Cream butter and sugar until light and fluffy. Add eggs; mix until well blended. Add combined 1 cup flour, cocoa, baking powder and salt. Mix until well blended. Stir in remaining 1 cup flour and chocolate-covered raisins. Cover; refrigerate until firm, 2 hours or overnight.

Preheat oven to 350°F. Coat hands with powdered sugar. Shape rounded teaspoonfuls of dough into 1-inch balls; roll in powdered sugar. Place 2 inches apart on greased cookie sheets. Bake 14 to 17 minutes or until firm to the touch. Remove to wire racks immediately. Cool completely.

Makes about 4 dozen cookies

Cocoa Crinkle Sandwiches

Almond Hearts

1 package DUNCAN HINES® Golden
    Sugar Cookie Mix
¾ cup ground almonds
2 egg yolks
⅓ cup CRISCO® Oil or CRISCO®
    PURITAN® Canola Oil
1½ tablespoons water
14 ounces (6 cubes) vanilla-flavored candy
    coating
    Pink candy coating, for garnish

1. Preheat oven to 375°F.

2. Combine cookie mix, ground almonds, egg yolks, oil and water in large bowl. Stir until thoroughly blended.

3. Divide dough in half. Roll half the dough between 2 sheets of waxed paper into 11-inch circle. Slide onto flat surface. Refrigerate about 15 minutes. Repeat with remaining dough. Loosen top sheet of waxed paper from dough. Turn over and remove second sheet of waxed paper. Cut dough with 2½-inch heart cookie cutter. Place cut-outs 2 inches apart on ungreased cookie sheets. (Roll leftover cookie dough to ⅛-inch thickness between sheets of waxed paper. Chill before cutting.) Repeat cutting with remaining dough circle. Bake at 375°F for 6 to 8 minutes or until light golden brown. Cool 1 minute on cookie sheets. Remove to cooling racks. Cool completely.

4. Place vanilla candy coating in 1-quart saucepan on low heat; stir until melted and smooth. Dip half of one heart cookie into candy coating. Allow excess to drip back into pan. Place cookie on waxed paper. Repeat with remaining cookies. Place pink candy coating in small saucepan on low heat. Stir until melted and smooth. Spoon into pastry bag fitted with small writing tip. Decorate tops of cookies as desired.   *Makes about 5 dozen cookies*

Cashew Clusters

9 ounces semi-sweet chocolate
½ cup CRAISINS® Sweetened Dried
    Cranberries
½ cup cashews

Melt chocolate in double boiler. Remove from heat and cool slightly. Stir in dried cranberries and nuts. Drop by teaspoonfuls onto cookie sheet. Let clusters harden at room temperature or chill in refrigerator.   *Makes about 16 clusters*

Mexican Wedding Cookies

1 cup pecan pieces or halves
1 cup (2 sticks) unsalted butter, softened
2 cups powdered sugar, divided
2 cups all-purpose flour, divided
2 teaspoons vanilla
¼ teaspoon salt

1. Place pecans in food processor. Process using on/off pulses until pecans are ground, but not pasty.

2. Beat butter and ½ cup powdered sugar in large bowl with electric mixer at medium speed until light and fluffy. Gradually add 1 cup flour, vanilla and salt. Beat at low speed until well blended. Stir in remaining 1 cup flour and ground nuts with spoon. Form dough into a ball; wrap in plastic wrap and refrigerate 1 hour or until firm.

3. Preheat oven to 350°F. Roll tablespoons of dough into 1-inch balls. Place 1 inch apart on *ungreased* cookie sheets. Bake 12 to 15 minutes or until pale golden brown. Let cookies stand on cookie sheets 2 minutes.

4. Meanwhile, place 1 cup powdered sugar in 13×9-inch glass dish. Transfer hot cookies to dish. Roll cookies in powdered sugar, coating well. Let cookies cool in sugar. Sift remaining ½ cup powdered sugar over sugar-coated cookies before serving. Store tightly covered at room temperature or freeze up to 1 month.

Makes about 4 dozen cookies

Double Chocolate Peanut Cookies made with Snickers® Bars

¾ cup margarine, softened
⅓ cup granulated sugar
⅓ cup firmly packed light brown sugar
1 large egg
1 teaspoon vanilla extract
1½ cups all-purpose flour
2 tablespoons cocoa powder
¾ teaspoon baking soda
¼ teaspoon salt
4 SNICKERS® Bars (2.07 ounces each), coarsely chopped

Preheat oven to 350°F.

In large mixing bowl, cream margarine and sugars. Add egg and vanilla; beat until light and fluffy. Combine flour, cocoa powder, baking soda and salt; gradually blend into creamed mixture. Stir in chopped Snickers® Bars until evenly blended. Drop by heaping tablespoonfuls about 2 inches apart onto ungreased cookie sheets. Bake 9 to 13 minutes. Cool 1 minute on cookie sheets; remove to wire cooling racks. Store in tightly covered container. *Makes about 3 dozen cookies*

Orange Pecan Gems

1 package DUNCAN HINES® Moist Deluxe Orange Supreme Cake Mix
1 container (8 ounces) vanilla low fat yogurt
1 egg
2 tablespoons butter or margarine, softened
1 cup finely chopped pecans
1 cup pecan halves

1. Preheat oven to 350°F. Grease baking sheets.

2. Combine cake mix, yogurt, egg, butter and chopped pecans in large bowl. Beat at low speed with electric mixer until blended. Drop by rounded teaspoonfuls 2 inches apart onto greased baking sheets. Press pecan half onto center of each cookie. Bake at 350°F for 11 to 13 minutes or until golden brown. Cool 1 minute on baking sheets. Remove to cooling racks. Cool completely. Store in airtight container. *Makes about 4½ to 5 dozen cookies*

Try to form cookies of equal size and shape so they will all finish baking at the same time.

Chocolate Dunking Biscotti

1⅓ cups all-purpose flour
⅓ cup unsweetened cocoa powder
1 teaspoon baking powder
½ teaspoon ground allspice
¼ teaspoon salt
¾ cup granulated sugar
2 eggs, lightly beaten
½ teaspoon almond extract

GLAZE (optional)
¼ cup powdered sugar
1 teaspoon water

Preheat oven to 350°F. Coat baking sheet with nonstick cooking spray. Sift together flour, cocoa powder, baking powder, allspice and salt in small bowl. Whisk together remaining ingredients in medium bowl. Add flour mixture; mix with hands to form dough. (Dough will be dry yet sticky.)

Divide dough in half; form 2 logs about 2 inches wide and 12 inches long on baking sheet. Bake 25 to 30 minutes. Remove from oven; cut logs into ½-inch slices. For drier biscotti, bake slices 10 minutes more at 300°F. For moister biscotti, omit second baking. For glaze, blend powdered sugar and water until smooth; drizzle over biscotti with spoon. *Makes about 2 dozen biscotti*

Favorite recipe from **The Sugar Association, Inc.**

Classic Refrigerator Sugar Cookies

1 cup (2 sticks) butter, softened
1 cup sugar
1 egg
1 teaspoon vanilla
2 cups all-purpose flour
2 teaspoons baking powder
   Dash nutmeg
¼ cup milk
   Colored sprinkles (optional)

Beat butter in large bowl with electric mixer at medium speed until smooth. Add sugar; beat until well blended. Add egg and vanilla; beat until well blended.

Combine flour, baking powder and nutmeg in medium bowl. Add flour mixture and milk alternately to butter mixture, beating at low speed after each addition until well blended.

Shape dough into 2 logs, each about 6 inches long and 2 inches in diameter. Roll logs in colored sprinkles, if desired, coating evenly (about ¼ cup sprinkles per roll). Or, leave rolls plain and decorate with melted chocolate after baking. Wrap each roll in plastic wrap. Refrigerate 2 to 3 hours or overnight.

Preheat oven to 350°F. Grease cookie sheets. Cut logs into ¼-inch-thick slices; place 1 inch apart on prepared cookie sheets. (Keep unbaked logs and sliced cookies chilled until ready to bake.) Bake 8 to 10 minutes or until edges are golden brown. Transfer to wire racks to cool. Store in airtight container. *Makes about 48 cookies*

Peanut Butter Jewels

1 package DUNCAN HINES® Peanut Butter
   Cookie Mix
1 egg
¼ cup CRISCO® Oil or CRISCO®
   PURITAN® Canola Oil
1 tablespoon water
⅓ cup granulated sugar
⅓ cup cocktail peanuts, finely chopped
   Strawberry jam
   Apricot preserves

1. Preheat oven to 375°F.

2. Combine cookie mix, peanut butter flavor packet from Mix, egg, oil and water in large bowl. Stir until thoroughly blended. Shape dough into 48 (1-inch) balls. Roll half the balls in sugar and half in chopped peanuts. Place 2 inches apart on ungreased baking sheets. Make indentation in center of each ball with finger or handle end of wooden spoon. Fill with ¼ teaspoon strawberry jam or apricot preserves. Bake at 375°F for 8 to 10 minutes or until light golden brown. Cool 1 minute on baking sheets. Remove to cooling racks. Cool completely. Store in airtight container.
Makes 4 dozen cookies

Tip: *For a delicious flavor variation, try seedless red raspberry or blackberry jam.*

Classic Refrigerator Sugar Cookies

Chocolate Walnut Meringues

3 egg whites
Pinch salt
¾ cup sugar
½ cup good-quality Dutch-processed cocoa
⅓ cup finely chopped California walnuts

Preheat oven to 350°F. Place egg whites and salt in large mixing bowl. Beat with electric mixer or wire whisk until soft peaks form. Gradually add sugar, beating until stiff peaks form. Sift cocoa over peaks and fold into egg white mixture with walnuts. Spoon mounds about 1 inch in diameter and about 1 inch apart onto parchment-lined baking sheets. Bake 20 minutes or until dry to the touch. Let cool completely before removing from baking sheets. Store in airtight container. *Makes 48 cookies*

Favorite recipe from **Walnut Marketing Board**

Mint Chocolate Macaroons

1½ cups (10-ounce package) NESTLÉ® TOLL HOUSE® Mint-Chocolate Morsels
3 egg whites
¼ cup granulated sugar
2¼ cups (7-ounce package) flaked or shredded coconut

MELT morsels in small, *heavy-duty* saucepan over *lowest possible* heat. When morsels begin to melt, remove from heat; stir. Return to heat for a few seconds at a time, stirring until smooth; cool to room temperature.

BEAT egg whites in large mixer bowl until foamy. Gradually add sugar; beat until stiff peaks form. Fold in melted chocolate and coconut. Drop by rounded tablespoon onto foil- or parchment paper-lined baking sheets.

BAKE in preheated 350°F. oven for 15 to 18 minutes. Cool on baking sheets for 5 minutes; remove to wire racks to cool completely.
Makes about 2½ dozen cookies

Spicy Oatmeal Raisin Cookies

1 package DUNCAN HINES® Moist Deluxe Spice Cake Mix
4 egg whites
1 cup quick-cooking oats (not instant or old-fashioned), uncooked
½ cup CRISCO® Oil or CRISCO® PURITAN® Canola Oil
½ cup raisins

1. Preheat oven to 350°F. Grease baking sheets.

2. Combine cake mix, egg whites, oats and oil in large mixer bowl. Beat on low speed with electric mixer until blended. Stir in raisins. Drop by rounded teaspoons onto greased baking sheets. Bake at 350°F for 7 to 9 minutes or until lightly browned. Cool 1 minute on baking sheets. Remove to cooling racks. Cool completely. Store in airtight container. *Makes about 4 dozen cookies*

Peanut Butter and Jelly Thumbprints

1½ cups all-purpose flour
½ cup sugar
½ teaspoon baking soda
¼ teaspoon salt
¾ cup PETER PAN® Creamy Peanut Butter
¼ cup butter, softened
¼ cup honey
1 tablespoon milk
Jelly (grape, apple or favorite flavor)

In large bowl, combine flour, sugar, baking soda and salt. Add peanut butter and butter; mix until crumbly. Stir in honey and milk. Shape into 1-inch balls. Place 2 inches apart on ungreased baking sheets. Press thumb into center of each ball; place *½ teaspoon* jelly in each thumbprint. Bake at 375°F for 8 to 10 minutes. Cool on baking sheet 1 minute before removing to wire racks. Store in airtight container.

Makes 2 dozen cookies

Domino® Sugar Cookies

1 cup DOMINO® Granulated Sugar
1 cup (2 sticks) butter or margarine, softened
1 egg
1 tablespoon vanilla
2¼ cups all-purpose flour
1 teaspoon baking soda
Additional DOMINO® Granulated Sugar

In large bowl, blend sugar and butter. Beat in egg and vanilla until light and fluffy. Mix in flour and baking soda. Divide dough in half. Shape each half into roll about 1½ inches in diameter. Wrap and refrigerate for 1 hour until chilled.* Cut rolls into ¼-inch slices. Place on ungreased baking sheet and sprinkle generously with additional sugar. Bake in 375°F oven for 10 to 12 minutes or until lightly browned around edges. Cool on wire rack.

Makes about 3 dozen cookies

__Tip:__ To chill dough quickly, place in freezer for 30 minutes.

Peanut Butter Chewies

1 BUTTER FLAVOR* CRISCO® Stick or
1 cup BUTTER FLAVOR CRISCO
all-vegetable shortening
1½ cups JIF® Creamy Peanut Butter
1½ cups firmly packed brown sugar
2 eggs
1 can (14 ounces) sweetened condensed milk
2 teaspoons vanilla
2 cups all-purpose flour
1 teaspoon baking soda
1 teaspoon salt
1½ cups chopped pecans

Butter Flavor Crisco is artificially flavored.

1. Preheat oven to 350°F.

2. Combine shortening, peanut butter and sugar in large bowl. Beat at medium speed of electric mixer until well blended. Beat in eggs, sweetened condensed milk and vanilla.

3. Combine flour, baking soda and salt. Mix into creamed mixture at low speed until just blended. Stir in nuts.

4. Drop rounded tablespoonfuls of dough 2 inches apart onto ungreased cookie sheets.

5. Bake at 350°F for 10 to 11 minutes or until lightly browned on bottom. Cool 2 minutes on cookie sheets. Remove to cooling rack.

Makes about 4 dozen cookies

Spiced Wafers

½ cup (1 stick) butter or margarine, softened
1 cup sugar
1 egg
2 tablespoons milk
1 teaspoon vanilla
1¾ cups all-purpose flour
2 teaspoons baking powder
1 teaspoon ground cinnamon
½ teaspoon ground nutmeg
¼ teaspoon ground cloves
Red colored sugar or red hot candies
(optional)

Beat butter in large bowl with electric mixer at medium speed until smooth. Add sugar; beat until well blended. Add egg, milk and vanilla; beat until well blended.

Combine flour, baking powder, cinnamon, nutmeg and cloves in medium bowl. Gradually add flour mixture to butter mixture at low speed. Blend well after each addition.

Shape dough into 2 logs, each about 6 inches long and 2 inches in diameter. Wrap each log in plastic wrap. Refrigerate 2 to 3 hours or overnight.

Preheat oven to 350°F. Grease cookie sheets. Cut logs into ¼-inch-thick slices; sprinkle with colored sugar or candies, if desired. (Or leave plain and decorate with icing later.) Place at least 2 inches apart on cookie sheets.

Bake 11 to 13 minutes or until edges are light brown. Transfer to wire racks to cool. Store in airtight container.

Makes about 48 cookies

Peanut Butter Chewies

Nutty Clusters

2 squares (1 ounce each) unsweetened chocolate
½ cup (1 stick) butter or margarine, softened
1 cup granulated sugar
1 egg
⅓ cup buttermilk
1 teaspoon vanilla
1¾ cups all-purpose flour
½ teaspoon baking soda
1 cup mixed salted nuts, coarsely chopped
Chocolate Icing (recipe follows)

Preheat oven to 400°F. Line cookie sheets with parchment paper or leave ungreased. Melt chocolate in top of double boiler over hot, not boiling, water. Remove from heat; cool. Beat butter and granulated sugar in large bowl until smooth. Beat in egg, melted chocolate, buttermilk and vanilla until light. Stir in flour, baking soda and nuts.

Drop dough by teaspoonfuls 2 inches apart onto cookie sheets. Bake 8 to 10 minutes or until almost no imprint remains when touched. Immediately remove cookies from cookie sheet to wire rack. While cookies bake, prepare Chocolate Icing. Frost cookies while still warm.

Makes about 4 dozen cookies

Chocolate Icing

2 squares (1 ounce each) unsweetened chocolate
2 tablespoons butter or margarine
2 cups powdered sugar
2 to 3 tablespoons water

Melt chocolate and butter in small heavy saucepan over low heat, stirring until completely melted. Add powdered sugar and water, mixing until smooth.

No-Bake Peanutty Cookies

2 cups Roasted Honey Nut SKIPPY® Creamy or SUPER CHUNK® Peanut Butter
2 cups graham cracker crumbs
1 cup confectioners' sugar
½ cup KARO® Light or Dark Corn Syrup
¼ cup semisweet chocolate chips, melted
Colored sprinkles (optional)

1. In large bowl, combine peanut butter, graham cracker crumbs, confectioners' sugar and corn syrup. Mix until smooth. Shape into 1-inch balls. Place on waxed paper-lined cookie sheet.

2. Drizzle melted chocolate over balls; roll in colored sprinkles if desired. Store covered in refrigerator. *Makes about 5 dozen cookies*

Nutty Clusters

Lemon Cookies

**1 package DUNCAN HINES® Moist Deluxe
Lemon Supreme Cake Mix**
2 eggs
**⅓ cup CRISCO® Oil or CRISCO®
PURITAN® Canola Oil**
1 tablespoon lemon juice
**¾ cup chopped nuts or flaked coconut
Confectioners sugar**

1. Preheat oven to 375°F. Grease baking sheets.

2. Combine cake mix, eggs, oil and lemon juice in
large bowl. Beat at low speed with electric mixer
until well blended. Add nuts. Shape into 1-inch
balls. Place 1 inch apart on greased baking sheets.
Bake at 375°F for 6 to 7 minutes or until lightly
browned. Cool 1 minute on baking sheets. Remove
to cooling racks. Sprinkle with confectioners sugar.
Cool completely. Store in airtight container.

Makes about 3 dozen cookies

Tip: *You can frost cookies with 1 cup confectioners
sugar mixed with 1 tablespoon lemon juice instead of
sprinkling cookies with confectioners sugar.*

Cocoa Snickerdoodles

1 cup (2 sticks) butter or margarine, softened
¾ cup packed brown sugar
**¾ cup plus 2 tablespoons granulated sugar,
divided**
2 eggs
2 cups uncooked rolled oats
1½ cups all-purpose flour
**¼ cup plus 2 tablespoons unsweetened cocoa
powder, divided**
1 teaspoon baking soda
2 tablespoons ground cinnamon

Preheat oven to 375°F. Lightly grease cookie sheets
or line with parchment paper.

Beat butter, brown sugar and ¾ cup granulated
sugar in large bowl until light and fluffy. Add eggs;
mix well. Combine oats, flour, ¼ cup cocoa and
baking soda in medium bowl. Stir into butter
mixture until blended.

Mix remaining 2 tablespoons granulated sugar,
remaining 2 tablespoons cocoa and cinnamon in
small bowl. Drop dough by rounded teaspoonfuls
into cinnamon mixture; toss to coat. Place 2 inches
apart on prepared cookie sheets.

Bake 8 to 10 minutes or until firm in center. *Do not
overbake.* Remove to wire racks to cool.

Makes about 4½ dozen cookies

Lemon Cookies

Finnish Spice Cookies

2 cups all-purpose flour
1½ teaspoons ground ginger
1½ teaspoons ground cinnamon
½ teaspoon ground cardamom
½ teaspoon ground cloves
⅔ cup packed light brown sugar
½ cup (1 stick) butter, softened
3 to 5 tablespoons hot water
½ teaspoon baking soda
   Prepared white icing (optional)

1. Place flour, ginger, cinnamon, cardamom and cloves in medium bowl; stir to combine.

2. Beat brown sugar and butter in large bowl with electric mixer at medium speed until light and fluffy. Place water and baking soda in cup; stir until baking soda dissolves. Beat into butter mixture. Gradually add flour mixture. Beat at low speed until dough forms. (If dough is too crumbly, add more water, 1 tablespoon at a time, until dough holds together.)

3. Form dough into 2 discs; wrap in plastic wrap and refrigerate until firm, 30 minutes or overnight. Preheat oven to 375°F. Grease cookie sheets.

4. Working with 1 disc at a time, unwrap dough and place on lightly floured surface. Roll out dough with lightly floured rolling pin to ⅛-inch thickness.

5. Cut dough with floured 3-inch pig-shaped cookie cutter. Place cutouts 1 inch apart on prepared cookie sheets. Gently press dough trimmings together; reroll and cut out more cookies. (Rerolled dough will produce slightly tougher cookies than first rolling.)

6. Bake 8 to 10 minutes or until firm and lightly browned. Remove cookies to wire racks; cool completely. Decorate cooled cookies with icing, if desired. Store tightly covered at room temperature or freeze up to 3 months.

Makes about 5 dozen cookies

Chocolate Candy Cookies

⅔ cup MIRACLE WHIP® Salad Dressing
1 two-layer devil's food cake mix
2 eggs
1 (8-ounce) package candy-coated chocolate candies

• Preheat oven to 375°F.

• Blend salad dressing, cake mix and eggs at low speed with electric mixer until moistened. Beat on medium speed 2 minutes. Stir in chocolate candies. (Dough will be stiff.)

• Drop by rounded teaspoonfuls, 2 inches apart, onto greased cookie sheets.

• Bake 9 to 11 minutes or until almost set. (Cookies will still appear soft.) Cool 1 minute; remove from cookie sheets.

Makes about 4½ dozen cookies

Finnish Spice Cookies

Chocolate-Dipped Almond Horns

1½ cups powdered sugar
1 cup (2 sticks) butter or margarine, softened
2 egg yolks
1½ teaspoons vanilla
2 cups all-purpose flour
½ cup ground almonds
1 teaspoon cream of tartar
1 teaspoon baking soda
1 cup semisweet chocolate chips, melted
  Powdered sugar

Preheat oven to 325°F. In large mixer bowl, combine powdered sugar and butter. Beat at medium speed, scraping bowl often, until creamy, 1 to 2 minutes. Add egg yolks and vanilla; continue beating until well mixed, 1 to 2 minutes. Reduce speed to low. Add flour, almonds, cream of tartar and baking soda. Continue beating, scraping bowl often, until well mixed, 1 to 2 minutes. Shape into 1-inch balls. Roll balls into 2-inch ropes; shape into crescents. Place 2 inches apart on cookie sheets. Flatten slightly with bottom of glass covered in waxed paper. Bake 8 to 10 minutes or until set. (Cookies will not brown.) Cool completely. Dip half of each cookie into chocolate; sprinkle remaining half with powdered sugar. Refrigerate until set. *Makes about 3 dozen cookies*

Hermits

MAZOLA NO STICK® cooking spray
3 cups flour
2 teaspoons pumpkin pie spice
¾ teaspoon baking powder
¾ teaspoon baking soda
¼ teaspoon salt
½ cup (1 stick) MAZOLA® Margarine or
  butter, softened
1 cup packed brown sugar
2 eggs
½ cup KARO® Dark Corn Syrup
1 cup raisins
1 cup coarsely chopped walnuts
2 tablespoons finely chopped crystallized
  ginger (optional)

1. Preheat oven to 350°F. Spray cookie sheets with cooking spray. In medium bowl combine flour, pumpkin pie spice, baking powder, baking soda and salt; set aside.

2. In large bowl with mixer at medium speed, beat margarine and brown sugar until fluffy. Beat in eggs and corn syrup. Reduce speed; beat in flour mixture until blended. Stir in raisins, walnuts and ginger. Drop by heaping teaspoonfuls 1½ inches apart on prepared cookie sheets.

3. Bake 12 minutes until golden and lightly browned at edges. Cool several minutes on cookie sheets. Remove; cool completely on wire rack.
Makes about 4 dozen cookies

Prep time: 25 minutes
Bake time: 12 minutes, plus cooling

Chocolate-Dipped Almond Horns

Pfeffernusse

3½ cups all-purpose flour
2 teaspoons baking powder
1½ teaspoons ground cinnamon
1 teaspoon ground ginger
½ teaspoon baking soda
½ teaspoon salt
½ teaspoon ground cloves
½ teaspoon ground cardamom
¼ teaspoon freshly ground black pepper
1 cup (2 sticks) butter, softened
1 cup granulated sugar
¼ cup dark molasses
1 large egg
Powdered sugar

1. Grease cookie sheets; set aside. Place flour, baking powder, cinnamon, ginger, baking soda, salt, cloves, cardamom and pepper in large bowl; stir to combine.

2. Beat butter and sugar in large bowl with electric mixer at medium speed until light and fluffy. Beat in molasses and egg. Gradually add flour mixture. Beat at low speed until dough forms. Form dough into a disc; wrap in plastic wrap and refrigerate until firm, 30 minutes or up to 3 days.

3. Preheat oven to 350°F. Roll dough into 1-inch balls. Place balls 2 inches apart on prepared cookie sheets. Bake 12 to 14 minutes or until golden brown.

4. Remove cookies to wire racks; dust with sifted powdered sugar. Cool completely. Store tightly covered at room temperature or freeze up to 3 months. *Makes about 5 dozen cookies*

Swiss Chocolate Crispies

1 package DUNCAN HINES® Moist Deluxe Swiss Chocolate Cake Mix
½ BUTTER FLAVOR* CRISCO® Stick or ½ cup BUTTER FLAVOR CRISCO all-vegetable shortening
½ cup butter or margarine, softened
2 eggs
2 tablespoons water
3 cups crispy rice cereal, divided

*Butter Flavor Crisco is artificially flavored.

1. Preheat oven to 350°F. Grease baking sheets.

2. Combine cake mix, shortening, butter, eggs and water in large bowl. Beat at low speed with electric mixer for 2 minutes. Fold in 1 cup cereal. Refrigerate 1 hour.

3. Crush remaining 2 cups cereal into coarse crumbs.

4. Shape dough into 1-inch balls. Roll in crushed cereal. Place about 1 inch apart on baking sheets. Bake at 350°F for 11 to 13 minutes. Cool 1 minute on baking sheets. Remove to wire racks. Cool completely. Store in airtight container.
Makes about 4 dozen cookies

Pfeffernusse

Chocolate Bunny Cookies

1 package (19.8 ounces) DUNCAN HINES®
    Chewy Fudge Brownie Mix
1 egg
¼ cup water
¼ cup CRISCO® Oil or CRISCO®
    PURITAN® Canola Oil
1⅓ cups pecan halves (96)
1 container (16 ounces) DUNCAN HINES®
    Creamy Homestyle Dark Chocolate
    Frosting
    Vanilla milk chips

1. Preheat oven to 350°F. Grease baking sheets.

2. Combine brownie mix, egg, water and oil in large bowl. Stir with spoon until well blended, about 50 strokes. Drop by 2 level teaspoonfuls 2 inches apart onto greased baking sheets. Place two pecan halves, flat-side up, onto each cookie for ears. Bake at 350°F for 10 to 12 minutes or until set. Cool 2 minutes on baking sheets. Remove to cooling racks. Cool completely.

3. Spread Dark Chocolate frosting on one cookie. Place vanilla milk chips, upside down, on frosting for eyes and nose. Dot each eye with Dark Chocolate frosting using toothpick. Repeat for remaining cookies. Allow frosting to set before storing between layers of waxed paper in airtight container.   *Makes 4 dozen cookies*

Tip: *For variety, frost cookies with DUNCAN HINES® Creamy Homestyle Vanilla Frosting and use semi-sweet chocolate chips for the eyes and noses.*

Lemon Buttermilk Baby Cakes

½ cup butter, softened
1 cup sugar
1 egg
¾ cup buttermilk
1 tablespoon grated lemon peel
1 tablespoon fresh lemon juice
½ teaspoon vanilla
2 cups plus 2 tablespoons all-purpose flour
½ teaspoon baking soda
½ teaspoon salt

Beat butter in large bowl until light and fluffy. Add sugar; beat until well blended. Add egg; mix until well blended. Stir in buttermilk, lemon peel, lemon juice and vanilla. Sift together flour, baking soda and salt in small bowl; gradually add to butter mixture. Chill dough at least 2 hours.

Preheat oven to 400°F. Drop small rounded teaspoons of dough onto lightly greased cookie sheets. Bake 6 to 8 minutes or until edges are lightly browned. Sprinkle pinch of sugar over each cookie; remove to wire racks to cool.

Makes approximately 5 dozen cookies

Tip: *Cookie dough can be frozen and baked in small batches when needed.*

Favorite recipe from **The Sugar Association, Inc.**

Chocolate Bunny Cookies

Dutch Chocolate Meringues

¼ cup finely chopped pecans
2½ tablespoons unsweetened cocoa powder
    (preferably Dutch process)
 3 large egg whites
¼ teaspoon salt
¾ cup sugar
    Powdered sugar (optional)

1. Preheat oven to 200°F. Line cookie sheets with foil; grease well. Set aside. Place pecans and cocoa in medium bowl; stir to combine.

2. Beat egg whites and salt in clean large bowl with electric mixer at high speed until light and foamy. Gradually beat in sugar until stiff peaks form.

3. Gently fold in pecan mixture until evenly blended.

4. Spoon batter into pastry bag fitted with large plain tip. Pipe 1-inch mounds 2 inches apart on prepared cookie sheets. Bake 1 hour. Turn oven off. *Do not open oven door;* let stand in oven until set, 2 hours or overnight.

5. When cookies are firm, carefully peel cookies from foil. Dust with powdered sugar, if desired. Store loosely covered at room temperature up to 2 days.   *Makes about 6 dozen cookies*

Meringue Mushrooms: *Pipe same number of 1-inch-tall "stems" as mounds. Bake as directed in step 4. When cookies are firm, attach "stems" to "caps" with melted chocolate. Dust with sifted unsweetened cocoa powder.*

Chocolate Malted Cookies

¾ cup firmly packed light brown sugar
⅔ CRISCO® Stick or ⅔ cup CRISCO
    all-vegetable shortening
 1 teaspoon vanilla
 1 egg
1¾ cups all-purpose flour
½ cup malted milk powder
⅓ cup unsweetened cocoa powder
¾ teaspoon baking soda
½ teaspoon salt
 2 cups malted milk balls, broken into large
    pieces*

*Place malted milk balls in heavy resealable plastic bag; break malted milk balls with rolling pin or back of heavy spoon.

1. Heat oven to 375°F. Place sheets of foil on countertop for cooling cookies.

2. Place brown sugar, shortening and vanilla in large bowl. Beat at medium speed of electric mixer until well blended. Add egg; beat well.

3. Combine flour, malted milk powder, cocoa, baking soda and salt. Add to shortening mixture; beat at low speed just until blended. Stir in malted milk pieces.

4. Drop dough by rounded measuring tablespoonfuls 2 inches apart onto ungreased baking sheets.

5. Bake one baking sheet at a time at 375°F for 7 to 9 minutes or until cookies are set. *Do not overbake.* Cool 2 minutes on baking sheets. Remove cookies to foil.   *Makes about 3 dozen cookies*

*Dutch Chocolate Meringues and
Meringue Mushrooms*

Peanut Butter & Jelly Cookies

1 package DUNCAN HINES® Peanut Butter Cookie Mix
¾ cup quick-cooking oats (not instant or old-fashioned)
1 egg
¼ cup CRISCO® Oil or CRISCO® PURITAN® Canola Oil
½ cup grape jelly
½ cup confectioners sugar
2 teaspoons water

1. Preheat oven to 375°F.

2. Combine cookie mix, peanut butter packet from Mix, oats, egg and oil in large bowl. Stir until thoroughly blended. Divide dough into 4 equal portions. Shape each portion into 12-inch-long log on waxed paper. Place logs on ungreased cookie sheets. Press back of spoon down center of each log to form indentation. Bake at 375°F for 10 to 12 minutes or until light golden brown. Press back of spoon down center of each log again. Cool 2 minutes on cookie sheets. Remove to cooling racks. Cool completely. Spoon 2 tablespoons jelly along indentation of each log.

3. Combine confectioners sugar and water in small bowl. Stir until smooth. Drizzle over each log. Allow glaze to set. Cut each log diagonally into 12 slices with large, sharp knife. Store between layers of waxed paper in airtight container.

Makes about 48 cookies

Double Almond Butter Cookies

2 cups softened butter
2½ cups powdered sugar, sifted, divided
4 cups flour
2¼ teaspoons vanilla, divided
⅔ cup BLUE DIAMOND® Blanched Almond Paste
¼ cup firmly packed light brown sugar
½ cup BLUE DIAMOND® Chopped Natural Almonds, toasted

Beat butter with 1 cup powdered sugar. Gradually beat in flour. Beat in 2 teaspoons vanilla. Cover and chill dough 30 minutes. Combine almond paste, brown sugar, almonds, and remaining ¼ teaspoon vanilla. Shape dough around ½ teaspoon almond paste mixture, forming 1-inch balls. Place on ungreased baking pans. Bake in preheated 350°F oven 15 minutes. Cool. Roll cookies in remaining 1½ cups powdered sugar or sift powdered sugar over cookies.

Makes 8 dozen cookies

Oatmeal Raisin Cookies

¾ cup all-purpose flour
¾ teaspoon salt
½ teaspoon baking soda
½ teaspoon ground cinnamon
¾ cup (1½ sticks) butter or margarine, softened
¾ cup granulated sugar
¾ cup packed light brown sugar
1 egg
1 tablespoon water
1 tablespoon vanilla, divided
3 cups uncooked quick or old-fashioned oats
1 cup raisins
½ cup powdered sugar
1 tablespoon milk

Preheat oven to 375°F. Grease cookie sheets; set aside. Combine flour, salt, baking soda and cinnamon in small bowl.

Beat butter, granulated sugar and brown sugar in large bowl with electric mixer at medium speed until light and fluffy. Add egg, water and 2 teaspoons vanilla; beat well. Add flour mixture; beat at low speed just until blended. Stir in oats with spoon. Stir in raisins. Drop tablespoonfuls of dough 2 inches apart onto prepared cookie sheets.

Bake 10 to 11 minutes or until edges are golden brown. Let cookies stand 2 minutes on cookie sheets; transfer to wire racks to cool completely.

For glaze, stir powdered sugar, milk and remaining 1 teaspoon vanilla in small bowl until smooth. Drizzle over cookies with fork or spoon. Store cookies tightly covered at room temperature or freeze up to 3 months.   *Makes about 48 cookies*

Luscious Cookie Drops made with Milky Way® Bars

3 MILKY WAY® Bars (2.15 ounces each), chopped, divided
2 tablespoons milk
½ cup butter or margarine, softened
⅓ cup packed light brown sugar
1 egg
½ teaspoon vanilla extract
1⅔ cups all-purpose flour
½ teaspoon baking soda
¼ teaspoon salt
½ cup chopped walnuts

Preheat oven to 350°F. Stir 1 Milky Way® Bar with milk in small saucepan over low heat until melted and smooth; cool. In large bowl, beat butter and brown sugar until creamy. Beat in egg, vanilla and melted Milky Way® Bar mixture. Combine flour, baking soda and salt in small bowl. Stir into chocolate mixture. Add remaining chopped Milky Way® Bars and nuts; stir gently. Drop dough by rounded teaspoonfuls onto ungreased cookie sheets.

Bake 12 to 15 minutes or until cookies are just firm to the touch. Cool on wire racks.

Makes about 2 dozen cookies

Prep time: 20 minutes
Bake time: 15 minutes

Oatmeal Raisin Cookies

Mini Pecan Tarts

TART SHELLS

  2 cups all-purpose flour
  1 teaspoon granulated sugar
    Pinch salt
1½ sticks cold butter or margarine, cut into
    pieces
⅓ cup ice water

FILLING

  1 cup powdered sugar
  ½ cup butter or margarine
  ⅓ cup dark corn syrup
  1 cup chopped pecans
  36 pecan halves

For tart shells, combine flour, granulated sugar and salt in large bowl. Using pastry blender or two knives, cut butter into dry ingredients until mixture resembles coarse cornmeal. Add water, 1 tablespoon at a time, kneading mixture until dough forms a ball. Wrap dough in plastic wrap; flatten dough and refrigerate at least 30 minutes.

Preheat oven to 375°F. Grease mini-muffin pans. Roll out dough on lightly floured surface to ⅛-inch thickness. Cut out 3-inch circles using cookie cutter; press into prepared mini-muffin cups and bake about 8 minutes or until very lightly browned. Remove from oven. *Reduce oven temperature to 350°F.*

For filling, combine powdered sugar, ½ cup butter and corn syrup in 2-quart saucepan. Cook over medium heat, stirring occasionally, until mixture comes to a full boil, 4 to 5 minutes. Remove from heat; stir in chopped pecans. Spoon into warm baked shells. Top each with pecan half. Bake 5 minutes. Cool completely; remove from pans.

Makes 3 dozen tarts

No-Bake Gingersnap Balls

  20 gingersnap cookies (about 5 ounces)
  3 tablespoons dark corn syrup
  2 tablespoons creamy peanut butter
  ⅓ cup powdered sugar

1. Place cookies in large resealable plastic food storage bag; crush finely with rolling pin or meat mallet.

2. Combine corn syrup and peanut butter in medium bowl. Add crushed gingersnaps; mix well. (Mixture should hold together without being sticky. If mixture is too dry, stir in additional tablespoon corn syrup.)

3. Roll mixture into 24 (1-inch) balls; coat with powdered sugar. *Makes 24 cookies*

No-Bake Gingersnap Balls

Peanut Butter Cut-Out Cookies

½ cup butter or margarine
1 cup REESE'S® Peanut Butter Chips
⅔ cup packed light brown sugar
1 egg
¾ teaspoon vanilla extract
1⅓ cups all-purpose flour
¾ teaspoon baking soda
½ cup finely chopped pecans
Chocolate Chip Glaze (recipe follows)

In medium saucepan, place butter and peanut butter chips; cook over low heat, stirring constantly, until melted. Pour into large bowl; add brown sugar, egg and vanilla, beating until well blended. Stir in flour, baking soda and pecans, blending well. Refrigerate 15 to 20 minutes or until firm enough to roll.

Heat oven to 350°F. Roll small portion of dough at a time on lightly floured board, or between 2 pieces of waxed paper to ¼-inch thickness. (Keep remaining dough in refrigerator.) With cookie cutters, cut dough into desired shapes; place on ungreased cookie sheets. Bake 7 to 8 minutes or until almost set (do not overbake). Cool 1 minute; remove from cookie sheets to wire racks. Cool completely. Drizzle Chocolate Chip Glaze onto each cookie; allow to set.

Makes about 3 dozen cookies

Chocolate Chip Glaze: In small microwave-safe bowl, place 1 cup HERSHEY'S Semi-Sweet Chocolate Chips and 1 tablespoon shortening (do not use butter, margarine or oil). Microwave at HIGH (100%) 1 minute; stir. If necessary, microwave an additional 15 seconds at a time, stirring after each heating, just until chips are melted when stirred. Makes about ⅔ cup glaze.

Peanut Gems

2½ cups all-purpose flour
1 teaspoon baking powder
⅛ teaspoon salt
1 cup (2 sticks) butter, softened
1 cup packed light brown sugar
2 eggs
2 teaspoons vanilla
1½ cups cocktail peanuts, finely chopped
Powdered sugar (optional)

Preheat oven to 350°F. Combine flour, baking powder and salt in small bowl. Beat butter in large bowl with electric mixer at medium speed until smooth. Gradually beat in brown sugar; increase speed to medium-high and beat until light and fluffy.

Beat in eggs, 1 at a time, until fluffy. Beat in vanilla. Gradually stir in flour mixture until blended. Stir in peanuts until blended. Drop heaping tablespoonfuls of dough about 1 inch apart onto *ungreased* cookie sheets; flatten slightly with hands.

Bake 12 minutes or until set. Let cookies stand on cookie sheets 5 minutes; transfer to wire racks to cool completely. Dust cookies with powdered sugar, if desired. Store in airtight container.

Makes 30 cookies

Peanut Gems

Bar Cookie Bonanza

Chippy Chewy Bars

½ cup (1 stick) butter or margarine
1½ cups graham cracker crumbs
1⅔ cups (10-ounce package) REESE'S® Peanut Butter Chips, divided
1½ cups MOUNDS® Sweetened Coconut Flakes
1 can (14 ounces) sweetened condensed milk (not evaporated milk)
1 cup HERSHEY'S Semi-Sweet Chocolate Chips or HERSHEY'S MINICHIPS Semi-Sweet Chocolate
1½ teaspoons shortening (do not use butter, margarine or oil)

1. Heat oven to 350°F.

2. Place butter in 13×9×2-inch baking pan. Heat in oven until melted. Remove pan from oven. Sprinkle graham cracker crumbs evenly over butter; press down with fork. Layer 1 cup peanut butter chips over crumbs; sprinkle coconut over peanut butter chips. Layer remaining ⅔ cup peanut butter chips over coconut; drizzle sweetened condensed milk evenly over top.

3. Bake 20 minutes or until lightly browned.

4. In small microwave-safe bowl, place chocolate chips and shortening. Microwave at HIGH (100%) 1 minute; stir. If necessary, microwave at HIGH an additional 15 seconds at a time, stirring after each heating, just until chips are melted when stirred. Drizzle evenly over top of baked mixture. Cool completely in pan on wire rack. Cut into bars.

Makes about 48 bars

Note: *For lighter drizzle, use ½ cup chocolate chips and ¾ teaspoon shortening. Microwave at HIGH 30 seconds to 1 minute; stir. If necessary, microwave at HIGH an additional 15 seconds at a time, stirring after each heating, just until chips are melted when stirred.*

Chippy Chewy Bars

Fruit and Oat Squares

1 cup all-purpose flour
1 cup uncooked quick oats
¾ cup packed light brown sugar
½ teaspoon baking soda
¼ teaspoon salt
¼ teaspoon ground cinnamon
⅓ cup margarine or butter, melted
¾ cup apricot, cherry or other fruit flavor
    preserves

1. Preheat oven to 350°F. Spray 9-inch square baking pan with nonstick cooking spray; set aside.

2. Combine flour, oats, brown sugar, baking soda, salt and cinnamon in medium bowl; mix well. Add margarine; stir with fork until mixture is crumbly.

3. Reserve ¾ cup crumb mixture for topping. Press remaining crumb mixture evenly onto bottom of prepared pan. Bake 5 to 7 minutes or until lightly browned.

4. Spread preserves onto crust; sprinkle with reserved crumb mixture.

5. Bake 20 to 25 minutes or until golden brown. Cool completely in pan on wire rack. Cut into 16 squares. *Makes 16 servings*

Chewy Rocky Road Bars

1½ cups finely crushed unsalted pretzels
¾ cup (1½ sticks) butter or margarine, melted
1 can (14 ounces) sweetened condensed milk
    (not evaporated milk)
2 cups miniature marshmallows
1 cup HERSHEY'S Butterscotch Chips
1 cup HERSHEY'S Semi-Sweet Chocolate
    Chips
1 cup MOUNDS® Sweetened Coconut Flakes
¾ cup chopped nuts

Heat oven to 350°F. In small bowl, combine pretzels and butter; spread mixture onto bottom of ungreased 13×9×2-inch baking pan. Pour sweetened condensed milk over crumb mixture; spread to edges of pan. Top with marshmallows, butterscotch chips, chocolate chips, coconut and nuts. Press toppings firmly into sweetened condensed milk. Bake 25 to 30 minutes or until lightly browned. Cool completely in pan on wire rack. Cut into bars. *Makes about 36 bars*

Note: 1⅔ cups (10-ounce package) HERSHEY'S Butterscotch Chips or 2 cups (12-ounce package) HERSHEY'S Semi-Sweet Chocolate Chips may be used instead of 1 cup of each flavor.

Fruit and Oat Squares

Marshmallow Krispie Bars

1 package (19.8 ounces) DUNCAN HINES®
   Chewy Fudge Brownie Mix
1 package (10½ ounces) miniature
   marshmallows
1½ cups semi-sweet chocolate chips
1 cup JIF® Creamy Peanut Butter
1 tablespoon butter or margarine
1½ cups crisp rice cereal

1. Preheat oven to 350°F. Grease bottom of 13×9-inch pan.

2. Prepare and bake brownies following package directions for basic recipe. Remove from oven. Sprinkle marshmallows on hot brownies. Return to oven. Bake for 3 minutes longer.

3. Place chocolate chips, peanut butter and butter in medium saucepan. Cook over low heat, stirring constantly, until chips are melted. Add rice cereal; mix well. Spread mixture over marshmallow layer. Refrigerate until chilled. Cut into bars.

Makes about 2 dozen bars

Tip: *For a special presentation, cut cookies into diamond shapes.*

Rainbow Blondies

1 cup (2 sticks) butter or margarine, softened
1½ cups firmly packed light brown sugar
1 large egg
1 teaspoon vanilla extract
2 cups all-purpose flour
½ teaspoon baking soda
1¾ cups "M&M's"® Semi-Sweet or Milk
   Chocolate Mini Baking Bits
1 cup chopped walnuts or pecans

Preheat oven to 350°F. Lightly grease 13×9×2-inch baking pan; set aside. In large bowl cream butter and sugar until light and fluffy; beat in egg and vanilla. In medium bowl combine flour and baking soda; add to creamed mixture just until combined. *Dough will be stiff.* Stir in "M&M's"® Chocolate Mini Baking Bits and nuts. Spread dough into prepared baking pan. Bake 30 to 35 minutes or until toothpick inserted in center comes out with moist crumbs. *Do not overbake.* Cool completely. Cut into bars. Store in tightly covered container.

Makes 24 bars

Marshmallow Krispie Bars

Luscious Lemon Bars

    2 cups all-purpose flour
    1 cup (2 sticks) butter
    ½ cup powdered sugar
    4 teaspoons finely grated lemon peel, divided
    ¼ teaspoon salt
    1 cup granulated sugar
    3 large eggs
    ⅓ cup fresh lemon juice
       Sifted powdered sugar

1. Preheat oven to 350°F. Grease 13×9-inch baking pan; set aside. Place flour, butter, powdered sugar, 1 teaspoon lemon peel and salt in food processor. Process until mixture forms coarse crumbs.

2. Press mixture evenly into prepared pan. Bake 18 to 20 minutes or until golden brown.

3. Beat granulated sugar, eggs, lemon juice and remaining 3 teaspoons lemon peel in medium bowl with electric mixer at medium speed until well blended.

4. Pour mixture evenly over warm crust. Return to oven; bake 18 to 20 minutes or until center is set and edges are golden brown. Remove pan to wire rack; cool completely.

5. Dust with sifted powdered sugar; cut into 2×1½-inch bars. Store tightly covered at room temperature. *Do not freeze.*   *Makes 3 dozen bars*

Banana Chocolate Chip Bars

    1 cup plus 2 tablespoons all-purpose flour
    1 cup plus 2 tablespoons rolled oats
    ¼ cup plus 2 tablespoons DOLE® Chopped
       Almonds, toasted
    ½ teaspoon baking soda
    ¼ teaspoon salt
    ¾ cup packed brown sugar
    ½ cup margarine
    2 small, ripe DOLE® Bananas, peeled
    ½ cup chocolate chips
    ½ teaspoon grated orange peel

• Combine flour, oats, almonds, baking soda and salt.

• Beat sugar and margarine until light and fluffy. Add flour mixture and beat until well combined. Press half of mixture in 8-inch square baking pan coated with vegetable spray. Bake in 350°F oven 10 to 12 minutes. Cool.

• Dice bananas (1½ cups). Combine with chocolate chips and orange peel. Spread over cooked crust. Top with remaining flour mixture. Press lightly. Bake 20 to 25 minutes until golden.

• Cut into bars.   *Makes 12 bars*

Prep time: 20 minutes
Bake time: 35 minutes

Luscious Lemon Bars

Easy Linzer Bars

2 cups flour
½ cup sugar
¾ teaspoon baking soda
½ teaspoon cinnamon
½ teaspoon grated lemon peel
½ cup (1 stick) MAZOLA® Margarine or
    butter
¼ cup KARO® Light Corn Syrup
½ cup seedless raspberry preserves
⅓ cup finely chopped walnuts
⅔ cup confectioners sugar
1 tablespoon milk

1. Preheat oven to 350°F. In large bowl combine flour, sugar, baking soda, cinnamon and lemon peel; set aside. In small saucepan heat margarine and corn syrup over low heat until margarine melts. Stir into flour mixture until blended. Divide dough into 5 equal pieces.

2. On large ungreased cookie sheet, pat each piece of dough into 14×1-inch rope. Combine raspberry preserves and walnuts. Make an indentation down center of each rope; fill with preserve mixture, mounding slightly.

3. Bake 12 to 14 minutes or until lightly browned. Remove from oven; immediately cut diagonally into 1-inch-wide slices.

4. In small bowl stir confectioners sugar and milk until smooth. Drizzle over warm cookies. Cool on wire racks. *Makes about 5 dozen cookies*

Prep time: 20 minutes
Bake time: 12 minutes, plus cooling

Pumpkin Harvest Bars

1¾ cups all-purpose flour
2 teaspoons baking powder
1 teaspoon grated orange peel
1 teaspoon ground cinnamon
½ teaspoon salt
½ teaspoon ground nutmeg
¼ teaspoon ground ginger
¼ teaspoon ground cloves
¾ cup sugar
½ cup MOTT'S® Natural Apple Sauce
½ cup solid-pack pumpkin
1 whole egg
1 egg white
2 tablespoons vegetable oil
½ cup raisins

1. Preheat oven to 350°F. Spray 13×9-inch baking pan with nonstick cooking spray.

2. In small bowl, combine flour, baking powder, orange peel, cinnamon, salt, nutmeg, ginger and cloves.

3. In large bowl, combine sugar, apple sauce, pumpkin, whole egg, egg white and oil.

4. Add flour mixture to apple sauce mixture; stir until well blended. Stir in raisins. Spread batter into prepared pan.

5. Bake 25 to 30 minutes or until toothpick inserted in center comes out clean. Cool on wire rack 15 minutes; cut into 16 bars.
Makes 16 servings

Pumpkin Harvest Bars

Chocolate Caramel Nut Bars

1 package (18¼ ounces) devil's food cake mix
¾ cup (1½ sticks) butter or margarine, melted
½ cup milk, divided
60 vanilla caramels
1 cup cashew pieces, coarsely chopped
1 cup semisweet chocolate chips

Preheat oven to 350°F. Grease 13×9-inch baking pan. Combine cake mix, butter and ¼ cup milk in medium bowl; mix well. Press half of batter into bottom of prepared pan.

Bake 7 to 8 minutes or until batter just begins to form crust. Remove from oven. Meanwhile, combine caramels and remaining ¼ cup milk in heavy medium saucepan. Cook over low heat, stirring often, about 5 minutes or until caramels are melted and mixture is smooth.

Pour melted caramel mixture over partially baked crust. Combine cashews and chocolate chips; sprinkle over caramel mixture.

Drop spoonfuls of remaining batter evenly over nut mixture. Return pan to oven; bake 18 to 20 minutes more or until top cake layer springs back when lightly touched. (Caramel center will be soft.) Cool on wire rack before cutting into squares or bars. (Bars can be frozen; let thaw 20 to 25 minutes before serving.) *Makes about 48 bars*

Strawberry Pecan Jumbles

1¼ cups all-purpose flour
½ cup CREAM OF WHEAT® Cereal (½-minute, 2½-minute or 10-minute stovetop cooking)
⅓ cup PLANTERS® Gold Measure Pecans, chopped
⅓ cup sugar
½ teaspoon DAVIS® Baking Powder
½ cup FLEISCHMANN'S® Margarine, melted
1 egg, slightly beaten
1 teaspoon vanilla extract
½ cup strawberry preserves*

*Any flavor preserves may be substituted.

In large bowl, combine flour, cereal, pecans, sugar and baking powder; stir in margarine, egg and vanilla until crumbly. Reserve ½ cup dough. Press remaining dough on bottom of greased 9×9×2-inch baking pan. Spread strawberry preserves evenly over dough. Crumble reserved dough over preserves. Bake at 375°F for 18 to 20 minutes or until golden brown. Cool completely in pan on wire rack. Cut into bars to serve. *Makes 18 bars*

Chocolate Caramel Nut Bars

Dish: Bar Cookies   **Recipe**   Serves:

Chocolate-Caramel-Nut Bars
1 package (18 1/4 ounces) devils food cake mix
3/4 cup butter or margarine, melted
1/2 cup milk, divided
60 vanilla caramels
1 cup cashew pieces, coarsely chopped
1 cup semisweet chocolate chips

PREHEAT oven to 350°F. Grease 13x9 inch ba[...]
Combine cake mix, butter and 1/4 cup milk in m[...]

Orange Coconut Cream Bars

- 1 (18¼-ounce) package yellow cake mix
- 1 cup quick-cooking or old-fashioned oats, uncooked
- ¾ cup chopped nuts
- ½ cup (1 stick) butter or margarine, melted
- 1 large egg
- 1 (14-ounce) can sweetened condensed milk
- 2 teaspoons grated orange zest
- 1 cup shredded coconut
- 1 cup "M&M's"® Semi-Sweet Chocolate Mini Baking Bits

Preheat oven to 375°F. Lightly grease 13×9×2-inch baking pan; set aside. In large bowl combine cake mix, oats, nuts, butter and egg until ingredients are thoroughly moistened and mixture resembles coarse crumbs. Reserve 1 cup mixture. Firmly press remaining mixture onto bottom of prepared pan; bake 10 minutes. In separate bowl combine condensed milk and orange zest; spread over baked base. Combine reserved crumb mixture, coconut and "M&M's"® Semi-Sweet Chocolate Mini Baking Bits; sprinkle evenly over condensed milk mixture and press in lightly. Continue baking 20 to 25 minutes or until golden brown. Cool completely. Cut into bars. Store in tightly covered container.

Makes 26 bars

Lemon Nut Bars

- 1⅓ cups flour
- ½ cup packed brown sugar
- ¼ cup granulated sugar
- ¾ cup butter or margarine
- 1 cup old-fashioned or quick oats, uncooked
- ½ cup chopped nuts
- 1 (8-ounce) package PHILADELPHIA BRAND® Cream Cheese, softened
- 1 egg
- 3 tablespoons lemon juice
- 1 tablespoon grated lemon peel

Preheat oven to 350°F. Stir together flour and sugars in medium bowl. Cut in butter until mixture resembles coarse crumbs. Stir in oats and nuts. Reserve 1 cup crumb mixture; press remaining crumb mixture onto bottom of greased 13×9-inch baking pan. Bake 15 minutes. Beat cream cheese, egg, lemon juice and peel in small bowl at medium speed with electric mixer until well blended. Pour over crust; sprinkle with reserved crumb mixture. Bake 25 minutes. Cool; cut into bars.

Makes about 36 bars

Prep time: 30 minutes
Bake time: 25 minutes

Orange Coconut Cream Bars

Wild Rice Applesauce Bars

BARS:
- 2 cups well-cooked wild rice
- 1 cup buttermilk or sour milk, divided
- 1 cup applesauce
- ¼ cup vegetable oil
- ¾ cup shortening
- 1 cup firmly packed brown sugar
- 3 eggs
- 2 teaspoons vanilla
- 2½ cups all-purpose flour
- 1 teaspoon baking soda
- 1 teaspoon salt
- 1 teaspoon cinnamon
- 1 cup chopped nuts

FROSTING:
- ½ cup butter or margarine, softened
- 4 cups powdered sugar
- ¼ cup cold strong coffee
- 2 teaspoons vanilla

Preheat oven to 350°F. Grease bottom of 15×10×1-inch jelly-roll pan. In medium bowl, combine wild rice, ½ cup buttermilk, applesauce and oil; set aside. In large bowl, combine shortening, brown sugar, eggs and vanilla; beat at high speed 5 minutes or until smooth and creamy. Add remaining ½ cup buttermilk; beat at low speed until well-blended. Add flour, baking soda, salt and cinnamon; beat at low speed until well-blended. Stir in wild rice mixture and nuts. Spread in prepared pan. Bake 20 to 25 minutes or until toothpick inserted in center comes out clean. Cool completely.

In medium bowl, combine all frosting ingredients; beat at high speed until smooth and creamy. Frost cooled bars. *Makes 48 bars*

Favorite recipe from **Minnesota Cultivated Wild Rice Council**

No-Fuss Bar Cookies

- 2 cups graham cracker crumbs (about 24 graham cracker squares)
- 1 cup semisweet chocolate chips
- 1 cup flaked coconut
- ¾ cup coarsely chopped walnuts
- 1 can (14 ounces) sweetened condensed milk

Preheat oven to 350°F. Combine crumbs, chips, coconut and walnuts in medium bowl; toss to blend. Add milk; mix until blended. Spread batter into greased 13×9-inch baking pan. Bake 15 to 18 minutes or until edges are golden brown. Let pan stand on wire rack until completely cooled. Cut into 2¼-inch squares. *Makes about 20 bars*

No-Fuss Bar Cookies

Heavenly Oat Bars

½ cup (1 stick) MAZOLA® Margarine,
    softened
½ cup packed brown sugar
½ cup KARO® Light or Dark Corn Syrup
 1 teaspoon vanilla
 3 cups uncooked quick or old-fashioned oats
 1 cup (6 ounces) semisweet chocolate chips
½ cup SKIPPY® Creamy Peanut Butter

1. Preheat oven to 350°F. Lightly grease 9-inch square baking pan.

2. In large bowl with mixer at medium speed, beat margarine, brown sugar, corn syrup and vanilla until blended and smooth. Stir in oats. Spread in prepared pan.

3. Bake 25 minutes or until center is just firm. Cool slightly on wire rack.

4. In small heavy saucepan over low heat, stir chocolate chips until melted and smooth. Remove from heat; stir in peanut butter until smooth. Spread over warm bars. Cool completely on wire rack before cutting. *Makes 24 bars*

Prep time: 15 minutes
Bake time: 25 minutes, plus cooling

Tips: To melt chocolate chips in microwave, place chips in dry microwavable bowl or glass measuring cup. Microwave on HIGH (100%), 1 minute; stir. Microwave 1 minute longer. Stir until chocolate is smooth.

For quick cleanup and easy cutting, line pan with foil, overlapping sides slightly. Grease foil lightly. When completely cool, lift out of pan by holding edges of foil. Peel off foil. Cut into bars.

Norwegian Almond Bars

1¾ cups all-purpose flour
 1 cup sugar
¼ cup ground almonds
 1 cup (2 sticks) butter or margarine, softened
 1 egg
 1 teaspoon ground cinnamon
½ teaspoon salt
 1 egg white
¾ cup sliced almonds

Preheat oven to 350°F. In large bowl combine flour, sugar, ground almonds, butter, egg, cinnamon and salt. Beat at low speed, scraping bowl often, until well mixed, 2 to 3 minutes. Divide dough in half. Place each half on separate cookie sheet; press to 1/16-inch thickness. In small bowl, beat egg white with fork until foamy. Brush over dough; sprinkle with almonds. Bake 12 to 15 minutes or until very lightly browned. Immediately cut into 2-inch squares and remove from cookie sheets. Cool; store in tightly covered container.

Makes 36 to 48 bars

Norwegian Almond Bars

Pecan Pie Bars

¾ cup (1½ sticks) butter or margarine
½ cup powdered sugar
1½ cups all-purpose flour
3 eggs
2 cups coarsely chopped pecans
1 cup granulated sugar
1 cup light corn syrup
2 tablespoons butter or margarine, melted
1 teaspoon vanilla

Preheat oven to 350°F. For crust, beat butter in large bowl with electric mixer at medium speed until smooth. Add powdered sugar; beat until well blended. Add flour gradually, beating at low speed after each addition. (Mixture will be crumbly but presses together easily.)

Press dough evenly into *ungreased* 13×9-inch baking pan. Press mixture slightly up sides of pan (less than ¼ inch) to form lip to hold filling.

Bake 20 to 25 minutes or until golden brown. Meanwhile, for filling, beat eggs lightly in medium bowl with fork. Add pecans, granulated sugar, corn syrup, melted butter and vanilla; mix well. Pour filling over partially baked crust. Return to oven; bake 35 to 40 minutes or until filling is set.

Loosen edges with knife. Cool completely on wire rack before cutting into squares. Cover and refrigerate until 10 to 15 minutes before serving time. *Do not freeze.*   *Makes about 48 bars*

Fruit and Chocolate Streusel Squares

1½ cups all-purpose flour
1½ cups quick or old-fashioned oats
½ cup granulated sugar
½ cup packed brown sugar
1 teaspoon baking powder
¼ teaspoon salt (optional)
1 cup (2 sticks) butter or margarine, softened
¾ cup raspberry, strawberry or apricot preserves
2 cups (12-ounce package) NESTLÉ® TOLL HOUSE® Semi-Sweet Chocolate Morsels
¼ cup chopped almonds
Powdered sugar (optional)

COMBINE flour, oats, granulated sugar, brown sugar, baking powder and salt in large bowl. Cut in butter with pastry blender or two knives; reserve *1 cup* oat mixture for topping. Press *remaining* oat mixture into greased 9-inch square baking pan. Spread preserves over crust; sprinkle with morsels.

COMBINE reserved oat mixture and nuts; sprinkle over morsels. Pat down lightly.

BAKE in preheated 375°F. oven for 30 to 35 minutes or until golden brown. Cool completely in pan on wire rack until chocolate is firm, or chill for 30 minutes to speed cooling. Sprinkle with powdered sugar.   *Makes 2½ dozen squares*

Pecan Pie Bars

Chocolate Chip Cookie Bars

1¼ cups firmly packed light brown sugar
¾ BUTTER FLAVOR* CRISCO® Stick or
    ¾ cup BUTTER FLAVOR CRISCO all-
    vegetable shortening
2 tablespoons milk
1 tablespoon vanilla
1 egg
1¾ cups all-purpose flour
1 teaspoon salt
¾ teaspoon baking soda
1 cup (6 ounces) semisweet chocolate chips
1 cup coarsely chopped pecans** (optional)

*Butter Flavor Crisco is artificially flavored.

**If pecans are omitted, add an additional ½ cup semisweet chocolate chips.

1. Heat oven to 350°F. Grease 13×9-inch baking pan. Place cooling rack on countertop.

2. Place brown sugar, shortening, milk and vanilla in large bowl. Beat at medium speed of electric mixer until well blended. Add egg; beat well.

3. Combine flour, salt and baking soda. Add to shortening mixture; beat at low speed just until blended. Stir in chocolate chips and pecans, if desired.

4. Press dough evenly onto bottom of prepared pan.

5. Bake at 350°F for 20 to 25 minutes or until lightly browned and firm in the center. *Do not overbake.* Cool completely on cooling rack. Cut into 2×1½-inch bars. *Makes about 3 dozen bars*

Rocky Road Peanut Butter Bars

3 quarts popped JOLLY TIME® Pop Corn
½ cup raisins
1 cup light corn syrup
1 tablespoon butter or margarine
½ cup peanut butter pieces
⅓ cup chunky or creamy peanut butter
¾ cup miniature marshmallows
½ cup peanuts
½ cup semi-sweet chocolate pieces
1 teaspoon vegetable shortening

Place popped pop corn and raisins in large bowl. In saucepan, heat corn syrup and butter to boiling. Boil 3 minutes. Remove from heat. Stir in peanut butter pieces and peanut butter until smooth. Pour mixture over pop corn, tossing gently to coat all pieces. Press into greased 9-inch square baking pan. Sprinkle marshmallows and peanuts over top, pressing lightly into pop corn mixture. Melt chocolate pieces and shortening over very low heat. Drizzle over top. Cool several hours before serving. Cut into 2¼×1-inch bars. *Makes 36 bars*

Chocolate Chip Cookie Bars

No-Bake Chocolate Oat Bars

1 cup (2 sticks) butter or margarine
½ cup firmly packed brown sugar
1 teaspoon vanilla
3 cups uncooked quick oats
1 cup semisweet chocolate chips
½ cup crunchy or creamy peanut butter

Grease 9-inch square baking pan. Melt butter in large saucepan over medium heat. Add sugar and vanilla; mix well. Stir in oats. Cook over low heat 2 to 3 minutes or until ingredients are well blended. Press half of mixture into prepared pan. Use back of large spoon to spread mixture evenly.

Melt chocolate chips in small heavy saucepan over low heat, stirring occasionally. Stir in peanut butter. Pour chocolate mixture over oat mixture in pan; spread evenly with knife or back of spoon. Crumble remaining oat mixture over chocolate layer, pressing in gently. Cover and refrigerate 2 to 3 hours or overnight.

Bring to room temperature before cutting into bars. (Bars can be frozen; let thaw at least 10 minutes before serving.)

Makes 32 bars

The Original Kellogg's® Rice Krispies Treats® Recipe

3 tablespoons margarine
1 package (10 ounces, about 40) regular marshmallows or 4 cups miniature marshmallows
6 cups KELLOGG'S® RICE KRISPIES® Cereal
Vegetable cooking spray

1. Melt margarine in large saucepan over low heat. Add marshmallows and stir until completely melted. Remove from heat.

2. Add Kellogg's® Rice Krispies® cereal. Stir until well coated.

3. Using buttered spatula or waxed paper, press mixture evenly into 13×9×2-inch pan coated with cooking spray. Cut into 2-inch squares when cool.

Makes 24 treats

Note: *Use fresh marshmallows for best results. Do not use diet or reduced fat margarine.*

Microwave Directions: Microwave margarine and marshmallows at HIGH 2 minutes in microwave-safe mixing bowl. Stir to combine. Microwave at HIGH 1 minute longer. Stir until smooth. Add cereal. Stir until well coated. Press into pan as directed in Step 3.

No-Bake Chocolate Oat Bars

Swirl of Chocolate Cheesecake Triangles

CRUST
2 cups graham cracker crumbs
½ cup (1 stick) butter or margarine, melted
⅓ cup granulated sugar

FILLING
2 packages (8 ounces each) cream cheese, softened
1 cup granulated sugar
¼ cup all-purpose flour
1½ cups (12-fluid-ounce can) CARNATION® Evaporated Milk
2 eggs
1 tablespoon vanilla extract
1 cup (6 ounces) NESTLÉ® TOLL HOUSE® Semi-Sweet Chocolate Morsels

FOR CRUST:
COMBINE graham cracker crumbs, butter and sugar in medium bowl; press onto bottom of ungreased 13×9-inch baking pan.

FOR FILLING:
BEAT cream cheese, sugar and flour in large mixer bowl until smooth. Gradually beat in evaporated milk, eggs and vanilla.

MICROWAVE morsels in medium, microwave-safe bowl on HIGH (100%) power for 1 minute; stir. Microwave at additional 10- to 20-second intervals, stirring until smooth. Stir 1 cup cream cheese mixture into chocolate. Pour remaining cream cheese mixture over crust. Pour chocolate mixture over cream cheese mixture; swirl mixture with spoon, pulling plain cream cheese mixture up to surface.

BAKE in preheated 325°F. oven for 40 to 45 minutes or until set. Cool to room temperature; chill until firm. Cut into 15 rectangles; cut each rectangle in half diagonally to form triangles.

Makes 2½ dozen triangles

Peanut Butter Bars

1 package DUNCAN HINES® Peanut Butter Cookie Mix
2 egg whites
¼ cup CRISCO® Oil or CRISCO® PURITAN® Canola Oil
½ cup chopped peanuts
1 cup confectioners sugar
2 tablespoons water
½ teaspoon vanilla extract

1. Preheat oven to 350°F.

2. Combine cookie mix, peanut butter packet from Mix, egg whites and oil in large bowl. Stir until thoroughly blended. Press into ungreased 13×9×2-inch pan. Sprinkle peanuts over dough. Press lightly.

3. Bake at 350°F for 18 to 20 minutes or until golden brown. Cool completely. Combine confectioners sugar, water and vanilla extract in small bowl. Stir until blended. Drizzle glaze over top. Cut into bars. *Makes 24 bars*

Peanut Butter Bars

Naomi's Revel Bars

1 cup (2 sticks) plus 2 tablespoons butter or
   margarine, softened, divided
2 cups packed brown sugar
2 eggs
2 teaspoons vanilla
2½ cups all-purpose flour
1 teaspoon baking soda
3 cups uncooked quick or old-fashioned oats
1 package (12 ounces) semisweet chocolate
   chips
1 can (14 ounces) sweetened condensed milk

Preheat oven to 325°F. Lightly grease 13×9-inch baking pan. Beat 1 cup butter and sugar in large bowl with electric mixer until blended. Add eggs; beat until light. Blend in vanilla.

Combine flour and baking soda in medium bowl; stir into butter mixture. Stir in oats. Spread ¾ of oat mixture evenly in prepared pan. Combine chocolate chips, milk and remaining 2 tablespoons butter in heavy small saucepan. Stir over low heat until chocolate is melted. Pour chocolate mixture evenly over oat mixture in pan. Dot with remaining oat mixture.

Bake 20 to 25 minutes or until edges are browned and center feels firm. Cool on wire rack. Cut into bars.
Makes about 36 bars

Roman Meal Apple Squares

2 cups flour
1¼ cups brown sugar
½ cup ROMAN MEAL® Apple Cinnamon
   Cereal
½ cup margarine
1 cup chopped nuts
1 cup plain nonfat yogurt
1 egg, beaten
1 teaspoon vanilla
2 teaspoons cinnamon
1 teaspoon baking soda
½ teaspoon salt
2 cups chopped, peeled apples

In mixing bowl combine flour, brown sugar, cereal and margarine. Blend at low speed until crumbly. Stir in nuts. Press about 2¾ cups mixture into bottom of ungreased 13×9×2-inch pan. To remaining mixture, add yogurt, egg, vanilla, cinnamon, baking soda and salt. Beat until thoroughly combined. Stir in apples. Spoon over bottom layer in pan. Bake at 350°F 35 to 40 minutes or until cake tests done. Garnish with whipped cream, if desired.
Makes 24 servings

Naomi's Revel Bars

Pumpkin Cheesecake Bars

BASE AND TOPPING
- 2 cups all-purpose flour
- ⅔ cup packed light brown sugar
- ½ cup (1 stick) butter or margarine
- 1 cup finely chopped pecans

PUMPKIN CREAM CHEESE FILLING
- 11 ounces (one 8-ounce package and one 3-ounce package) cream cheese, softened
- 1¼ cups granulated sugar
- 1½ teaspoons vanilla extract
- 1½ teaspoons ground cinnamon
- ½ teaspoon ground allspice
- ¾ cup LIBBY'S® Solid Pack Pumpkin
- 3 eggs
- Glazed Pecans (recipe follows)

FOR BASE AND TOPPING:
COMBINE flour and brown sugar in medium bowl. Cut in butter with pastry blender or two knives until mixture resembles coarse crumbs; stir in nuts. Reserve *1½ cups* mixture for topping; press remaining mixture onto bottom of ungreased 13×9-inch baking pan. Bake in preheated 350°F. oven for 15 minutes.

FOR PUMPKIN CREAM CHEESE FILLING:
BEAT cream cheese, granulated sugar, vanilla, cinnamon and allspice in large mixer bowl until smooth. Beat in pumpkin and eggs. Spread over crust; sprinkle with *reserved* topping. Bake in 350°F.

oven for 25 to 30 minutes or until center is set. Cool in pan on wire rack; chill for several hours or until firm. Cut into bars; place Glazed Pecan half on each bar. *Makes 32 bar cookies*

Glazed Pecans: PLACE waxed paper under greased wire rack. Bring ¼ cup dark corn syrup to a boil in medium saucepan; boil, stirring occasionally, for 1 minute. Remove from heat; stir in 30 pecan halves. Remove pecan halves to wire rack. Turn right side up; separate. Cool.

Chocolate Pecan Pie Squares

- Bar Cookie Crust (page 125)
- 1½ cups KARO® Light or Dark Corn Syrup
- 1 cup (6 ounces) semisweet chocolate chips
- 1 cup sugar
- 4 eggs, slightly beaten
- 1½ teaspoons vanilla
- 2½ cups coarsely chopped pecans

1. Preheat oven to 350°F. Prepare Bar Cookie Crust according to recipe directions.

2. In large heavy saucepan combine corn syrup and chocolate chips. Stir over low heat just until chocolate melts. Remove from heat. Blend in sugar, eggs and vanilla. Stir in pecans. Pour over hot crust; spread evenly.

3. Bake 30 minutes or until filling is firm around edges and slightly firm in center. Cool completely on wire rack before cutting. *Makes 24 squares*

Prep time: 30 minutes
Bake time: 30 minutes, plus cooling

Crispy Chocolate Bars

1 package (6 ounces, 1 cup) semi-sweet chocolate morsels
1 package (6 ounces, 1 cup) butterscotch morsels
½ cup peanut butter
5 cups KELLOGG'S CORN FLAKES® cereal
Vegetable cooking spray

1. In large saucepan, combine chocolate and butterscotch chips and peanut butter. Stir over low heat until smooth. Remove from heat.

2. Add Kellogg's Corn Flakes® cereal. Stir until well coated.

3. Using buttered spatula or waxed paper, press mixture evenly into 9×9×2-inch pan coated with cooking spray. Cut into bars when cool.

Makes 16 bars

Bar Cookie Crust

MAZOLA NO STICK® Corn Oil Cooking Spray
2 cups flour
½ cup (1 stick) cold MAZOLA® Margarine or butter, cut into pieces
⅓ cup sugar
¼ teaspoon salt

1. Preheat oven to 350°F. Spray 13×9-inch baking pan with cooking spray.

2. In large bowl with mixer at medium speed, beat flour, margarine, sugar and salt until mixture resembles coarse crumbs. Press firmly into bottom and ¼ inch up sides of prepared pan.

3. Bake 15 minutes or until golden brown. Top with desired filling. Complete as recipe directs.

Prep time: 10 minutes
Bake time: 15 minutes

Chocolate Chip Walnut Bars

Bar Cookie Crust (page 125)
2 eggs
½ cup KARO® Light or Dark Corn Syrup
½ cup sugar
2 tablespoons MAZOLA® Margarine or butter, melted
1 cup (6 ounces) semisweet chocolate chips
¾ cup chopped walnuts

1. Preheat oven to 350°F. Prepare Bar Cookie Crust.

2. Meanwhile, in medium bowl beat eggs, corn syrup, sugar and margarine until well blended. Stir in chocolate chips and walnuts. Pour over hot crust; spread evenly.

3. Bake 15 to 18 minutes or until set. Cool completely on wire rack. Cut into 2×1½-inch bars.

Makes about 32 bars

Prep time: 30 minutes
Bake time: 30 minutes, plus cooling

Special Treat No-Bake Squares

½ cup plus 1 teaspoon butter or margarine,
    divided
¼ cup granulated sugar
¼ cup unsweetened cocoa
 1 large egg
¼ teaspoon salt
1½ cups graham cracker crumbs
¾ cup flaked coconut
½ cup chopped pecans
⅓ cup butter or margarine, softened
 1 package (3 ounces) cream cheese, softened
 1 teaspoon vanilla
 1 cup powdered sugar
 1 (2-ounce) dark sweet or bittersweet candy
    bar, broken into ½-inch pieces

Line 9-inch square pan with foil, shiny side up, allowing a 2-inch overhang on sides. Set aside.

For crust, combine ½ cup butter, granulated sugar, cocoa, egg and salt in medium saucepan. Cook over medium heat, stirring constantly, until mixture thickens, about 2 minutes. Remove from heat; stir in graham cracker crumbs, coconut and pecans. Press evenly into prepared pan.

For filling, beat ⅓ cup softened butter, cream cheese and vanilla in small bowl until smooth. Gradually beat in powdered sugar. Spread over crust; refrigerate 30 minutes.

For glaze, combine candy bar and remaining 1 teaspoon butter in small resealable plastic bag; seal. Microwave at HIGH (100%) 50 seconds. Turn bag

over; heat at HIGH 40 to 50 seconds or until melted. Knead bag until candy bar is smooth. Cut off tiny corner of bag; drizzle chocolate over filling. Refrigerate until firm, about 20 minutes. Remove foil from pan. Cut into 1½-inch squares.

Makes about 25 squares

Nutty Chocolate Chunk Bars

 3 eggs
 1 cup JACK FROST® Granulated Sugar
 1 cup JACK FROST® Brown Sugar, packed
 1 cup oat bran
 1 cup crunchy peanut butter
¾ cup butter
 2 teaspoons baking soda
 2 teaspoons vanilla
3½ cups quick-cooking oats
 1 cup Spanish peanuts
 1 package (12 ounces) semi-sweet chocolate
    chunks

In large bowl, beat eggs, granulated sugar and brown sugar. Add oat bran, peanut butter, butter, baking soda and vanilla. Mix well. Stir in oats, peanuts and chocolate chunks. Spread mixture into greased 15×10×2-inch pan. Bake in 350°F oven 20 to 25 minutes.

Makes 36 bars

Special Treat No-Bake Squares

Oatmeal Chocolate Cherry Bars

½ cup (1 stick) butter or margarine, softened
¼ cup solid vegetable shortening
1 cup firmly packed light brown sugar
1 large egg
1 teaspoon vanilla extract
2½ cups quick-cooking or old-fashioned oats, uncooked
1 cup all-purpose flour
1 teaspoon baking soda
1¾ cups "M&M's"® Chocolate Mini Baking Bits, divided
1 cup dried cherries, plumped*

*To plump cherries, pour 1½ cups boiling water over cherries and let stand 10 minutes. Drain well and use as directed.

Preheat oven to 350°F. Lightly grease 13×9×2-inch baking pan; set aside. In large bowl cream butter and shortening until light and fluffy; beat in sugar, egg and vanilla. In medium bowl combine oats, flour and baking soda; blend into creamed mixture. Stir in *1¼ cups "M&M's"® Chocolate Mini Baking Bits* and cherries. Spread batter evenly in prepared pan; top with remaining *½ cup "M&M's"® Chocolate Mini Baking Bits*. Bake 25 to 30 minutes or until toothpick inserted in center comes out clean. Cool completely. Cut into squares. Store in tightly covered container.   *Makes 24 bars*

Variation: To make cookies, drop dough by rounded tablespoonfuls about 2 inches apart onto lightly greased cookie sheets; place 4 to 5 pieces of remaining ½ cup "M&M's"® Chocolate Mini Baking Bits on top of each

cookie. Bake 13 to 15 minutes. Cool 2 to 3 minutes on cookie sheets; remove to wire racks to cool completely. Store in tightly covered container. Makes about 4 dozen cookies.

Apple Crumb Squares

2 cups QUAKER® Oats (Quick or Old Fashioned), uncooked
1½ cups all-purpose flour
1 cup packed brown sugar
¾ cup butter or margarine, melted
1 teaspoon ground cinnamon
½ teaspoon baking soda
½ teaspoon salt (optional)
¼ teaspoon ground nutmeg
1 cup applesauce
½ cup chopped nuts

Preheat oven to 350°F. In large bowl, combine all ingredients except applesauce and nuts; mix until crumbly. Reserve 1 cup oats mixture. Press remaining mixture on bottom of greased 13×9-inch pan. Bake 13 to 15 minutes; cool. Spread applesauce over partially baked crust; sprinkle with nuts. Sprinkle reserved 1 cup oats mixture over top. Bake 13 to 15 minutes or until golden brown. Cool in pan on wire rack; cut into 2-inch squares.
Makes about 24 squares

Oatmeal Chocolate Cherry Bars

Mystical Layered Bars

⅓ cup margarine or butter
1 cup graham cracker crumbs
½ cup old-fashioned or quick oats
1 can (14 ounces) sweetened condensed milk
1 cup flaked coconut
¾ cup semisweet chocolate chips
¾ cup raisins
1 cup coarsely chopped pecans

Preheat oven to 350°F. Melt margarine in 13×9-inch baking pan. Remove pan from oven.

Sprinkle graham cracker crumbs and oats evenly over margarine; press down with fork. Drizzle condensed milk over oats. Layer coconut, chocolate chips, raisins and pecans over milk.

Bake 25 to 30 minutes or until lightly browned. Cool in pan on wire rack 5 minutes; cut into 2×1½-inch bars. Cool completely in pan on wire rack.

Store tightly covered at room temperature or freeze up to 3 months.

Makes 3 dozen bars

> Butter-rich bar cookies and brownies are the perfect choice for bake sales—they freeze very well so they can be made in advance whenever you have some time to spare.

Peanut Butter Cereal Treats

4 cups favorite ready-to-eat breakfast cereal*
  or combination of cereals
½ cup sugar
½ cup KARO® Light or Dark Corn Syrup
½ cup SKIPPY® SUPER CHUNK® or Creamy
  Peanut Butter

*If using flake cereal, increase amount to 5 cups.

1. Line 8- or 9-inch square baking pan with plastic wrap. Pour cereal into large bowl; set aside.

2. In medium saucepan combine sugar and corn syrup. Stirring occasionally, bring to a boil over medium heat; boil 1 minute. Remove from heat. Add peanut butter; stir until completely melted.

3. Pour over cereal; stir to coat well. Press evenly into prepared pan.

4. Cool about 15 minutes. Invert onto cutting board; remove plastic wrap. Cut into squares.

Makes 36 squares

Microwave Directions: Prepare pan as directed above. Pour cereal into large bowl. In 2-quart microwavable bowl combine sugar, corn syrup and peanut butter. Microwave at HIGH (100% power), 3½ to 4 minutes or until mixture is smooth and sugar is dissolved, stirring twice.

Mystical Layered Bars

Reese's® Bits Blondies

⅔ cup butter or margarine, softened
1 cup packed light brown sugar
½ cup granulated sugar
¾ cup REESE'S® Creamy or REESE'S®
    Crunchy Peanut Butter
2 eggs
1 teaspoon vanilla extract
⅓ cup milk
1¾ cups all-purpose flour
1 teaspoon baking powder
1⅓ cups (10-ounce package) REESE'S® Bits for
    Baking, divided
    Chocolate Brownie Frosting (recipe follows)

1. Heat oven to 325°F. Grease 13×9×2-inch baking pan.

2. In large bowl, beat butter, brown sugar, granulated sugar and peanut butter until creamy. Add eggs and vanilla; beat well. Gradually beat in milk. Gradually beat in flour and baking powder, beating thoroughly. Stir in 1 cup baking bits. Spread batter into prepared pan.

3. Bake 40 to 45 minutes or until wooden pick inserted in center comes out clean. Cool completely in pan on wire rack. Meanwhile, prepare Chocolate Brownie Frosting; spread over top of blondies. Sprinkle remaining ⅓ cup bits on top. Cut into bars. *Makes about 36 bars*

Chocolate Brownie Frosting

¼ cup (½ stick) butter or margarine, softened
¼ cup HERSHEY'S Cocoa
1 tablespoon light corn syrup
2 tablespoons milk
1 teaspoon vanilla extract
1½ cups powdered sugar

In medium bowl, beat butter, cocoa, corn syrup, milk and vanilla until smooth. Gradually add powdered sugar, beating until spreading consistency. *Makes about 1¼ cups frosting*

Grape Gingerbread Bars

1 package (14.5 ounces) gingerbread and
    cookie mix
⅓ cup chopped walnuts
½ cup lukewarm water
1 egg
1½ cups California seedless grapes

Combine gingerbread mix and walnuts; mix well. Stir in water and egg until well mixed. Spread batter in bottom of greased 15×10×1-inch jelly-roll pan. Place grapes on batter. Bake at 350°F about 20 minutes or until wooden pick inserted near center comes out clean. Cool in pan. Cut into bars. *Makes 24 bars*

Favorite recipe from **California Table Grape Commission**

Peachy Oatmeal Bars

CRUMB MIXTURE
 1½ cups all-purpose flour
 1 cup quick oats
 ½ cup sugar
 ¾ cup (1½ sticks) margarine, melted
 ½ teaspoon baking soda
 ¼ teaspoon salt
 2 teaspoons almond extract

FILLING
 ¾ cup peach preserves
 ⅓ cup flaked coconut

Preheat oven to 350°F. For crumb mixture, in large bowl combine all crumb mixture ingredients. Beat at low speed, scraping bowl often, until mixture is crumbly, 1 to 2 minutes. Reserve ¾ cup crumb mixture; press remaining crumb mixture onto bottom of greased 9-inch square baking pan.

For filling, spread peach preserves to within ½ inch of edge of crumb mixture; sprinkle reserved crumb mixture and coconut over top. Bake 22 to 27 minutes or until edges are lightly browned. Cool completely. Cut into bars. *Makes 24 to 30 bars*

Strawberry Streusel Bars

CRUMB MIXTURE
 2 cups all-purpose flour
 1 cup sugar
 ¾ cup pecans, coarsely chopped
 1 cup (2 sticks) butter or margarine, softened
 1 egg

FILLING
 1 jar (10 ounces) strawberry preserves

Preheat oven to 350°F. For crumb mixture, in large bowl combine all crumb mixture ingredients. Beat at low speed, scraping bowl often, 2 to 3 minutes or until mixture is crumbly. Reserve 1 cup crumb mixture; press remaining crumb mixture onto bottom of greased 9-inch square baking pan.

For filling, spread preserves to within ½ inch of edge of crumb mixture. Sprinkle reserved crumb mixture over preserves. Bake 42 to 50 minutes or until lightly browned. Cool completely. Cut into bars. *Makes about 24 bars*

Top to bottom: Peachy Oatmeal Bars and Strawberry Streusel Bars

Gooey Caramel Chocolate Bars

2 cups all-purpose flour
1 cup granulated sugar
¼ teaspoon salt
2 cups (4 sticks) butter or margarine, divided
1 cup packed light brown sugar
⅓ cup light corn syrup
1 cup (6 ounces) semisweet chocolate chips

Preheat oven to 350°F. Line 13×9-inch baking pan with foil. Combine flour, granulated sugar and salt in medium bowl; stir until blended. Cut in 14 tablespoons (1¾ sticks) butter until mixture resembles coarse crumbs. Press into bottom of prepared pan.

Bake 18 to 20 minutes until lightly browned around edges. Remove pan to wire rack; cool completely.

Combine 1 cup butter, brown sugar and corn syrup in heavy medium saucepan. Cook over medium heat 5 to 8 minutes until mixture boils, stirring frequently. Boil gently 2 minutes, without stirring. Immediately pour over cooled base; spread evenly to edges of pan with metal spatula. Cool completely.

Melt chocolate in double boiler over hot (not boiling) water. Stir in remaining 2 tablespoons butter. Pour over cooled caramel layer and spread evenly to edges of pan with metal spatula. Refrigerate 10 to 15 minutes until chocolate begins to set. Remove; cool completely. Cut into bars.

Makes 3 dozen bars

Chocolate Iced Shortbread

1 cup (2 sticks) butter or margarine, softened
½ cup granulated sugar
1 teaspoon vanilla extract
2 cups all-purpose flour
1¾ cups "M&M's"® Semi-Sweet Chocolate Mini Baking Bits, divided
1 cup prepared chocolate frosting

Preheat oven to 350°F. Lightly grease 13×9×2-inch baking pan. In large bowl cream butter, sugar and vanilla until light and fluffy. Add flour; mix to form stiff dough. Stir in *1 cup "M&M's"® Semi-Sweet Chocolate Mini Baking Bits.* Press dough into prepared pan. Bake 18 to 20 minutes or until firm. Cool completely. Spread with chocolate frosting; sprinkle with remaining *¾ cup "M&M's"® Semi-Sweet Chocolate Mini Baking Bits.* Cut into bars. Store in tightly covered container.

Makes 32 bars

Chocolate Iced Shortbread

Viennese Meringue Bars

   1 cup (2 sticks) butter or margarine, softened
1¼ cups sugar, divided
   2 egg yolks
   ¼ teaspoon salt
2¼ cups all-purpose flour
   1 cup seedless raspberry jam
1½ cups mini semisweet chocolate chips
   3 egg whites
   ½ cup slivered almonds, toasted

Preheat oven to 350°F. Beat butter and ½ cup sugar in large bowl with electric mixer at medium speed until light and fluffy. Beat in egg yolks and salt. Gradually add flour. Beat at low speed until well blended.

With buttered fingers, pat dough evenly into ungreased 15×10-inch jelly-roll pan. Bake 22 to 25 minutes or until light golden brown. Remove from oven; immediately spread jam over crust. Sprinkle evenly with chocolate chips.

For meringue topping, beat egg whites in large bowl with electric mixer on high speed until foamy. Gradually beat in remaining ¾ cup sugar until stiff peaks form. Gently stir in almonds with rubber spatula.

Spoon meringue over chocolate chips; spread evenly with small spatula. Bake 20 to 25 minutes or until golden brown. Cool completely on wire rack. Cut into bars.   *Makes about 2 dozen bars*

Banana Split Bars

   ⅓ cup margarine or butter, softened
   1 cup sugar
   1 egg
   1 banana, mashed
   ½ teaspoon vanilla
1¼ cups all-purpose flour
   1 teaspoon CALUMET® Baking Powder
   ¼ teaspoon salt
   ⅓ cup chopped nuts
   2 cups KRAFT® Miniature Marshmallows
   1 cup BAKER'S® Semi-Sweet Real Chocolate Chips
   ⅓ cup maraschino cherries, drained and quartered

Heat oven to 350°F.

Beat margarine and sugar until light and fluffy. Add egg, banana and vanilla; mix well. Mix in flour, baking powder and salt. Stir in nuts. Pour batter into greased 13×9-inch pan.

Bake 20 minutes. Remove from oven. Sprinkle with marshmallows, chips and cherries. Bake 10 to 15 minutes longer or until wooden pick inserted in center comes out clean. Cool in pan; cut into bars.
Makes about 24 bars

Prep time: 25 minutes
Bake time: 30 to 35 minutes

Viennese Meringue Bar

Praline Bars

¾ cup (1½ sticks) butter or margarine, softened
1 cup sugar, divided
1 teaspoon vanilla, divided
1½ cups flour
2 packages (8 ounces each) PHILADELPHIA BRAND® Cream Cheese, softened
2 eggs
½ cup almond brickle chips
3 tablespoons caramel ice cream topping

MIX butter, ½ cup of the sugar and ½ teaspoon of the vanilla with electric mixer on medium speed until light and fluffy. Gradually add flour, mixing on low speed until blended. Press onto bottom of 13×9-inch baking pan. Bake at 350°F for 20 to 23 minutes or until lightly browned.

MIX cream cheese, remaining ½ cup sugar and ½ teaspoon vanilla with electric mixer on medium speed until well blended. Add eggs; mix well. Blend in chips. Pour over crust. Dot top of cream cheese mixture with caramel topping. Cut through batter with knife several times for marble effect.

BAKE at 350°F for 30 minutes. Cool in pan on wire rack. Refrigerate. Cut into bars.

Makes 2 dozen bars

Monkey Bars

3 cups miniature marshmallows
½ cup honey
⅓ cup butter or margarine
¼ cup peanut butter
2 teaspoons vanilla
¼ teaspoon salt
2 cups rolled oats, uncooked
4 cups crispy rice cereal
½ cup flaked coconut
¼ cup peanuts

Combine marshmallows, honey, butter, peanut butter, vanilla and salt in medium saucepan. Cook marshmallow mixture over low heat, stirring constantly, until melted and smooth. Combine oats, rice cereal, coconut and peanuts in 13×9-inch baking pan. Pour marshmallow mixture over dry ingredients. Mix until thoroughly coated. Press mixture firmly into pan. *Makes 2 dozen bars*

Favorite recipe from **National Honey Board**

To measure honey or syrup, lightly spray measuring cup with nonstick cooking spray before measuring so the liquid will not stick to the cup.

Praline Bars

Rich Chocolate Chip Toffee Bars

2⅓ cups all-purpose flour
⅔ cup packed light brown sugar
¾ cup (1½ sticks) butter or margarine
1 egg, slightly beaten
2 cups (12-ounce package) HERSHEY'S
    Semi-Sweet Chocolate Chips, divided
1 cup coarsely chopped nuts
1 can (14 ounces) sweetened condensed milk
    (not evaporated milk)
1¾ cups (10-ounce package) SKOR® English
    Toffee Bits, divided

1. Heat oven to 350°F. Grease 13×9×2-inch baking pan.

2. In large bowl, stir together flour and brown sugar. Cut in butter with pastry blender until mixture resembles coarse crumbs. Add egg; mix well. Stir in 1½ cups chocolate chips and nuts. Reserve 1½ cups mixture. Press remaining crumb mixture onto bottom of prepared pan.

3. Bake 10 minutes. Pour sweetened condensed milk evenly over hot crust. Top with 1½ cups toffee bits. Sprinkle reserved crumb mixture and remaining ½ cup chips over top.

4. Bake 25 to 30 minutes or until golden brown. Sprinkle with remaining ¼ cup toffee bits. Cool completely in pan on wire rack. Cut into bars.

Makes about 36 bars

Chocolate Pecan Popcorn Bars

3 quarts popped corn
2 cups pecan halves or coarsely chopped
    pecans
2 cups (12 ounces) semisweet chocolate chips
¾ cup sugar
¾ cup KARO® Light or Dark Corn Syrup
2 tablespoons MAZOLA® Margarine

1. Preheat oven to 300°F. In large roasting pan combine popped corn and pecans; set aside.

2. In medium saucepan combine chocolate chips, sugar, corn syrup and margarine. Stirring occasionally, bring to boil over medium-high heat; boil 1 minute.

3. Pour over popcorn mixture; toss to coat well. Bake 30 minutes, stirring twice.

4. Spoon into 13×9-inch baking pan. Press warm mixture firmly and evenly into pan. Cool 5 minutes. Invert onto cutting board; cut into bars.

Makes about 30 bars

Prep time: 15 minutes
Bake time: 30 minutes

Rich Chocolate Chip Toffee Bars

Caramel Marshmallow Bars

CRUMB MIXTURE

1¼ cups all-purpose flour
¼ cup graham cracker crumbs
½ cup sugar
½ cup (1 stick) butter or margarine, softened
¼ teaspoon salt
½ cup chopped salted peanuts

FILLING

¾ cup caramel ice cream topping
½ cup salted peanuts
½ cup miniature marshmallows
½ cup milk chocolate chips

Preheat oven to 350°F. For crumb mixture, in small mixer bowl combine flour, graham cracker crumbs, sugar, butter and salt. Beat at low speed, scraping bowl often, until mixture is crumbly, 1 to 2 minutes. Stir in nuts. Reserve ¾ cup crumb mixture. Press remaining crumb mixture on bottom of greased and floured 9-inch square baking pan. Bake 10 to 12 minutes or until lightly browned.

For filling, spread caramel topping evenly over hot crust. Sprinkle nuts, marshmallows and chocolate chips over top. Crumble ¾ cup reserved crumb mixture over top. Continue baking 10 to 12 minutes or until marshmallows just start to brown. Cool on rack about 30 minutes. Cover; refrigerate 1 to 2 hours or until firm. Cut into bars.

Makes about 30 bars

Raspberry Coconut Layer Bars

1⅔ cups graham cracker crumbs
½ cup (1 stick) butter or margarine, melted
2⅔ cups (7-ounce package) flaked coconut
1¼ cups (14-ounce can) CARNATION® Sweetened Condensed Milk
1 cup raspberry jam or preserves
⅓ cup finely chopped walnuts, toasted
½ cup NESTLÉ TOLL® HOUSE® Semi-Sweet Chocolate Morsels, melted
¼ cup (1½ ounces) NESTLÉ® Premier White Baking Bar, melted

COMBINE graham cracker crumbs and butter in medium bowl. Spread evenly over bottom of 13×9-inch baking pan; press in firmly. Sprinkle with coconut; pour sweetened condensed milk evenly over coconut.

BAKE in preheated 350°F. oven for 20 to 25 minutes or until lightly browned; cool for 15 minutes.

SPREAD jam over coconut layer; chill for 3 to 4 hours or until firm. Sprinkle with nuts. Drizzle with melted morsels and baking bar; chill. Cut into 3×1½-inch bars.

Makes 24 bar cookies

Caramel Marshmallow Bars

Chocolate Marbled Blondies

½ cup (1 stick) butter or margarine, softened
½ cup firmly packed light brown sugar
1 large egg
2 teaspoons vanilla extract
1½ cups all-purpose flour
1¼ teaspoons baking soda
1 cup "M&M's"® Chocolate Mini Baking Bits, divided
4 ounces cream cheese, softened
2 tablespoons granulated sugar
1 large egg yolk
¼ cup unsweetened cocoa powder

Preheat oven to 350°F. Lightly grease 9×9×2-inch baking pan; set aside. In large bowl cream butter and brown sugar until light and fluffy; beat in egg and vanilla. In medium bowl combine flour and baking soda; blend into creamed mixture. Stir in ⅔ cup "M&M's"® Chocolate Mini Baking Bits; set aside. *Dough will be stiff.* In separate bowl beat together cream cheese, granulated sugar and egg yolk until smooth; stir in cocoa powder until well blended. Place chocolate-cheese mixture in six equal portions evenly onto bottom of prepared pan. Place reserved dough around cheese mixture and swirl slightly with tines of fork. Pat down evenly on top. Sprinkle with remaining ⅓ cup "M&M's"® Chocolate Mini Baking Bits. Bake 25 to 30 minutes until toothpick inserted in center comes out with moist crumbs. Cool completely. Cut into bars. Store in refrigerator in tightly covered container.

Makes 16 bars

Chocolate Scotcheroos

1 cup light corn syrup
1 cup sugar
1 cup peanut butter
6 cups KELLOGG'S® RICE KRISPIES® cereal
1 package (6 ounces, 1 cup) semisweet chocolate chips
1 package (6 ounces, 1 cup) butterscotch chips
Vegetable cooking spray

Combine corn syrup and sugar in large saucepan. Cook over medium heat, stirring frequently, until sugar dissolves and mixture begins to boil. Remove from heat. Stir in peanut butter; mix well. Add Kellogg's® Rice Krispies® cereal. Stir until well coated. Press mixture into 13×9-inch baking pan coated with cooking spray. Set aside.

Melt chocolate and butterscotch chips together in small saucepan over low heat, stirring constantly. Spread evenly over cereal mixture. Let stand until firm. Cut into 2×1-inch bars when cool.

Makes 4 dozen bars

Chocolate Marbled Blondies

Blueberry Cheesecake Bars

**1 package DUNCAN HINES® Bakery Style
   Blueberry Muffin Mix**
¼ cup cold butter or margarine
⅓ cup finely chopped pecans
1 (8-ounce) package cream cheese, softened
½ cup sugar
1 egg
3 tablespoons lemon juice
1 teaspoon grated lemon peel

1. Preheat oven to 350°F. Grease 9-inch square pan.

2. Rinse blueberries from Mix with cold water and drain.

3. Place muffin mix in medium bowl; cut in butter with pastry blender or two knives. Stir in pecans. Press into bottom of prepared pan. Bake 15 minutes or until set.

4. Combine cream cheese and sugar in medium bowl. Beat until smooth. Add egg, lemon juice and lemon peel. Beat well. Spread over baked crust. Sprinkle with blueberries. Sprinkle topping packet from Mix over blueberries. Return to oven. Bake 35 to 40 minutes or until filling is set. Cool completely. Refrigerate until ready to serve. Cut into bars.

Makes about 16 bars

Almond Toffee Squares

1 cup (2 sticks) margarine or butter, softened
1 cup firmly packed brown sugar
1 egg
1 teaspoon vanilla
2 cups all-purpose flour
¼ teaspoon salt
**2 (4-ounce) packages BAKER'S®
   GERMAN'S® Sweet Chocolate, broken
   into squares**
½ cup toasted slivered almonds
**½ cup lightly toasted BAKER'S® ANGEL
   FLAKE® Coconut**

Preheat oven to 350°F.

Beat margarine, sugar, egg and vanilla. Mix in flour and salt. Press into greased 13×9-inch pan.

Bake for 30 minutes or until edges are golden brown. Remove from oven. Immediately sprinkle with chocolate squares. Cover with foil; let stand 5 minutes or until chocolate is softened.

Spread chocolate evenly over entire surface; sprinkle with almonds and coconut. Cut into squares while still warm. Cool on wire rack.

Makes about 26 squares

Prep time: 20 minutes
Bake time: 30 minutes

Blueberry Cheesecake Bars

Mini Kisses Praline Bars

2 cups all-purpose flour
1⅓ cups packed light brown sugar, divided
½ cup (1 stick) plus ⅔ cup butter, divided
1 cup coarsely chopped pecans
1¾ cups (10-ounce package) HERSHEY'S MINI KISSES™ Chocolate

1. Heat oven to 350°F.

2. In large bowl, stir together flour and 1 cup brown sugar; cut in ½ cup butter with pastry blender until fine crumbs form. Press mixture into 13×9×2-inch baking pan; sprinkle with pecans.

3. In small saucepan, place remaining ⅔ cup butter and remaining ⅓ cup brown sugar; cook over medium heat, stirring constantly, until mixture boils. Continue boiling, stirring constantly, 30 seconds, until sugar dissolves; drizzle evenly over pecans and crust.

4. Bake 18 to 22 minutes until topping is bubbly and golden; remove from oven. Immediately sprinkle Mini Kisses Chocolate over top. Cool completely in pan on wire rack. Cut into bars.

Makes about 36 bars

Tip: *Bloom, the gray film that sometimes appears on chocolate and chocolate chips, occurs when chocolate is exposed to varying temperatures or has been stored in damp conditions. Bloom does not affect the taste or quality of the chocolate.*

Double Chocolate Crispy Bars

6 cups crispy rice cereal
½ cup peanut butter
⅓ cup butter or margarine
2 squares (1 ounce each) unsweetened chocolate
1 package (8 ounces) marshmallows
1 cup (6 ounces) semisweet chocolate chips *or*
 6 ounces bittersweet chocolate, chopped
6 ounces white chocolate, chopped
2 teaspoons shortening, divided

Preheat oven to 350°F. Line 13×9-inch pan with waxed paper. Spread cereal on cookie sheet; toast in oven 10 minutes or until crispy. Place in large bowl. Meanwhile, combine peanut butter, butter and unsweetened chocolate in large heavy saucepan. Stir over low heat until chocolate is melted. Add marshmallows; stir until melted and smooth. Pour chocolate mixture over cereal; mix until evenly coated. Press firmly into prepared pan.

Place semisweet and white chocolates in separate bowls. Add 1 teaspoon shortening to each bowl. Place bowls over very warm water; stir until chocolates are melted. Spread top of bars with melted semisweet chocolate; cool until chocolate is set. Turn bars out of pan onto sheet of waxed paper, chocolate side down. Remove waxed paper from bottom of bars; spread white chocolate over surface. Cool until chocolate is set. Cut into 2×1½-inch bars with sharp, thin knife.

Makes about 3 dozen bars

Mini Kisses Praline Bars

Best-Selling Brownies

Outrageous Brownies

½ cup MIRACLE WHIP® Salad Dressing
2 eggs, beaten
¼ cup cold water
1 (21.5-ounce) package fudge brownie mix
3 (7-ounce) milk chocolate bars, divided
    Walnut halves (optional)

Preheat oven to 350°F. Mix together salad dressing, eggs and water until well blended. Stir in brownie mix, mixing just until moistened.

Coarsely chop two chocolate bars; stir into brownie mixture. Pour into greased 13×9-inch baking pan.

Bake 30 to 35 minutes or until edges begin to pull away from sides of pan. Immediately top with 1 chopped chocolate bar. Let stand about 5 minutes or until melted; spread evenly over brownies. Garnish with walnut halves, if desired. Cool. Cut into squares.   *Makes about 24 brownies*

Prep time: 10 minutes
Bake time: 35 minutes

Extra Moist & Chunky Brownies

1 (8-ounce) package cream cheese, softened
1 cup sugar
1 egg
1 teaspoon vanilla extract
¾ cup all-purpose flour
1 (4-serving size) package ROYAL® Chocolate
    or Dark 'N' Sweet Chocolate Pudding &
    Pie Filling
4 (1-ounce) semisweet chocolate squares,
    chopped

In large bowl with electric mixer at high speed, beat cream cheese, sugar, egg and vanilla until smooth; blend in flour and pudding mix. Spread in greased 8×8-inch microwavable dish; top with chocolate. Microwave at HIGH 8 to 10 minutes or until toothpick inserted in center comes out clean, rotating ½ turn every 2 minutes. Cool in pan.
Makes 16 brownies

Outrageous Brownies

Peanut Butter Brownie Squares

1 package (19.8 ounces) DUNCAN HINES® Chewy Fudge Brownie Mix

FROSTING
1½ cups confectioners sugar
⅓ cup peanut butter
¼ cup plus 2 tablespoons milk
2 tablespoons butter, softened

DRIZZLE
⅓ cup semi-sweet chocolate chips
1 tablespoon CRISCO® all-vegetable shortening

1. Preheat oven to 350°F. Grease bottom only of 13×9×2-inch pan.

2. Prepare and bake brownies following package directions for cake-like brownies. Cool 5 to 10 minutes.

3. **For frosting,** combine confectioners sugar, peanut butter, milk and butter in small bowl. Beat at medium speed with electric mixer until blended. Spread over warm brownies.

4. **For drizzle,** place chocolate chips and shortening in small resealable plastic bag; seal. Microwave at HIGH (100% power) for 1 minute or until melted. Snip pinpoint hole in bottom corner of bag. Drizzle over frosting. Allow chocolate drizzle to set before cutting into bars.   *Makes 24 brownies*

Praline Brownies

BROWNIES
1 package DUNCAN HINES® Chocolate Lovers' Milk Chocolate Chunk Brownie Mix
2 eggs
⅓ cup water
⅓ cup CRISCO® Oil or CRISCO® PURITAN® Canola Oil
¾ cup chopped pecans

TOPPING
¾ cup firmly packed brown sugar
¾ cup chopped pecans
¼ cup butter or margarine, melted
2 tablespoons milk
½ teaspoon vanilla extract

1. Preheat oven to 350°F. Grease 9-inch square pan.

2. **For brownies,** combine brownie mix, eggs, water, oil and ¾ cup pecans in large bowl. Stir with spoon until well blended, about 50 strokes. Spread in prepared pan. Bake at 350°F for 35 to 40 minutes. Remove from oven.

3. **For topping,** combine brown sugar, ¾ cup pecans, melted butter, milk and vanilla extract in medium bowl. Stir with spoon until well blended. Spread over hot brownies. Return to oven. Bake for 15 minutes longer or until topping is set. Cool completely. Cut into bars.

Makes about 16 brownies

Peanut Butter Brownie Squares

Rocky Road Brownies

½ cup (1 stick) butter or margarine
½ cup unsweetened cocoa
1 cup sugar
1 egg
½ cup all-purpose flour
¼ cup buttermilk
1 teaspoon vanilla
1 cup miniature marshmallows
1 cup coarsely chopped walnuts
1 cup (6 ounces) semisweet chocolate chips

Preheat oven to 350°F. Lightly grease 8-inch square pan. Combine butter and cocoa in heavy medium saucepan over low heat, stirring constantly until smooth. Remove from heat; stir in sugar, egg, flour, buttermilk and vanilla. Mix until smooth. Spread batter evenly in prepared pan. Bake 25 minutes or until center feels dry. (Do not overbake or brownies will be dry.) Remove from oven; sprinkle marshmallows, walnuts and chocolate chips over the top. Return to oven for 3 to 5 minutes or just until topping is warmed enough to hold together. Cool in pan on wire rack. Cut into 2-inch squares.

Makes 16 brownies

Moist and Minty Brownies

1¼ cups all-purpose flour
½ teaspoon baking soda
¼ teaspoon salt
¾ cup granulated sugar
½ cup (1 stick) butter or margarine
2 tablespoons water
1½ cups (10-ounce package) NESTLÉ® TOLL HOUSE® Mint-Chocolate Morsels, *divided*
1 teaspoon vanilla extract
2 eggs

COMBINE flour, baking soda and salt in small bowl. Combine sugar, butter and water in medium saucepan. Bring *just to a boil* over medium heat, stirring constantly; remove from heat.* Add *1 cup* morsels and vanilla; stir until smooth. Add eggs, one at a time, stirring well after each addition. Stir in flour mixture and *remaining* morsels. Spread into greased 9-inch square baking pan.

BAKE in preheated 350°F oven for 20 to 30 minutes or until center is set. Cool in pan on wire rack (center will sink). *Makes 16 brownies*

*Or, combine sugar, butter and water in medium microwave-safe bowl. Microwave on HIGH (100%) power for 3 minutes, stirring halfway through cooking time. Stir until smooth. Proceed as above.

Rocky Road Brownies

Oatmeal Brownie Gems

2¾ cups quick-cooking or old-fashioned oats,
    uncooked
1 cup all-purpose flour
1 cup firmly packed light brown sugar
1 cup coarsely chopped walnuts
1 teaspoon baking soda
1 cup (2 sticks) butter or margarine, melted
1¾ cups "M&M's"® Semi-Sweet Chocolate
    Mini Baking Bits
1 (19- to 21-ounce) package fudge brownie
    mix, prepared according to package
    directions for fudge-like brownies

Preheat oven to 350°F. In large bowl combine oats, flour, sugar, nuts and baking soda; add butter until mixture forms coarse crumbs. Toss in "M&M's"® Semi-Sweet Chocolate Mini Baking Bits until evenly distributed. Reserve 3 cups mixture. Pat remaining mixture onto bottom of 15×10×1-inch pan to form crust. Pour prepared brownie mix over crust, carefully spreading into thin layer. Sprinkle reserved crumb mixture over top of brownie mixture; pat down lightly. Bake 25 to 30 minutes or until toothpick inserted in center comes out with moist crumbs. Cool completely. Cut into bars. Store in tightly covered container.

Makes 48 bars

Chocolate Peanut Brownie Bars

2 eggs
1 cup sugar
⅔ cup butter, melted
1 teaspoon vanilla
¾ cup flour
⅓ cup unsweetened cocoa powder
1 teaspoon baking powder
½ teaspoon salt
1½ cups coarsely chopped, peeled and cored
    apples or Bartlett pears
1 cup chopped dry-roasted peanuts, divided
½ cup peanut butter morsels

Preheat oven to 350°F. Beat eggs in large bowl until fluffy. Blend in sugar, butter and vanilla, beating until sugar is dissolved.

Combine flour, cocoa, baking powder and salt in separate bowl. Stir into egg mixture until dry ingredients are just moistened. Carefully fold in apples or pears, ½ cup peanuts and peanut butter morsels.

Pour into greased 8-inch baking pan; sprinkle with remaining ½ cup peanuts. Bake 30 to 35 minutes or until toothpick inserted into center comes out clean. Remove to wire rack to cool completely. Cut into squares.

Makes 16 bars

Favorite recipe from **Texas Peanut Producers Board**

Oatmeal Brownie Gems

Recipe for Oatmeal Brownie Gems

From — Josephine

— Serves —

Ingredients:

2 3/4 cups quick-cooking or old
   fashioned oats, uncooked
1 cup all-purpose flour
1 cup firmly packed brown sugar
1 tsp. baking soda
1 cup chocolate chips

Sour Cream Walnut Brownies

BROWNIES

1 package DUNCAN HINES® Walnut
    Brownie Mix
¾ cup dairy sour cream
1 egg
1 teaspoon water

CHOCOLATE DRIZZLE

½ cup semi-sweet chocolate chips
2 teaspoons CRISCO® all-vegetable
    shortening

1. Preheat oven to 350°F. Grease 13×9-inch pan.

2. For brownies, combine brownie mix, sour cream, egg and water in large bowl. Stir with spoon until well blended, about 50 strokes. Spread in prepared pan. Sprinkle with walnut packet from Mix. Bake at 350°F for 25 to 28 minutes or until set.

3. For chocolate drizzle, place chocolate chips and shortening in small resealable plastic bag; seal. Place bag in bowl of hot water for several minutes. Dry with paper towel. Knead until blended and chocolate is smooth. Snip pinpoint hole in corner of bag. Drizzle chocolate over brownies. Cool completely. Cut into bars.

Makes about 24 brownies

White Chocolate Chunk Brownies

4 squares (1 ounce each) unsweetened
    chocolate, coarsely chopped
½ cup (1 stick) butter or margarine
2 large eggs
1¼ cups granulated sugar
1 teaspoon vanilla
½ cup all-purpose flour
½ teaspoon salt
1 (6-ounce) white baking bar, cut into ¼-inch
    pieces
½ cup coarsely chopped walnuts (optional)
    Powdered sugar for garnish

Preheat oven to 350°F. Melt unsweetened chocolate and butter in small, heavy saucepan over low heat, stirring constantly; set aside. Beat eggs in large bowl; gradually add granulated sugar, beating at medium speed about 4 minutes until very thick and lemon colored. Beat in chocolate mixture and vanilla. Beat in flour and salt just until blended. Stir in baking bar pieces and walnuts. Spread evenly into greased 8-inch square baking pan. Bake 30 minutes or until edges just begin to pull away from sides of pan and center is set. Remove pan to wire rack; cool completely. Cut into 2-inch squares. Sprinkle with powdered sugar, if desired.

Makes about 16 brownies

Sour Cream Walnut Brownies

All American Heath® Brownies

⅓ cup butter or margarine
1 square (1 ounce) unsweetened chocolate
1 cup sugar
2 eggs
1 teaspoon vanilla
1 cup flour
½ teaspoon baking powder
¼ teaspoon salt
1 package (6 ounces) HEATH® Bits

Preheat oven to 350°F. Grease bottom of 8-inch square baking pan.

In 1½-quart saucepan, melt butter and chocolate over low heat, stirring occasionally. Blend in sugar. Add eggs, 1 at a time, beating after each addition. Blend in vanilla. In small bowl, mix together flour, baking powder and salt; add to chocolate mixture and blend. Spread batter in prepared pan.

Bake 20 minutes. Remove from oven; sprinkle with Heath® Bits. Cover tightly with foil and cool completely on wire rack. Remove foil; cut into bars.

Makes about 12 brownies

Raspberry Fudge Brownies

½ cup (1 stick) butter or margarine
3 squares (1 ounce each) bittersweet chocolate*
1 cup sugar
2 eggs
1 teaspoon vanilla
¾ cup all-purpose flour
¼ teaspoon baking powder
   Dash salt
½ cup sliced or slivered almonds
½ cup raspberry preserves
1 cup (6 ounces) milk chocolate chips

*Bittersweet chocolate is available in specialty food stores. One square unsweetened chocolate plus 2 squares semisweet chocolate may be substituted.

Preheat oven to 350°F. Butter and flour 8-inch square pan. Melt butter and bittersweet chocolate in heavy small saucepan over low heat. Remove from heat; cool. Beat sugar, eggs and vanilla in large bowl until light. Beat in chocolate mixture. Stir in flour, baking powder and salt until just blended. Spread ¾ of batter in prepared pan; sprinkle almonds over top. Bake 10 minutes. Remove from oven; spread preserves over almonds. Carefully spoon remaining batter over preserves, smoothing top. Bake 25 to 30 minutes or just until top feels firm. Remove from oven; sprinkle chocolate chips over top. Let stand several minutes until chips melt, then spread evenly over brownies. Cool completely in pan on wire rack. When chocolate is set, cut into 2-inch squares. *Makes 16 brownies*

Raspberry Fudge Brownies

One Bowl™ Brownies

4 squares BAKER'S® Unsweetened Chocolate
¾ cup (1½ sticks) margarine or butter
2 cups sugar
3 eggs
1 teaspoon vanilla
1 cup all-purpose flour
1 cup chopped nuts (optional)

Preheat oven to 350°F.

Microwave chocolate and margarine in large microwavable bowl on HIGH 2 minutes or until margarine is melted. **Stir until chocolate is completely melted.**

Stir sugar into melted chocolate mixture. Mix in eggs and vanilla until well blended. Stir in flour and nuts. Spread in greased 13×9-inch pan.

Bake for 30 to 35 minutes or until wooden pick inserted into center comes out with fudgy crumbs. **Do not overbake.** Cool in pan; cut into squares.

Makes about 24 brownies

Prep time: 10 minutes
Bake time: 30 to 35 minutes

Peanut Butter Swirl Brownies: *Prepare One Bowl™ Brownie batter as directed, reserving 1 tablespoon of the margarine and 2 tablespoons of the sugar. Add reserved ingredients to ⅔ cup peanut butter; mix well.*

Place spoonfuls of peanut butter mixture over brownie batter. Swirl with knife to marbleize. Bake for 30 to 35 minutes or until wooden pick inserted into center comes out with fudgy crumbs. Cool in pan; cut into squares. Makes about 24 brownies.

Prep time: 15 minutes
Bake time: 30 to 35 minutes

Rocky Road Brownies: *Prepare One Bowl™ Brownies as directed. Bake for 30 minutes. Sprinkle 2 cups KRAFT® Miniature Marshmallows, 1 cup BAKER'S® Semi-Sweet Real Chocolate Chips and 1 cup chopped nuts over brownies immediately. Continue baking 3 to 5 minutes or until topping begins to melt together. Cool in pan; cut into squares. Makes about 24 brownies.*

Prep time: 15 minutes
Bake time: 35 minutes

One Bowl™ Brownies

Brownie Kiss Cups

1 package (19.8 ounces) DUNCAN HINES®
  Chewy Fudge Brownie Mix
1 egg
⅓ cup water
⅓ cup CRISCO® Oil or CRISCO®
  PURITAN® Canola Oil
25 milk chocolate candy kisses, unwrapped

1. Preheat oven to 350°F. Place 25 (2-inch) foil liners in muffin pans or on cookie sheets.

2. Combine brownie mix, egg, water and oil in large bowl. Stir with spoon until well blended, about 50 strokes. Fill each liner with 2 measuring tablespoonfuls batter. Bake at 350°F for 17 to 20 minutes. Remove from oven. Place 1 milk chocolate candy kiss on each cupcake. Bake 1 minute longer. Cool 5 to 10 minutes in pans. Remove to cooling racks. Cool completely.

Makes 25 brownie cups

Toffee Chunk Brownie Cookies

1 cup (2 sticks) butter
4 ounces unsweetened chocolate, coarsely
  chopped
1½ cups sugar
2 eggs
1 tablespoon vanilla
3 cups all-purpose flour
⅛ teaspoon salt
1½ cups coarsely chopped chocolate-covered
  toffee bars

Preheat oven to 350°F. Melt butter and chocolate in large saucepan over low heat, stirring until smooth. Remove from heat; cool slightly.

Stir sugar into chocolate mixture until smooth. Stir in eggs until well blended. Stir in vanilla until smooth. Stir in flour and salt just until mixed. Fold in chopped toffee. Drop heaping tablespoonfuls of dough 1½ inches apart onto *ungreased* cookie sheets.

Bake 12 minutes or until just set. Let cookies stand on cookie sheets 5 minutes; transfer to wire racks to cool completely. Store in airtight container.

Makes 36 cookies

Brownie Kiss Cups

Bamboozlers

1 cup all-purpose flour
¾ cup packed light brown sugar
¼ cup unsweetened cocoa powder
1 egg
2 egg whites
5 tablespoons margarine, melted
¼ cup skim milk
¼ cup honey
1 teaspoon vanilla
2 tablespoons semisweet chocolate chips
2 tablespoons coarsely chopped walnuts
    Powdered sugar (optional)

1. Preheat oven to 350°F. Grease and flour 8-inch square baking pan; set aside.

2. Combine flour, brown sugar and cocoa in medium bowl. Blend together egg, egg whites, margarine, milk, honey and vanilla in medium bowl. Add to flour mixture; mix well. Pour into prepared baking pan; sprinkle with chocolate chips and walnuts.

3. Bake brownies until they spring back when lightly touched in center, about 30 minutes. Cool completely in pan on wire rack. Sprinkle with powdered sugar just before serving.

Makes 12 servings

Peanutters: *Substitute peanut butter chips for chocolate chips and peanuts for walnuts.*

Butterscotch Babies: *Substitute butterscotch chips for chocolate chips and pecans for walnuts.*

Brownie Sundaes: *Serve brownies on dessert plates. Top each brownie with a scoop of vanilla ice cream and 2 tablespoons nonfat chocolate or caramel sauce.*

Double Fudge Saucepan Brownies

⅔ cup all-purpose flour
¼ teaspoon baking soda
¼ teaspoon salt
½ cup sugar
2 tablespoons butter or margarine
2 tablespoons water
2 cups (12-ounce package) HERSHEY'S Semi-Sweet Chocolate Chips, divided
2 eggs, slightly beaten
1 teaspoon vanilla extract
½ cup chopped nuts (optional)

Heat oven to 325°F. Grease 9-inch square baking pan. In bowl, stir together flour, baking soda and salt. In medium saucepan, combine sugar, butter and water. Cook over low heat, stirring constantly, until mixture comes to boil. Remove from heat; immediately add 1 cup chocolate chips, stirring until melted. Stir in eggs and vanilla until blended. Gradually add flour mixture, blending well. Stir in remaining 1 cup chips and nuts, if desired. Pour batter into prepared pan. Bake 25 to 30 minutes or until brownies begin to pull away from sides of pan. Cool completely in pan on wire rack. Cut into squares. *Makes about 1½ dozen brownies*

Bamboozlers

Double "Topped" Brownies

BROWNIES
> 1 package DUNCAN HINES® Chocolate
> Lovers' Double Fudge Brownie Mix
> 2 eggs
> ⅓ cup water
> ¼ cup CRISCO® Oil or CRISCO®
> PURITAN® Canola Oil
> ½ cup flaked coconut
> ½ cup chopped nuts

FROSTING
> 3 cups confectioners sugar
> ⅓ cup butter or margarine, softened
> 1½ teaspoons vanilla extract
> 2 to 3 tablespoons milk

TOPPING
> 3 squares (3 ounces) unsweetened chocolate
> 1 tablespoon butter or margarine

1. Preheat oven to 350°F. Grease bottom of 13×9-inch pan.

2. For brownies, combine brownie mix, fudge packet from Mix, eggs, water and oil in large bowl. Stir with spoon until well blended, about 50 strokes. Stir in coconut and nuts. Spread in prepared pan. Bake at 350°F for 27 to 30 minutes or until set. Cool completely.

3. For frosting, combine confectioners sugar, ⅓ cup butter and vanilla extract. Stir in milk, 1 tablespoon at a time, until frosting is spreading consistency. Spread over brownies. Refrigerate until frosting is firm, about 30 minutes.

4. For topping, melt chocolate and 1 tablespoon butter in small bowl over hot water; stir until smooth. Drizzle over frosting. Refrigerate until chocolate is firm, about 15 minutes. Cut into bars.

Makes about 48 brownies

Blonde Brickle Brownies

> 1⅓ cups all-purpose flour
> ½ teaspoon baking powder
> ¼ teaspoon salt
> 2 eggs
> ½ cup granulated sugar
> ½ cup packed brown sugar
> ⅓ cup butter or margarine, melted
> 1 teaspoon vanilla extract
> ¼ teaspoon almond extract
> 1 package (7.5 ounces) BITS 'O BRICKLE®,
> divided
> ½ cup chopped pecans (optional)

Preheat oven to 350°F. Grease 8-inch square baking pan. Mix flour, baking powder and salt in small bowl; set aside. Beat eggs in large bowl. Gradually beat in granulated sugar and brown sugar until thick and creamy. Add melted butter, vanilla and almond extract; mix well. Gently stir in flour mixture until moistened. Fold in ⅔ cup Bits 'O Brickle® and pecans, if desired. Pour into prepared pan.

Bake 30 minutes. Remove from oven; immediately sprinkle remaining Bits 'O Brickle® over top. Cool completely in pan on wire rack. Cut into squares.

Makes about 16 brownies

Double "Topped" Brownies

Brownies with Peanut Butter Chips

1¼ cups (2½ sticks) butter or margarine, melted
1¾ cups sugar
4 eggs
2 teaspoons vanilla extract
1⅔ cups all-purpose flour
⅔ cup HERSHEY'S Cocoa
½ teaspoon baking powder
½ teaspoon salt
1⅔ cups (10-ounce package) REESE'S Peanut
    Butter Chips, divided
    Peanut Butter Chip Glaze (recipe follows)

1. Heat oven to 350°F. Grease 13×9×2-inch baking pan.

2. In large bowl, stir together butter and sugar. Add eggs and vanilla; beat with spoon or whisk until well blended. Stir together flour, cocoa, baking powder and salt; add to butter mixture, stirring until well blended. Reserve ½ cup peanut butter chips for glaze. Stir remaining chips into batter. Spread batter into prepared pan.

3. Bake 30 to 35 minutes or until wooden pick inserted in center comes out clean. Cool completely in pan on wire rack. Meanwhile, prepare Peanut Butter Chip Glaze; drizzle over brownies. Let stand until glaze is set. Cut into squares.

Makes about 32 brownies

Peanut Butter Chip Glaze: In small microwave-safe bowl, place ½ cup REESE'S Peanut Butter Chips (reserved from brownies), 2 tablespoons butter or margarine and 2 tablespoons milk. Microwave at HIGH (100%) 45 seconds; stir. If necessary, microwave at HIGH an additional 15 seconds at a time, stirring after each heating, just until chips are melted when stirred. Gradually add ¼ cup powdered sugar, beating with whisk until smooth.

For easy removal of brownies and bar cookies (and no cleanup), line the baking pan with foil and leave at least 3 inches of overhang on each end.

Brownies with Peanut Butter Chips

Chocolatey Rocky Road Brownies

BROWNIES
1 cup (2 sticks) butter or margarine
4 squares (1 ounce each) unsweetened chocolate
1½ cups granulated sugar
1 cup all-purpose flour
3 eggs
1½ teaspoons vanilla
½ cup salted peanuts, chopped

FROSTING
¼ cup butter or margarine
1 (3-ounce) package cream cheese
1 square (1 ounce) unsweetened chocolate
¼ cup milk
2¾ cups powdered sugar
1 teaspoon vanilla
2 cups miniature marshmallows
1 cup salted peanuts

Preheat oven to 350°F. For brownies, combine 1 cup butter and 4 squares chocolate in large saucepan. Cook over medium heat, stirring constantly, until melted, 5 to 7 minutes. Remove from heat. Add granulated sugar, flour, eggs and 1½ teaspoons vanilla; mix well. Stir in ½ cup chopped peanuts. Spread into greased 13×9-inch baking pan. Bake 20 to 25 minutes or until brownie starts to pull away from sides of pan. Cool completely.

For frosting, combine ¼ cup butter, cream cheese, 1 square chocolate and milk in large saucepan. Cook over medium heat, stirring occasionally, 6 to 8 minutes or until melted. Remove from heat; add powdered sugar and 1 teaspoon vanilla. Beat with hand mixer until smooth. Stir in marshmallows and 1 cup peanuts. Immediately spread frosting over cooled brownies. Cool completely; cut into bars.

Makes about 4 dozen brownies

Philly® Marble Brownies

1 package (21½ ounces) brownie mix
1 package (8 ounces) PHILADELPHIA BRAND® Cream Cheese, softened
⅓ cup sugar
½ teaspoon vanilla
1 egg
1 cup BAKER'S® Semi-Sweet Real Chocolate Chips

PREPARE brownie mix as directed on package. Spread batter in greased 13×9-inch baking pan.

MIX cream cheese, sugar and vanilla with electric mixer on medium speed until well blended. Add egg; mix well. Pour over brownie batter; cut through batter with knife several times for marble effect. Sprinkle with chips.

BAKE at 350°F for 35 to 40 minutes or until cream cheese mixture is lightly browned. Cool in pan on wire rack. Cut into squares. *Makes 2 dozen*

Prep time: 20 minutes plus cooling
Baking time: 40 minutes

Chocolatey Rocky Road Brownies

Caramel Fudge Brownies

1 jar (12 ounces) hot caramel ice cream topping
1¼ cups all-purpose flour, divided
¼ teaspoon baking powder
    Dash salt
**4 squares (1 ounce each) unsweetened
    chocolate, coarsely chopped**
¾ cup (1½ sticks) margarine or butter
2 cups sugar
3 eggs
2 teaspoons vanilla
¾ cup semisweet chocolate chips
¾ cup chopped pecans

Preheat oven to 350°F. Lightly grease 13×9-inch baking pan. Combine caramel topping and ¼ cup flour in small bowl; set aside. Combine remaining 1 cup flour, baking powder and salt in small bowl; mix well.

Place unsweetened chocolate and margarine in medium microwavable bowl. Microwave at HIGH 2 minutes or until margarine is melted; stir until chocolate is completely melted. Stir sugar into melted chocolate with mixing spoon. Add eggs and vanilla; stir until combined. Add flour mixture, stirring until well blended. Spread chocolate mixture evenly into prepared pan.

Bake 25 minutes. Immediately after removing brownies from oven, spread caramel mixture over brownies. Sprinkle top evenly with chocolate chips and pecans.

Return pan to oven; bake 20 to 25 minutes or until topping is golden brown and bubbling. (Do not overbake.) Cool brownies completely in pan on wire rack. Cut into 2×1½-inch bars. Store tightly covered at room temperature or freeze up to 3 months. *Makes 3 dozen brownies*

Sensational Peppermint Pattie Brownies

24 small (1½-inch) YORK® Peppermint Patties
1½ cups (3 sticks) butter or margarine, melted
3 cups sugar
1 tablespoon vanilla extract
5 eggs
2 cups all-purpose flour
1 cup HERSHEY'S Cocoa
1 teaspoon baking powder
1 teaspoon salt

Heat oven to 350°F. Remove wrappers from peppermint patties. Grease 13×9×2-inch baking pan. In large bowl with spoon or whisk, stir together butter, sugar and vanilla. Add eggs; stir until well blended. Stir together flour, cocoa, baking powder and salt; gradually add to butter mixture, blending well. Reserve 2 cups batter. Spread remaining batter into prepared pan. Arrange peppermint patties about ½ inch apart in single layer over batter. Spread reserved batter over patties. Bake 50 to 55 minutes or until brownies begin to pull away from sides of pan. Cool completely in pan on wire rack. Cut into squares.
Makes about 36 brownies

Caramel Fudge Brownies

Double-Decker Confetti Brownies

¾ cup (1½ sticks) butter or margarine, softened
1 cup granulated sugar
1 cup firmly packed light brown sugar
3 large eggs
1 teaspoon vanilla extract
2½ cups all-purpose flour, divided
2½ teaspoons baking powder
½ teaspoon salt
⅓ cup unsweetened cocoa powder
1 tablespoon butter or margarine, melted
1 cup "M&M's"® Semi-Sweet Chocolate Mini Baking Bits, divided

Preheat oven to 350°F. Lightly grease 13×9×2-inch baking pan; set aside. In large bowl cream butter and sugars until light and fluffy; beat in eggs and vanilla. In medium bowl combine *2¼ cups flour,* baking powder and salt; blend into creamed mixture. Divide batter in half. Blend together cocoa powder and melted butter; stir into one half of the dough. Spread cocoa dough evenly into prepared baking pan. Stir remaining *¼ cup flour* and *½ cup "M&M's"® Semi-Sweet Chocolate Mini Baking Bits* into remaining dough; spread evenly over cocoa dough in pan. Sprinkle with remaining *½ cup "M&M's"® Semi-Sweet Chocolate Mini Baking Bits.* Bake 25 to 30 minutes or until edges start to pull away from sides of pan. Cool completely. Cut into bars. Store in tightly covered container.

Makes 24 brownies

Chewy Chocolate Brownies

¾ cup granulated sugar
½ cup (1 stick) butter or margarine
2 tablespoons water
4 bars (2 ounces *each*) NESTLÉ® TOLL HOUSE® Semi-Sweet Baking Chocolate, broken into pieces
2 eggs
2 teaspoons vanilla extract
1 cup all-purpose flour
¼ teaspoon baking soda
¼ teaspoon salt
½ cup chopped nuts (optional)

MICROWAVE sugar, butter and water in large, microwave-safe bowl on HIGH (100%) power for 3 minutes or until mixture boils, stirring once. Add baking bars; stir until melted.

STIR in eggs one at a time until well blended. Stir in vanilla. Add flour, baking soda and salt; stir well. Stir in nuts. Pour into greased 13×9-inch baking pan.

BAKE in preheated 350°F. oven for 16 to 20 minutes or until wooden pick inserted in center comes out still slightly sticky. Cool in pan on wire rack.

Makes about 2 dozen brownies

For Saucepan Method:
BRING sugar, butter and water in medium saucepan just to a boil, stirring constantly. Remove from heat. Proceed as above.

Double-Decker Confetti Brownies

Caramel-Layered Brownies

4 squares BAKER'S® Unsweetened Chocolate
¾ cup (1½ sticks) margarine or butter
2 cups sugar
3 eggs
1 teaspoon vanilla
1 cup all-purpose flour
1 cup BAKER'S® Semi-Sweet Real Chocolate Chips
1½ cups chopped nuts
1 package (14 ounces) caramels
⅓ cup evaporated milk

HEAT oven to 350°F. MICROWAVE chocolate and margarine in large microwavable bowl on HIGH 2 minutes or until margarine is melted. **Stir until chocolate is completely melted.**

STIR sugar into melted chocolate mixture. Mix in eggs and vanilla until well blended. Stir in flour. Remove 1 cup of batter; set aside. Spread remaining batter in greased 13×9-inch pan. Sprinkle with chips and 1 cup of the nuts.

MICROWAVE caramels and milk in same bowl on HIGH 4 minutes, stirring after 2 minutes. Stir until caramels are completely melted and smooth. Spoon over chips and nuts, spreading to edges of pan. Gently spread reserved batter over caramel mixture. Sprinkle with the remaining ½ cup nuts.

BAKE for 40 minutes or until toothpick inserted into center comes out with fudgy crumbs. **Do not overbake.** Cool in pan; cut into squares.

Makes about 24 brownies

Prep time: 20 minutes
Baking time: 40 minutes

Peanut Butter Marbled Brownies

4 ounces cream cheese, softened
½ cup peanut butter
2 tablespoons sugar
1 egg
1 package (20 to 22 ounces) brownie mix plus ingredients to prepare mix
¾ cup lightly salted cocktail peanuts

Preheat oven to 350°F. Lightly grease 13×9-inch baking pan; set aside. Beat cream cheese, peanut butter, sugar and egg in medium bowl with electric mixer at medium speed until blended; set aside.

Prepare brownie mix according to package directions. Spread brownie mixture evenly in prepared pan. Spoon peanut butter mixture in dollops over brownie mixture. Swirl peanut butter mixture into brownie mixture with tip of knife. Sprinkle peanuts on top; lightly press peanuts down.

Bake 30 to 35 minutes or until toothpick inserted into center comes out almost clean. (Do not overbake.) Cool brownies completely in pan on wire rack; cut into 2-inch squares. Store tightly covered at room temperature or freeze up to 3 months.

Makes 2 dozen brownies

Peanut Butter Marbled Brownies

Mini Brownie Cups

¼ cup (½ stick) light corn oil spread
 2 egg whites
 1 egg
¾ cup sugar
⅔ cup all-purpose flour
⅓ cup HERSHEY'S Cocoa
½ teaspoon baking powder
¼ teaspoon salt
   Mocha Glaze (recipe follows)

Heat oven to 350°F. Line small muffin cups
(1¾ inches in diameter) with paper bake cups
or spray with vegetable cooking spray. In small
saucepan over low heat, melt corn oil spread; cool
slightly. In small bowl, on medium speed of electric
mixer, beat egg whites and egg until foamy;
gradually add sugar, beating until slightly thickened
and light in color. Stir together flour, cocoa, baking
powder and salt; gradually add to egg mixture,
beating until blended. Gradually add corn oil
spread, beating just until blended. Fill muffin cups
⅔ full with batter. Bake 15 to 18 minutes or until
wooden pick inserted in center comes out clean.
Remove from pan to wire rack. Cool completely.
Prepare Mocha Glaze; drizzle over tops of brownie
cups. Let stand until glaze is set.

Makes 24 servings

Mocha Glaze

¾ teaspoon HERSHEY'S Cocoa
¼ cup powdered sugar
¼ teaspoon powdered instant coffee
 2 teaspoons hot water
¼ teaspoon vanilla extract

In small bowl, stir together cocoa and powdered
sugar. Dissolve coffee in water; gradually add to
sugar mixture, stirring until well blended. Stir in
vanilla.

To safely separate eggs, crack one egg at a
time into a small cup or bowl before
transferring it to the mixing bowl. This will
prevent any egg yolk from accidentally
dropping into a bowl of egg whites. (The fat
in egg yolks will prevent egg whites from
reaching their full volume when beaten.)

Mini Brownie Cups

Chewy Brownie Cookies

1½ cups firmly packed light brown sugar
⅔ CRISCO® Stick or ⅔ cup CRISCO all-
  vegetable shortening
1 tablespoon water
1 teaspoon vanilla
2 eggs
1½ cups all-purpose flour
⅓ cup unsweetened cocoa powder
½ teaspoon salt
¼ teaspoon baking soda
2 cups (12 ounces) semisweet chocolate chips

1. Heat oven to 375°F. Place sheets of foil on countertop for cooling cookies.

2. Place brown sugar, shortening, water and vanilla in large bowl. Beat at medium speed of electric mixer until well blended. Add eggs; beat well.

3. Combine flour, cocoa, salt and baking soda. Add to shortening mixture; beat at low speed just until blended. Stir in chocolate chips.

4. Drop dough by rounded measuring tablespoonfuls 2 inches apart onto ungreased baking sheet.

5. Bake one baking sheet at a time at 375°F for 7 to 9 minutes or until cookies are set. *Do not overbake.* Cool 2 minutes on baking sheet. Remove cookies to foil to cool completely.

Makes about 3 dozen cookies

Decadent Blonde Brownies

½ cup (1 stick) butter or margarine, softened
¾ cup granulated sugar
¾ cup packed light brown sugar
2 large eggs
2 teaspoons vanilla
1½ cups all-purpose flour
1 teaspoon baking powder
½ teaspoon salt
1 package (10 ounces) semisweet chocolate chunks
1 jar (3½ ounces) macadamia nuts, coarsely chopped

Preheat oven to 350°F. Beat butter, granulated sugar and brown sugar in large bowl with electric mixer at medium speed until light and fluffy. Beat in eggs and vanilla. Add combined flour, baking powder and salt. Stir until well blended. Stir in chocolate chunks and macadamia nuts. Spread evenly into greased 13×9-inch baking pan.

Bake 25 to 30 minutes or until golden brown. Remove pan to wire rack; cool completely. Cut into 3¼×1½-inch bars.

Makes about 2 dozen brownies

Chewy Brownie Cookies

Classic Cupcakes & Muffins

Captivating Caterpillar Cupcakes

1 package DUNCAN HINES® Moist Deluxe
White Cake Mix
3 egg whites
1¼ cups water
⅓ cup CRISCO® Oil or CRISCO®
PURITAN® Canola Oil
½ cup decorating star decors, divided
1 container (16 ounces) DUNCAN HINES®
Creamy Homestyle Vanilla Frosting
Green food coloring
6 chocolate sandwich cookies, finely crushed
(see Tip)
½ cup candy-coated chocolate pieces
⅓ cup assorted jelly beans
Assorted nonpareil decors

1. Preheat oven to 350°F. Line 24 (2½-inch) muffin cups with paper baking cups.

2. Combine cake mix, egg whites, water and oil in large bowl. Beat at low speed with electric mixer until moistened. Beat at medium speed for 2 minutes. Fold in ⅓ cup star decors. Fill paper liners about half full. Bake 18 to 23 minutes or until toothpick inserted in center comes out clean. Cool in pans 5 minutes. Remove cupcakes to cooling racks. Cool completely.

3. Tint Vanilla frosting with green food coloring. Frost one cupcake. Sprinkle ½ teaspoon chocolate cookie crumbs on frosting. Arrange 4 candy-coated chocolate pieces to form caterpillar body. Place jelly bean at one end to form head. Attach remaining star and nonpareil decors with dots of frosting to form eyes. Repeat with remaining cupcakes.

Makes 24 cupcakes

Tip: *To finely crush chocolate sandwich cookies, place cookies in a resealable plastic bag. Remove excess air from bag; seal. Press rolling pin on top of cookies to break into pieces. Continue pressing until evenly crushed.*

Captivating Caterpillar Cupcakes

Chocolate Cheesecake Cupcakes

CUPCAKES

2 cups (12-ounce package) NESTLÉ® TOLL
    HOUSE® Semi-Sweet Chocolate
    Morsels, *divided*
1½ cups all-purpose flour
1 teaspoon baking soda
½ teaspoon salt
½ cup granulated sugar
⅓ cup vegetable oil
1 egg
1 teaspoon vanilla extract
1 cup water

FILLING

2 packages (3 ounces *each*) cream cheese,
    softened
¼ cup granulated sugar
1 egg
⅛ teaspoon salt

FOR CUPCAKES:

MICROWAVE *½ cup* morsels in small, microwave-safe bowl on HIGH (100%) power for 45 seconds; stir. Microwave at additional 10- to 20-second intervals, stirring until smooth; cool to room temperature.

COMBINE flour, baking soda and salt in small bowl. Beat sugar, oil, egg and vanilla in large mixer bowl until blended. Beat in melted chocolate; gradually beat in flour mixture alternately with water (batter will be thin).

FOR FILLING:

BEAT cream cheese, sugar, egg and salt in small mixer bowl until creamy. Stir in *1 cup* morsels.

TO ASSEMBLE:

SPOON batter into 16 greased or paper-lined muffin cups, filling ½ full. Spoon filling by rounded tablespoons over batter. Spoon remaining batter over filling. Bake in preheated 350°F. oven for 20 to 25 minutes or until wooden pick inserted in center comes out clean. While still hot, sprinkle with *remaining ½ cup* morsels. Let stand for 5 minutes or until morsels are shiny; spread to frost. Remove to wire racks to cool completely.

Makes 16 cupcakes

To soften cream cheese, remove wrapper and place cream cheese on a microwavable plate. Microwave at MEDIUM (50% power) for 1 to 1½ minutes for an 8-ounce package or 30 to 45 seconds for a 3-ounce package.

Chocolate Cheesecake Cupcakes

Coconut Cupcakes

1 package DUNCAN HINES® Moist Deluxe
    Butter Recipe Golden Cake Mix
3 eggs
1 cup (8 ounces) dairy sour cream
⅔ cup cream of coconut
¼ cup butter or margarine, softened
2 containers (16 ounces each) DUNCAN
    HINES® Creamy Homestyle Cream
    Cheese Frosting
2½ cups toasted coconut (see Tip)

1. Preheat oven to 375°F. Place 36 (2½-inch) paper liners in muffin cups.

2. Combine cake mix, eggs, sour cream, cream of coconut and butter in large bowl. Beat at low speed until blended. Beat at medium speed 4 minutes. Fill paper liners half full. Bake 17 to 19 minutes or until toothpick inserted in center comes out clean. Cool in pans 5 minutes. Remove to cooling racks. Cool completely.

3. Frost cupcakes; sprinkle with toasted coconut.

Makes 36 cupcakes

Tip: To toast coconut, spread evenly on baking sheet. Toast in 350°F oven for 3 minutes. Stir and toast 1 to 2 minutes longer or until light golden brown.

Polka Dot Cupcakes

TOPPING
½ cup (4 ounces) cream cheese, softened
1 egg
2 tablespoons granulated sugar
⅔ cup NESTLÉ® TOLL HOUSE®
    Semi-Sweet Chocolate Mini Morsels

CUPCAKES
1 package (16 ounces) pound cake mix
1 cup LIBBY'S® Solid Pack Pumpkin
⅓ cup water
2 eggs
2 teaspoons pumpkin pie spice
1 teaspoon baking soda

FOR TOPPING:

BEAT cream cheese, egg and granulated sugar in small mixer bowl until smooth. Stir in morsels.

FOR CUPCAKES:

COMBINE cake mix, pumpkin, water, eggs, pumpkin pie spice and baking soda in large mixer bowl; beat on medium speed for 3 minutes. Pour batter into paper-lined muffin cups, filling ¾ full. Spoon about 1 tablespoon topping over batter.

BAKE in preheated 325°F. oven for 25 to 30 minutes or until wooden toothpick inserted in center comes out clean. Cool in pans on wire racks for 10 minutes. Remove to wire racks to cool completely.

Makes 18 cupcakes

Coconut Cupcakes

Bread Pudding Snacks

1¼ cups 2% milk
½ cup cholesterol-free egg substitute
⅓ cup sugar
1 teaspoon vanilla
⅛ teaspoon ground nutmeg (optional)
⅛ teaspoon salt
4 cups (½-inch) cinnamon or cinnamon-raisin bread cubes (about 6 bread slices)
1 tablespoon margarine or butter, melted

1. Combine milk, egg substitute, sugar, vanilla, nutmeg and salt in medium bowl; mix well. Add bread; mix until well moistened. Let stand at room temperature 15 minutes.

2. Preheat oven to 350°F. Line 12 medium-sized muffin cups with paper liners. Spoon bread mixture evenly into prepared cups; drizzle evenly with margarine.

3. Bake 30 to 35 minutes or until snacks are puffed and golden brown. Remove to wire rack to cool completely. *Makes 12 servings*

Note: Snacks will puff up in the oven and fall slightly upon cooling.

Cream-Filled Banana Cupcakes

Cream Cheese Filling (recipe follows)
1 package (18.5 ounces) banana cake mix (with pudding in the mix)
¾ cup finely chopped nuts
2 tablespoons sugar

Prepare Cream Cheese Filling; set aside. Heat oven to 350°F. Prepare cake batter according to package directions. Fill paper-lined muffin cups (2½ inches in diameter) ½ full with batter. Spoon about 1 teaspoonful filling into center of each cupcake.

Combine nuts and sugar; sprinkle about 1 teaspoonful over top of each cupcake. Bake 20 minutes or until wooden pick inserted in cake portion comes out clean. Cool on wire rack.

Makes about 3 dozen cupcakes

Cream Cheese Filling

1 package (8 ounces) cream cheese, softened
⅓ cup sugar
1 egg
1 cup HERSHEY'S MINI CHIPS® Semi-Sweet Chocolate

In small bowl combine cream cheese, sugar and egg; beat until smooth. Stir in small chocolate chips.

Bread Pudding Snacks

Peanut Butter Brownie Cups

BROWNIE CUPS
- **1 package DUNCAN HINES® Double Fudge Brownie Mix**
- **2 eggs**
- **⅓ cup water**
- **¼ cup CRISCO® Oil or CRISCO® PURITAN® Canola Oil**

TOPPING
- **⅓ cup sugar**
- **⅓ cup light corn syrup**
- **½ cup peanut butter**

CHOCOLATE GLAZE
- **¾ cup semi-sweet chocolate chips**
- **3 tablespoons butter or margarine**
- **1 tablespoon light corn syrup**
- **3 tablespoons chopped peanuts, for garnish**

1. Preheat oven to 350°F. Place 24 (2-inch) foil liners on baking sheets.

2. For brownie cups, combine brownie mix, fudge packet from Mix, eggs, water and oil in large bowl. Stir with spoon until well blended, about 50 strokes. Place 2 level measuring tablespoons batter in each foil liner. Bake 20 to 22 minutes or until firm. Cool completely.

3. For topping, combine sugar and ⅓ cup corn syrup in small heavy saucepan. Bring to a boil on medium heat. Stir in peanut butter. Drop by rounded teaspoonfuls onto each brownie cup.

4. For chocolate glaze, combine chocolate chips, butter and 1 tablespoon corn syrup in small heavy saucepan. Cook, stirring constantly, on low heat until melted. Spoon 1 rounded teaspoonful chocolate glaze onto peanut butter topping. Sprinkle with chopped peanuts. Refrigerate 15 minutes or until chocolate is firm.

Makes 24 brownie cups

Quick Pumpkin Cupcakes

- **1 package (16 ounces) pound cake mix**
- **2 eggs**
- **1 cup LIBBY'S® Solid Pack Pumpkin**
- **⅓ cup water**
- **2 teaspoons pumpkin pie spice**
- **1 teaspoon baking soda**
- **Prepared vanilla frosting**

COMBINE cake mix, eggs, pumpkin, water, pumpkin pie spice and baking soda in large mixer bowl; beat on medium speed for 3 minutes. Pour batter into paper-lined muffin cups, filling ¾ full.

BAKE in preheated 325°F. oven for 25 to 30 minutes or until wooden pick inserted in center comes out clean. Cool in pan on wire rack for 10 minutes. Remove to wire rack to cool completely. Spread cupcakes with frosting.

Makes 14 cupcakes

Peanut Butter Brownie Cups

Sour Cream Coffeecake Cupcakes

1 cup (2 sticks) butter, softened (do not use margarine)
2 cups plus 4 teaspoons sugar, divided
2 eggs
1 cup sour cream
1 teaspoon vanilla
2 cups all-purpose flour
1 teaspoon salt
½ teaspoon baking soda
1 cup chopped black walnuts
1 teaspoon ground cinnamon

1. Preheat oven to 350°F. Insert paper liners into 18 muffin cups.

2. Beat together butter and 2 cups sugar in large bowl. Add eggs, 1 at a time, beating well after each addition. Blend in sour cream and vanilla.

3. Combine flour, salt and baking soda in medium bowl. Add to butter mixture; mix well.

4. Combine remaining 4 teaspoons sugar, walnuts and cinnamon in small bowl. Fill prepared muffin cups ⅓ full with batter; sprinkle with ⅔ of walnut mixture. Cover with remaining batter. Sprinkle with remaining walnut mixture.

5. Bake 25 to 30 minutes or until toothpick inserted into center comes out clean. Remove cupcakes from pan; cool on wire rack.

Makes about 1½ dozen cupcakes

Quick Chocolate Cupcakes

1½ cups all-purpose flour
¾ cup sugar
¼ cup HERSHEY'S Cocoa
1 teaspoon baking soda
½ teaspoon salt
1 cup water
¼ cup vegetable oil
1 tablespoon white vinegar
1 teaspoon vanilla extract

Heat oven to 375°F. Line muffin cups (2½ inches in diameter) with paper bake cups. In medium bowl, stir together flour, sugar, cocoa, baking soda and salt. Add water, oil, vinegar and vanilla; beat with whisk just until batter is smooth and ingredients are well blended. Fill muffin cups ⅔ full with batter. Bake 16 to 18 minutes or until wooden pick inserted in center comes out clean. Remove from pans to wire racks. Cool completely. Frost as desired. *Makes 1½ dozen cupcakes*

Sour Cream Coffeecake Cupcakes

Black Bottom Cheesecake Cups

CHEESECAKE FILLING
1 container (8 ounces) fat free cream cheese
¼ cup sugar
1 egg

CHOCOLATE BATTER
1½ cups all-purpose flour
¾ cup sugar
⅓ cup unsweetened cocoa powder
1 teaspoon baking soda
½ teaspoon salt
1 cup water
⅓ cup Prune Purée (recipe follows) or prepared prune butter *or* 1 jar (2½ ounces) first-stage baby food prunes
1 tablespoon instant espresso coffee powder *or* 2 tablespoons instant coffee granules
1 tablespoon white vinegar
2 teaspoons vanilla
½ cup semisweet chocolate chips

ALMOND TOPPING
¼ cup finely chopped blanched almonds
2 tablespoons sugar

Preheat oven to 350°F. Line eighteen 2¾-inch (⅓-cup capacity) muffin cups with cupcake liners. Coat liners lightly with vegetable cooking spray. To make filling, in small mixer bowl, beat filling ingredients at medium speed until smooth; set aside.

To make chocolate batter, in large bowl, combine first five batter ingredients. In medium bowl, beat water, prune purée, espresso powder, vinegar and vanilla until blended. Mix into flour mixture. Spoon into muffin cups, dividing equally. Top each with heaping teaspoonful of cream cheese mixture. Sprinkle with chocolate chips.

To make topping, mix almonds and sugar; sprinkle over chocolate chips. Bake cupcakes in center of oven about 25 minutes or until pick inserted into chocolate portion comes out clean. Cool in pans 5 minutes; remove from pans to wire racks to cool completely. *Makes 18 cupcakes*

Prune Purée: Combine 1⅓ cups (8 ounces) pitted prunes and 6 tablespoons hot water in container of food processor or blender. Pulse on and off until prunes are finely chopped and smooth. Store leftovers in a covered container in the refrigerator for up to two months. Makes 1 cup.

Favorite recipe from **California Prune Board**

Black Bottom Cheesecake Cups

Fudge 'n' Banana Cupcakes

1 package DUNCAN HINES® Moist Deluxe
    Devil's Food Cake Mix
3 large eggs
½ cup CRISCO® Oil or CRISCO®
    PURITAN® Canola Oil
1⅓ cups water
½ cup (1 stick) butter or margarine
2 ounces (2 squares) unsweetened chocolate
1 pound confectioners sugar
½ cup half-and-half
1 teaspoon vanilla extract
4 medium bananas
2 tablespoons lemon juice

1. Preheat oven to 350°F. Line 24 muffin cups with paper baking cups. Combine cake mix, eggs, oil and water in large mixer bowl. Prepare, bake and cool cupcakes as directed on package.

2. For frosting,* melt butter and chocolate in heavy saucepan over low heat. Remove from heat. Add confectioners sugar alternately with half-and-half, mixing until smooth after each addition. Beat in vanilla extract. Add more confectioners sugar to thicken or half-and-half to thin as needed.

3. Using small paring knife, remove cone-shaped piece from top center of each cupcake. Dot top of each cone with frosting. Frost top of each cupcake spreading frosting down into cone-shaped hole. Slice bananas and dip in lemon juice. Stand three banana slices in each hole. Set cone-shaped pieces, pointed side up, on banana slices.

Makes 24 cupcakes

*Or use 1 can DUNCAN HINES® Creamy Homestyle Chocolate Frosting.

Lemon Poppy Seed Cupcakes

CUPCAKES
1 package DUNCAN HINES® Moist Deluxe
    Lemon Supreme Cake Mix
3 eggs
1⅓ cups water
⅓ cup CRISCO® Oil or CRISCO®
    PURITAN® Canola Oil
3 tablespoons poppy seed

LEMON FROSTING
1 container (16 ounces) DUNCAN HINES®
    Creamy Homestyle Vanilla Frosting
1 teaspoon grated lemon peel
¼ teaspoon lemon extract
3 to 4 drops yellow food coloring
    Yellow and orange gumdrops, for garnish

1. Preheat oven to 350°F. Place 30 (2½-inch) paper liners in muffin cups.

2. For cupcakes, combine cake mix, eggs, water, oil and poppy seed in large bowl. Beat at medium speed of electric mixer 2 minutes. Fill paper liners about half full. Bake 18 to 21 minutes or until toothpick inserted in center comes out clean. Cool in pans 5 minutes. Remove to cooling racks. Cool completely.

3. For Lemon Frosting, combine Vanilla frosting, lemon peel and lemon extract in small bowl. Tint with yellow food coloring to desired color. Frost cupcakes with lemon frosting. Decorate with gumdrops.

Makes 30 cupcakes

Lemon Poppy Seed Cupcakes

Chocolate Surprise Cupcakes

FILLING
 1 package (8 ounces) PHILADELPHIA BRAND® Cream Cheese, softened
 ⅓ cup granulated sugar
 1 egg
 ½ cup BAKER'S® Semi-Sweet Real Chocolate Chips

CUPCAKES
 2 squares BAKER'S® Unsweetened Chocolate, melted
 ⅓ cup vegetable oil
 1¼ cups all-purpose flour
 1 cup granulated sugar
 ¾ cup water
 1 egg
 1 teaspoon vanilla
 ½ teaspoon baking soda
 ¼ teaspoon salt
  Powdered sugar (optional)

HEAT oven to 350°F.

BEAT cream cheese, ⅓ cup granulated sugar and 1 egg until smooth. Stir in chips; set aside.

BEAT melted chocolate, oil, flour, 1 cup granulated sugar, water, 1 egg, vanilla, baking soda and salt in large bowl with wire whisk or fork until smooth. Spoon ½ the batter evenly into 18 greased or paper-lined muffin cups. Top each with 1 tablespoon Filling. Spoon the remaining batter evenly over Filling.

BAKE 30 to 35 minutes or until toothpick inserted into center comes out clean. Remove from pans to cool on wire racks. Sprinkle with powdered sugar, if desired.

Makes 18 cupcakes

Prep time: 15 minutes
Baking time: 30 to 35 minutes

Cool melted chocolate to room temperature before adding it to the batter. Chocolate that is too warm may melt the fat in the batter, which will affect the texture of the final product.

Chocolate Surprise Cupcakes

Apple Streusel Mini Muffins

¼ cup chopped pecans
2 tablespoons brown sugar
1 tablespoon all-purpose flour
2 teaspoons butter or margarine, melted
1 package (7 ounces) apple cinnamon muffin mix plus ingredients to prepare mix
½ cup shredded peeled apple

1. Preheat oven to 425°F. Coat 18 mini muffin cups with nonstick cooking spray.

2. Combine pecans, brown sugar and flour in small bowl. Drizzle with butter; toss until mixture is moistened.

3. Prepare muffin mix according to package directions. Stir in apple. Fill each muffin cup ⅔ full. Sprinkle approximately 1 teaspoon pecan mixture on top of each muffin. Bake 12 to 15 minutes or until golden brown. Cool slightly. Serve warm.

Makes 18 mini muffins

Note: *For regular-size muffins, grease 6 (2½-inch) muffin cups. Prepare topping and batter as directed. Fill muffin cups ⅔ full of batter. Sprinkle approximately 1 tablespoon pecan mixture on top of each muffin. Bake 18 to 20 minutes or until golden brown. Makes 6 regular-size muffins.*

Banana Blueberry Muffins

2 extra-ripe, medium DOLE® Bananas, peeled
6 tablespoons margarine
6 tablespoons brown sugar
1 egg
1½ cups all-purpose flour
½ teaspoon baking powder
½ teaspoon baking soda
½ teaspoon salt
½ teaspoon grated lemon peel
1 cup frozen blueberries, rinsed, drained

• Purée bananas in blender (1 cup).

• Beat margarine and sugar until light and fluffy. Mix in bananas and egg.

• Combine flour, baking powder, baking soda, salt and lemon peel. Blend into banana mixture just until moistened. Fold in blueberries.

• Line 6 large muffin cups with paper liners. Coat lightly with vegetable spray. Divide batter evenly.

• Bake in 375°F oven 20 to 25 minutes.

Makes 6 muffins

Prep time: 20 minutes
Bake time: 25 minutes

Apple Streusel Mini Muffins

Raisin Zucchini Muffins

1 egg
¾ cup nonfat milk
½ cup brown sugar, packed
⅓ cup vegetable oil
1½ cups shredded zucchini
2 tablespoons grated orange peel
2 cups all-purpose flour
1 tablespoon baking powder
¼ teaspoon *each* **salt, cinnamon, ginger, nutmeg**
⅛ teaspoon ground cloves
1 cup DOLE® Raisins
½ cup DOLE® Chopped Almonds, toasted

• Beat egg, milk, brown sugar and oil. Stir in zucchini and orange peel.

• Combine remaining ingredients. Stir into zucchini mixture just until moistened.

• Spoon into 12 muffin cups coated with cooking spray. Bake in 375°F oven 25 minutes. Serve warm.

Makes 12 muffins

Prep time: 20 minutes
Bake time: 25 minutes

Orange Brunch Muffins

3 cups buttermilk baking mix
¾ cup all-purpose flour
⅔ cup granulated sugar
2 eggs, lightly beaten
½ cup plain yogurt
½ cup orange juice
1 tablespoon grated orange peel
2 cups (12-ounce package) NESTLÉ® TOLL HOUSE® Premier White Morsels, *divided*
½ cup chopped macadamia nuts or walnuts

COMBINE baking mix, flour and sugar in large bowl. Add eggs, yogurt, orange juice and orange peel; stir just until blended. Stir in *1⅓ cups* morsels. Spoon into 12 to 14 paper-lined muffin cups. Sprinkle with nuts. BAKE in preheated 375°F. oven for 18 to 22 minutes or until wooden pick inserted in center comes out clean. Cool in pans for 10 minutes; remove to wire racks to cool slightly. MICROWAVE *remaining* morsels in heavy-duty plastic bag on MEDIUM-HIGH (70%) power for 1 minute; knead. Microwave for additional 10- to 20-second intervals, kneading until smooth. Cut tiny corner from bag; squeeze to drizzle over muffins while still slightly warm. Serve warm.

Makes 12 to 14 muffins

Cherries and Cream Muffins

2½ cups frozen unsweetened tart cherries,
    divided
1 cup granulated sugar
½ cup butter or margarine
2 eggs
1 teaspoon almond extract
½ teaspoon vanilla extract
2 cups all-purpose flour
2 teaspoons baking powder
½ teaspoon salt
½ cup light cream, half-and-half or milk

Cut cherries in halves while frozen. Set aside to thaw and drain. In large bowl, beat sugar and butter until light and fluffy. Add eggs, almond extract and vanilla, beating well. Crush ½ cup cherries with fork; stir into batter.

Combine flour, baking powder and salt. Fold half the flour mixture into batter with spatula, then half the cream. Fold in remaining flour and cream. Fold in remaining cherry halves. Portion batter evenly into 12 paper-lined or lightly greased muffin cups (2¾ inches in diameter). Sprinkle with additional sugar.

Bake in preheated 375°F oven 20 to 30 minutes or until golden brown. *Makes 12 muffins*

Favorite recipe from **Cherry Marketing Institute, Inc.**

Banana Scotch Muffins

1 extra-ripe, large DOLE® Banana, peeled
1 egg, beaten
½ cup sugar
¼ cup milk
¼ cup vegetable oil
1 teaspoon vanilla extract
1 cup all-purpose flour
1 cup quick-cooking rolled oats
1 teaspoon baking powder
½ teaspoon baking soda
½ teaspoon salt
½ cup butterscotch chips

• Purée banana in blender (⅔ cup); combine with egg, sugar, milk, oil and vanilla.

• Combine flour, oats, baking powder, baking soda and salt.

• Stir banana mixture into dry ingredients with butterscotch chips until just blended. Spoon batter into greased muffin cups. Bake in 400°F oven 12 to 15 minutes. *Makes 12 muffins*

Prep time: 20 minutes
Bake time: 15 minutes

Glazed Strawberry Lemon Streusel Muffins

Lemon Streusel Topping (recipe follows)
Lemony Glaze (recipe follows)
1½ **cups all-purpose flour**
½ **cup sugar**
2 **teaspoons baking powder**
1 **teaspoon ground cinnamon**
¼ **teaspoon salt**
½ **cup milk**
½ **cup (1 stick) butter or margarine, melted**
1 **egg**
1½ **cups fresh strawberries, chopped**
1 **teaspoon grated lemon peel**

Preheat oven to 375°F. Paper-line 12 (2½-inch) muffin cups. Prepare Lemon Streusel Topping and Lemony Glaze; set aside.

Combine flour, sugar, baking powder, cinnamon and salt in large bowl. Combine milk, butter and egg in small bowl until well blended. Stir into flour mixture just until moistened. Fold in strawberries and lemon peel. Spoon evenly into prepared muffin cups. Sprinkle Lemon Streusel Topping evenly over tops of muffins.

Bake 20 to 25 minutes or until toothpick inserted in center comes out clean. Remove from pan. Cool on wire rack 10 minutes. Drizzle Lemony Glaze over tops of warm muffins. Serve warm or cool completely.
Makes 12 muffins

Lemon Streusel Topping: Combine ¼ cup chopped pecans, ¼ cup packed brown sugar, 2 tablespoons all-purpose flour, ½ teaspoon ground cinnamon and ½ teaspoon grated lemon peel in medium bowl. Add 1 tablespoon melted butter or margarine, stirring until crumbly.

Lemony Glaze: Combine ½ cup powdered sugar and 1 tablespoon fresh lemon juice in small bowl, stirring until smooth.

Be sure to wash lemons thoroughly before using their peel. For easier grating, run the lemon diagonally across a grater rather than up and down. One medium lemon will yield two to three teaspoons grated peel.

Glazed Strawberry Lemon Streusel Muffins

Blueberry Muffins

1 cup fresh or thawed, frozen blueberries
1¾ cups plus 1 tablespoon all-purpose flour, divided
2 teaspoons baking powder
1 teaspoon grated lemon peel
½ teaspoon salt
½ cup MOTT'S® Apple Sauce
½ cup sugar
1 whole egg
1 egg white
2 tablespoons vegetable oil
¼ cup skim milk

1. Preheat oven to 375°F. Line 12 (2½-inch) muffin cups with paper liners or spray with nonstick cooking spray.

2. In small bowl, toss blueberries with 1 tablespoon flour.

3. In large bowl, combine remaining 1¾ cups flour, baking powder, lemon peel and salt.

4. In another small bowl, combine apple sauce, sugar, whole egg, egg white and oil.

5. Stir apple sauce mixture into flour mixture alternately with milk. Mix just until moistened. Fold in blueberry mixture.

6. Spoon evenly into prepared muffin cups.

7. Bake 20 minutes or until toothpick inserted in center comes out clean. Immediately remove from pan; cool on wire rack 10 minutes. Serve warm or cool completely. *Makes 12 servings*

Favorite Corn Muffins

1 cup all-purpose flour
¾ cup cornmeal
¼ cup bran
2 teaspoons baking powder
1½ teaspoons salt
½ teaspoon baking soda
1 cup sour cream
2 eggs
¼ cup honey
¼ cup (½ stick) butter, melted

Preheat oven to 425°F. Coat 12-cup muffin pan generously with butter. Combine flour, cornmeal, bran, baking powder, salt and baking soda in large bowl. Beat sour cream, eggs, honey and butter in medium bowl until well blended. Add sour cream mixture to flour mixture; stir just until dry ingredients are evenly moistened. Spoon batter into prepared muffin cups. Bake 15 to 20 minutes. Cool in pan 5 minutes before removing. Serve warm.

Makes 12 muffins

Favorite recipe from **Wisconsin Milk Marketing Board**

Blueberry Muffins

Snacking Surprise Muffins

1½ cups all-purpose flour
½ cup sugar
1 cup fresh or frozen blueberries
2½ teaspoons baking powder
1 teaspoon ground cinnamon
¼ teaspoon salt
1 egg, beaten
⅔ cup buttermilk
¼ cup (½ stick) margarine or butter, melted
3 tablespoons peach preserves

TOPPING
1 tablespoon sugar
¼ teaspoon ground cinnamon

1. Preheat oven to 400°F. Line 12 medium muffin cups with paper liners; set aside.

2. Combine flour, ½ cup sugar, blueberries, baking powder, 1 teaspoon cinnamon and salt in medium bowl. Combine egg, buttermilk and margarine in small bowl. Add to flour mixture; mix just until moistened.

3. Spoon about 1 tablespoon batter into each muffin cup. Drop a scant teaspoonful of preserves into center of batter in each cup; top with remaining batter.

4. Combine 1 tablespoon sugar and ¼ teaspoon cinnamon in small bowl; sprinkle evenly over batter.

5. Bake 18 to 20 minutes or until lightly browned. Remove muffins to wire rack to cool completely.

Makes 12 servings

Toffee Crunch Muffins

1½ cups all-purpose flour
⅓ cup packed brown sugar
2 teaspoons baking powder
½ teaspoon baking soda
½ teaspoon salt
½ cup milk
½ cup sour cream
3 tablespoons butter or margarine, melted
1 egg, beaten
1 teaspoon vanilla
3 bars (1.4 ounces each) chocolate-covered toffee, chopped and divided

Preheat oven to 400°F. Grease or paper-line 36 (1¾-inch) mini-muffin cups; set aside.

Combine flour, sugar, baking powder, baking soda and salt in large bowl. Combine milk, sour cream, butter, egg and vanilla in small bowl until well blended. Stir into flour mixture just until moistened. Fold in two-thirds of toffee. Spoon into prepared muffin cups, filling almost full. Sprinkle remaining toffee evenly over tops of muffins.

Bake 16 to 18 minutes or until toothpick inserted in center comes out clean. Remove from pans. Cool on wire racks 10 minutes. Serve warm or cool completely.

Makes 36 mini muffins

Apple 'n' Walnut Spiced Muffins

1 cup raisins
   Hot water
2 cups all-purpose flour
1 cup oatmeal
⅔ cup sugar
2½ teaspoons baking powder
½ teaspoon salt
½ teaspoon ground cinnamon
½ teaspoon ground allspice
¼ teaspoon ground nutmeg
4 to 5 small apples
1 egg
2 egg whites
¼ cup canola or vegetable oil
½ cup chopped California walnuts

Preheat oven to 350°F. Grease muffin pans or coat with nonstick cooking spray. Place raisins in small bowl; cover with hot water. Let stand 10 minutes; drain well and set aside.

Meanwhile, in medium bowl, combine flour, oatmeal, sugar, baking powder, salt, cinnamon, allspice and nutmeg. Mix well; set aside.

Peel and core apples. Grate coarsely to make about 2 generous cups, lightly packed. Combine apples, egg, egg whites, oil and walnuts in medium bowl; beat until well blended. Add apple mixture and raisins to flour mixture; stir just until blended and moistened. (Batter will be very stiff.)

Spoon batter into prepared muffin pans, filling cups about three-fourths full. Bake for 20 to 25 minutes or until toothpick inserted in center comes out clean. Cool 5 minutes in pan; remove and serve warm. *Makes 12 muffins*

Favorite recipe from **Walnut Marketing Board**

Orange Almond Muffins

1½ cups flour
1 teaspoon baking powder
1 teaspoon baking soda
½ teaspoon salt
1 orange (about 8 ounces)
1 cup BLUE DIAMOND® Blanched Almond Paste
½ cup granulated sugar
¼ cup butter, melted
1 egg
½ cup plus 1½ tablespoons orange juice, divided
1 teaspoon vanilla extract
¼ teaspoon almond extract
1 cup powdered sugar, sifted

Sift flour, baking powder, baking soda and salt; set aside. Peel and dice orange; set aside. Beat almond paste and granulated sugar until mixture resembles coarse cornmeal. Beat in butter until smooth. Beat in diced orange, egg, ½ cup orange juice, vanilla and almond extracts. Stir in flour mixture just until combined.* *Do not overmix.* Divide batter evenly among 12 greased 2½-inch muffin cups.

Bake at 400°F for 15 to 20 minutes or until golden brown. Cool in pan 5 minutes. Rap pan sharply on side to remove muffins from pan; cool right side up on wire rack. Meanwhile, combine powdered sugar and remaining 1½ tablespoons orange juice. If necessary, add more orange juice until glaze is of desired consistency. Drizzle over muffins.

Makes 12 muffins

*To prepare batter in food processor, combine almond paste and sugar and mix with on-off pulses until mixture resembles coarse cornmeal. Add diced orange; process until orange is finely chopped. Add butter, egg, ½ cup orange juice, vanilla and almond extracts. Process until well blended. Add flour mixture, processing just until ingredients are incorporated.

Carrot and Cream Cheese Muffins

---

  1 cup bran cereal
  ½ cup boiling water
  2 eggs
  2 cups buttermilk
  2 cups quick-cooking oats
  1 cup JACK FROST® Granulated Sugar
  1 cup JACK FROST® Brown Sugar, packed
  ½ cup vegetable oil
2½ cups all-purpose flour
2½ teaspoons baking soda
  ½ teaspoon salt
  1 cup shredded carrots
  ½ cup chopped walnuts
    Cream Cheese Filling (recipe follows)

In small bowl, mix bran cereal and boiling water, set aside to cool. In large bowl beat eggs. Stir in buttermilk, oats, granulated sugar, brown sugar and oil; mix well. Add flour, baking soda, and salt; stir just until moistened. Stir in cooled bran mixture, carrots and walnuts. Grease muffin pans or line with paper liners. Fill muffin cups ⅔ full. Place 1 tablespoon Cream Cheese Filling over batter; top with 2 to 3 tablespoons batter. Bake in 350°F oven for 18 to 20 minutes. (Batter can be refrigerated up to 1 week to bake smaller batches at different times.)

Makes 24 muffins

Cream Cheese Filling

  ⅔ cup JACK FROST® Confectioners Sugar
  1 (8-ounce) package cream cheese

In small bowl, beat confectioners sugar and cream cheese until smooth.

Lemon Poppy Seed Muffins

3 cups all-purpose flour
1 cup sugar
3 tablespoons poppy seeds
1 tablespoon grated lemon peel
2 teaspoons baking powder
1 teaspoon baking soda
½ teaspoon salt
1 container (16 ounces) plain low-fat yogurt
½ cup fresh lemon juice
¼ cup vegetable oil
2 eggs, beaten
1½ teaspoons vanilla

Preheat oven to 400°F. Grease 12 (3½-inch) large muffin cups; set aside.

Combine flour, sugar, poppy seeds, lemon peel, baking powder, baking soda and salt in large bowl. Combine yogurt, lemon juice, oil, eggs and vanilla in small bowl until well blended. Stir into flour mixture just until moistened. Spoon into prepared muffin cups, filling two-thirds full.

Bake 25 to 30 minutes or until toothpick inserted in center comes out clean. Cool in pans on wire racks 5 minutes. Remove from pans; cool on wire racks 10 minutes. Serve warm or cool completely.

Makes 12 jumbo muffins

The Original Kellogg's All-Bran Muffin™

1¼ cups all-purpose flour
½ cup sugar
1 tablespoon baking powder
¼ teaspoon salt
2 cups KELLOGG'S® ALL-BRAN® Cereal
1¼ cups low fat milk
1 egg
¼ cup vegetable oil
Vegetable cooking spray

1. Stir together flour, sugar, baking powder and salt. Set aside.

2. In large mixing bowl, combine Kellogg's® All-Bran® cereal and milk. Let stand about 5 minutes or until cereal softens. Add egg and oil. Beat well. Add flour mixture, stirring only until combined. Portion batter evenly into twelve 2½-inch muffin pan cups coated with cooking spray.

3. Bake at 400°F about 20 minutes or until lightly browned. Serve warm. *Makes 12 muffins*

For muffins with reduced calories, fat and cholesterol: *Use 2 tablespoons sugar, 2 tablespoons oil, replace low fat milk with 1¼ cups skim milk, and substitute 2 egg whites for 1 egg. Prepare and bake as directed.*

Lemon Poppy Seed Muffins

Cranberry Pecan Muffins

1½ cups fresh or frozen cranberries
¼ cup light corn syrup
1 package DUNCAN HINES® Cinnamon
    Muffin Mix
1 egg
¾ cup water or milk
½ cup chopped pecans

1. Preheat oven to 400°F. Place 14 (2½-inch) paper liners in muffin cups. Place cranberries and corn syrup in heavy saucepan. Cook on medium heat, stirring occasionally, until cranberries pop and mixture is slightly thickened. Drain cranberries in tea strainer; set aside.

2. Empty muffin mix in medium bowl. Break up any lumps. Add egg and water. Stir until moistened, about 50 strokes. Stir in cranberries and pecans. Knead swirl packet from Mix for 10 seconds before opening. Cut off 1 end of swirl packet. Squeeze contents over top of batter. Swirl into batter with knife or spatula. *Do not completely mix in.* Spoon batter into muffin cups (see Tip). Sprinkle with contents of topping packet from Mix. Bake at 400°F for 18 to 22 minutes or until toothpick inserted into center comes out clean. Cool in pans 5 to 10 minutes. Serve warm or cool completely. *Makes 14 muffins*

Tip: *Fill an equal number of muffin cups in each muffin pan with batter. For more even baking, fill empty muffin cups with ½ inch of water.*

Potato Parmesan Muffins

1 medium COLORADO potato, peeled and
    coarsely chopped
½ cup water
¼ cup milk
1⅔ cup all-purpose flour
3 tablespoons sugar
3 to 4 tablespoons grated Parmesan cheese,
    divided
2 teaspoons baking powder
½ teaspoon dried basil leaves, crushed
¼ teaspoon baking soda
¼ cup vegetable oil
1 egg, beaten

In small saucepan, cook potato in water, covered, over medium heat about 10 minutes or until tender. Do not drain. Mash until smooth *or* place mixture in blender container and blend until smooth. Add enough milk to make 1 cup. In large bowl, combine flour, sugar, 2 tablespoons Parmesan, baking powder, basil and baking soda; mix well. Combine potato mixture, oil and egg; add to flour mixture, stirring just until moistened. Spoon into greased or paper-lined muffin cups. Sprinkle tops with remaining Parmesan. Bake at 400°F for 20 minutes or until lightly browned. Remove from pan and cool on wire rack. *Makes 10 muffins*

Favorite recipe from **Colorado Potato Administrative Committee**

Cranberry Pecan Muffins

German Chocolate Muffins

German Chocolate Topping (recipe follows)
1 package (18.25 ounces) pudding-included
German chocolate cake mix

Preheat oven to 400°F. Grease 12 (3½-inch) large muffin cups; set aside. Prepare German Chocolate Topping; set aside.

Prepare cake mix according to package directions, *reducing* water by ¼ cup. Spoon into prepared muffin cups, filling half full. Sprinkle German Chocolate Topping evenly over tops of muffins.

Bake 20 to 25 minutes or until toothpick inserted in center comes out clean. Cool in pan on wire rack 5 minutes. Remove from pan. Cool on wire rack 10 minutes. Serve warm or cool completely.

Makes 12 jumbo muffins

German Chocolate Topping: Combine 3 tablespoons *each* chopped pecans, flaked coconut and packed brown sugar in small bowl until well blended.

Country Spice Muffins

1½ cups 100% bran cereal
1 cup milk
¼ cup FLEISCHMANN'S® Margarine, melted
1 egg, slightly beaten
1½ cups all-purpose flour
½ cup firmly packed light brown sugar
1 tablespoon DAVIS® Baking Powder
1 teaspoon ground cinnamon
1 teaspoon ground nutmeg
1 cup shredded carrots
1 cup dried cherries or diced dried fruit mix
½ cup PLANTERS® Gold Measure Walnuts, chopped

In small bowl, mix bran, milk, margarine and egg; let stand 5 minutes. In another bowl, blend flour, brown sugar, baking powder, cinnamon and nutmeg; stir in bran mixture just until blended. Stir in carrots, dried cherries or fruit mix and walnuts. Spoon batter into 12 greased 2½-inch muffin-pan cups. Bake at 400°F for 15 to 20 minutes or until done. Serve warm.

Makes 12 muffins

German Chocolate Muffins

Cranberry Cappuccino Muffins

1¾ cups all-purpose flour
⅔ cup sugar
3 tablespoons unsweetened cocoa
1 tablespoon instant coffee
1½ teaspoons baking powder
¾ teaspoon salt
½ teaspoon baking soda
½ teaspoon ground cinnamon
¾ cup milk
6 tablespoons oil
1 egg
1¼ cups coarsely chopped OCEAN SPRAY®
Fresh or Frozen Cranberries

Preheat oven to 375°F. Grease 12-cup muffin pan.

Combine flour, sugar, cocoa, coffee, baking powder, salt, baking soda and cinnamon in medium bowl. Combine milk, oil and egg in separate bowl. Add liquid ingredients to dry ingredients, mixing just until dry ingredients are moistened. Stir in cranberries.

Fill each muffin cup ⅔ full. Bake for 25 minutes or until toothpick inserted into center comes out clean. *Makes 1 dozen muffins*

White Chocolate Chunk Muffins

2½ cups all-purpose flour
1 cup packed brown sugar
⅓ cup unsweetened cocoa powder
2 teaspoons baking soda
½ teaspoon salt
1⅓ cups buttermilk
6 tablespoons butter or margarine, melted
2 eggs, beaten
1½ teaspoons vanilla
1½ cups chopped white chocolate

Preheat oven to 400°F. Grease 12 (3½-inch) large muffin cups; set aside.

Combine flour, sugar, cocoa, baking soda and salt in large bowl. Combine buttermilk, butter, eggs and vanilla in small bowl until blended. Stir into flour mixture just until moistened. Fold in white chocolate. Spoon into prepared muffin cups, filling half full.

Bake 25 to 30 minutes or until toothpick inserted in center comes out clean. Cool in pan on wire rack 5 minutes. Remove from pan; cool on wire rack 10 minutes. Serve warm or cool completely. *Makes 12 jumbo muffins*

Black Magic Banana Cupcakes

2 extra-ripe, medium DOLE® Bananas, peeled
1 egg
½ cup buttermilk
¼ cup vegetable oil
½ teaspoon vanilla extract
1 cup sugar
¾ cup plus 2 tablespoons all-purpose flour
6 tablespoons unsweetened cocoa
1 teaspoon baking soda
¼ teaspoon baking powder
¼ teaspoon salt

• Purée bananas in blender (1 cup).

• Mix bananas, egg, buttermilk, oil and vanilla.

• Combine sugar, flour, cocoa, baking soda, baking powder and salt; add to banana mixture. Stir just until moistened.

• Line 12 muffin cups with paper liners. Lightly coat with vegetable spray. Fill two-thirds full with batter.

• Bake in 350°F oven 25 minutes.

Makes 12 cupcakes

Prep time: 20 minutes
Bake time: 25 minutes

Upside Down Banana Pecan Muffins

½ cup packed light brown sugar
⅓ cup butter, softened
⅔ cup chopped pecans
2 cups all-purpose flour
½ cup sugar
1 tablespoon baking powder
1 teaspoon ground cinnamon
½ teaspoon salt
2 eggs
½ cup WESSON® Vegetable Oil
2 ripe bananas, mashed
1 teaspoon vanilla extract

In small bowl, combine brown sugar and butter; stir in pecans. Place *1 tablespoon* nut mixture into 14 greased muffin cups; set aside. In medium bowl, combine flour, sugar, baking powder, cinnamon and salt. In small bowl, beat together eggs, oil, bananas and vanilla. Stir oil mixture into flour mixture just until all ingredients are moistened. Fill prepared muffin cups with batter. Bake at 375°F for 20 minutes or until muffins test done with wooden pick. To serve, invert muffins onto plate.

Makes 14 muffins

Nutmeg Strawberry Muffins

2 cups stemmed and halved (quartered if large) California strawberries (about 1 pint basket)
2 cups plus 1 tablespoon sugar, divided
½ cup plus 1 tablespoon cornmeal, divided
3¼ teaspoons ground nutmeg, divided
3 cups flour
1 teaspoon salt
1 teaspoon baking soda
1¼ cups vegetable oil
4 eggs, beaten
1 cup chopped walnuts

Preheat oven to 375°F. Toss strawberries with 1 tablespoon sugar in medium bowl; set aside. Combine 1 tablespoon sugar, 1 tablespoon cornmeal and ¼ teaspoon nutmeg for topping; set aside. Combine flour, remaining sugar, ½ cup cornmeal, 3 teaspoons nutmeg, salt and baking soda in large bowl. Add oil and eggs to strawberry mixture; mix gently. Add strawberry mixture and walnuts to flour mixture; mix just until dry ingredients are moistened. Measure ⅓ cup batter into 24 paper-lined or greased 2¾-inch muffin cups. Sprinkle reserved topping mixture evenly over muffins. Bake in center of oven about 25 minutes or until springy to the touch and toothpick inserted into centers comes out clean. Cooled muffins can be wrapped and frozen up to 2 months.

Makes 24 muffins

Nutmeg Strawberry Bread: *Prepare batter as directed above. Pour into two greased 8×4-inch loaf pans; sprinkle loaves with topping mixture. Bake in preheated 375°F oven about 1 hour and 10 minutes or until toothpick inserted into center comes out clean. Cool on rack.* *Makes 2 loaves*

Favorite recipe from **California Strawberry Commission**

Honey Maid® Graham Muffins

2 Stay Fresh Packs HONEY MAID® Honey Grahams, finely rolled (about 3 cups crumbs)
¼ cup sugar
2 teaspoons baking powder
1 cup skim milk
1 egg, slightly beaten
2 tablespoons honey

In medium bowl, combine crumbs, sugar and baking powder. Stir in milk, egg and honey just until moistened. Spoon batter into 9 greased 2½-inch muffin-pan cups.

Bake at 400°F for 15 to 18 minutes or until toothpick inserted in center comes out clean. Let stand 5 minutes; remove from pan. Serve warm.

Makes 9 muffins

Apple Butter Spice Muffins

½ cup sugar
1 teaspoon ground cinnamon
¼ teaspoon ground nutmeg
⅛ teaspoon ground allspice
½ cup pecans or walnuts, chopped
2 cups all-purpose flour
2 teaspoons baking powder
¼ teaspoon salt
1 cup milk
¼ cup vegetable oil
1 egg
¼ cup apple butter

Preheat oven to 400°F. Grease 12 (2½-inch) muffin cups; set aside.

Combine sugar, cinnamon, nutmeg and allspice in large bowl. Toss 2 tablespoons sugar mixture with pecans in small bowl; set aside. Add flour, baking powder and salt to remaining sugar mixture. Combine milk, oil and egg in medium bowl; stir into flour mixture just until moistened.

Spoon 1 tablespoon batter into each prepared muffin cup. Spoon 1 teaspoon apple butter into each cup. Spoon remaining batter over apple butter. Sprinkle reserved pecan mixture evenly over tops of muffins.

Bake 20 to 25 minutes or until toothpick inserted in center comes out clean. Remove from pan; cool completely.

Makes 12 muffins

Swiss Coconut Banana Muffins

½ cup milk
2 teaspoons lemon juice
3 cups all-purpose flour
4 teaspoons baking powder
1 teaspoon baking soda
½ teaspoon salt
⅔ cup butter, softened
⅔ cup sugar
3 large eggs
1 teaspoon vanilla
½ cup cream of coconut
3 ripe bananas, mashed (1 cup)
2 cups (8 ounces) finely shredded Wisconsin Swiss cheese, divided

Combine milk and lemon juice; set aside. Sift flour, baking powder, baking soda and salt together. In large bowl, beat butter and sugar with electric mixer until creamy. Add eggs, 1 at a time, beating well after each addition. Add vanilla, cream of coconut, bananas and milk mixture. Add flour mixture and blend just until moistened. Stir in cheese, reserving ¼ cup cheese to sprinkle over muffins, if desired. Fill greased or paper-lined muffin cups ½ to ⅔ full. Sprinkle with reserved cheese. Bake at 375°F 30 to 35 minutes.

Makes 2 dozen muffins

Favorite recipe from **Wisconsin Milk Marketing Board**

Apple Butter Spice Muffins

Bittersweet Chocolate Pound Cake

CAKE

2 cups all-purpose flour
1 teaspoon baking soda
1 teaspoon baking powder
1½ cups water
2 tablespoons freeze dried coffee
4 bars (8 ounces) NESTLÉ® TOLL HOUSE® Unsweetened Baking Chocolate, broken into pieces, *divided*
2 cups granulated sugar
1 cup (2 sticks) butter, softened
1 teaspoon vanilla extract
3 eggs

CHOCOLATE GLAZE

3 tablespoons butter or margarine
1½ cups sifted powdered sugar
2 to 3 tablespoons water
1 teaspoon vanilla extract
Powdered sugar (optional)

COMBINE flour, baking soda and baking powder in small bowl. Bring water and coffee to a boil in small saucepan; remove from heat. Add *3 bars (6 ounces)* baking chocolate; stir until smooth.

BEAT sugar, butter and vanilla in large mixer bowl until creamy. Add eggs; beat on high speed for 5 minutes. Beat in flour mixture alternately with chocolate mixture. Pour into well-greased 10-inch bundt pan.

BAKE in preheated 325°F. oven for 50 to 60 minutes or until long wooden pick inserted near center comes out clean. Cool in pan on wire rack for 30 minutes. Invert onto wire rack; cool completely. Drizzle with Chocolate Glaze; sprinkle with powdered sugar.

FOR CHOCOLATE GLAZE: MELT *remaining baking bar (2 ounces)* and butter in small, heavy duty saucepan over low heat, stirring until smooth. Remove from heat. Stir in powdered sugar alternately with water until desired consistency. Stir in vanilla.

Makes 12 servings

Bittersweet Chocolate Pound Cake

German Chocolate Cake

CAKE

1 package (4 ounces) sweet chocolate baking bar, chopped
½ cup boiling water
1 package DUNCAN HINES® Moist Deluxe White Cake Mix
3 eggs
¼ cup butter or margarine, softened

FROSTING

⅔ cup sugar
⅔ cup evaporated milk
2 egg yolks
⅓ cup butter or margarine
1⅓ cups flaked coconut
1 cup chopped pecans
½ teaspoon vanilla extract
1 container (16 ounces) DUNCAN HINES® Creamy Homestyle Chocolate Frosting

1. Preheat oven to 350°F. Grease and flour two 9-inch round cake pans.

2. For cake, place chocolate in 2-cup glass measuring cup. Add ½ cup boiling water. Stir until chocolate is melted. Add additional water to equal 1¼ cups liquid. Combine cake mix, eggs, chocolate liquid mixture and ¼ cup butter in large bowl. Beat at low speed with electric mixer until moistened. Beat at medium speed for 2 minutes. Divide evenly between pans. Bake at 350°F for 27 to 32 minutes or until toothpick inserted in center comes out clean. Cool following package directions.

3. For frosting, combine sugar, evaporated milk, egg yolks and ⅓ cup butter in medium saucepan. Cook on medium heat, stirring constantly, until mixture comes to a boil. Remove from heat. Add coconut, pecans and vanilla extract. Stir until thick. Cool 15 minutes.

4. To assemble, place one cake layer on serving plate. Spread with half the coconut frosting. Top with second cake layer. Spread Chocolate frosting on sides of cake. Spread remaining coconut frosting on top of cake. *Makes 12 to 16 servings*

Tip: Store leftover Chocolate frosting tightly covered in refrigerator. Spread frosting between graham crackers for a quick snack.

To transport cakes to a bake sale without ruining the frosting, arrange several toothpicks or uncooked spaghetti noodles in the top of the cake before covering it with foil or plastic wrap. This will prevent the wrap from sticking to the frosting.

German Chocolate Cake

Deep Dark Chocolate Cake with Mocha Frosting

CAKE
1¾ cups all-purpose flour
1½ cups granulated sugar
  1 tablespoon baking powder
  1 teaspoon salt
1¼ cups sour cream
 ⅔ cup WESSON® Vegetable Oil
  3 eggs
  3 ounces unsweetened baking chocolate, melted and cooled
1½ teaspoons vanilla extract

FROSTING
  1 (1-pound) box powdered sugar
  6 tablespoons butter, softened
  2 tablespoons unsweetened cocoa
  1 tablespoon instant coffee combined with 2 tablespoons hot water
2½ tablespoons milk
  1 teaspoon vanilla extract

In large bowl, combine flour, granulated sugar, baking powder and salt. Add sour cream, oil, eggs, chocolate and vanilla; beat 2 minutes with electric mixer. Pour batter into 2 greased and floured 8-inch cake pans. Bake at 350°F for 30 to 35 minutes or until wooden pick inserted in center comes out clean. Let stand in pans 10 minutes; cool completely on wire racks before frosting.

In medium bowl, beat all frosting ingredients until smooth and creamy. Frost cake on serving plate.

Makes 1 (8-inch) layer cake

Chocolate-Chocolate Cake

1 package (8 ounces) PHILADELPHIA BRAND® Cream Cheese, softened
1 cup BREAKSTONE'S® or KNUDSEN® Sour Cream
½ cup coffee-flavored liqueur or water
2 eggs
1 package (2-layer size) chocolate cake mix
1 package (4-serving size) JELL-O® Chocolate Flavor Instant Pudding and Pie Filling
1 cup BAKER'S Semi-Sweet Real Chocolate Chips

MIX cream cheese, sour cream, liqueur and eggs with electric mixer on medium speed until well blended. Add cake mix and pudding mix; beat until well blended. Fold in chips. (Batter will be stiff.)

POUR into greased and floured 12-cup fluted tube pan.

BAKE at 325°F for 1 hour to 1 hour and 5 minutes or until toothpick inserted near center comes out clean. Cool 5 minutes. Remove from pan. Cool completely on wire rack. Sprinkle with powdered sugar before serving. Garnish, if desired.

Makes 10 to 12 servings

Chocolate-Chocolate Cake

Deep Dark Chocolate Cake

2 cups sugar
1¾ cups all-purpose flour
¾ cup HERSHEY'S Cocoa or HERSHEY'S
    European Style Cocoa
1½ teaspoons baking powder
1½ teaspoons baking soda
1 teaspoon salt
2 eggs
1 cup milk
½ cup vegetable oil
2 teaspoons vanilla extract
1 cup boiling water
    One-Bowl Buttercream Frosting
    (recipe follows)

Heat oven to 350°F. Grease and flour two 9-inch round baking pans.* In large bowl, stir together sugar, flour, cocoa, baking powder, baking soda and salt. Add eggs, milk, oil and vanilla; beat on medium speed of electric mixer 2 minutes. Stir in water. (Batter will be thin.) Pour batter evenly into prepared pans. Bake 30 to 35 minutes or until wooden pick inserted in center comes out clean. Cool 10 minutes; remove from pans to wire racks. Cool completely. Prepare One-Bowl Buttercream Frosting; spread between layers and over top and sides of cake.   *Makes 8 to 10 servings*

*One 13×9×2-inch baking pan may be substituted for 9-inch round baking pans. Prepare as directed above. Bake 35 to 40 minutes. Cool completely in pan on wire rack. Frost as desired.

One-Bowl Buttercream Frosting

6 tablespoons butter or margarine, softened
2⅔ cups powdered sugar
½ cup HERSHEY'S Cocoa or HERSHEY'S
    European Style Cocoa
⅓ cup milk
1 teaspoon vanilla extract

In medium bowl, beat butter. Blend in powdered sugar and cocoa alternately with milk, beating well after each addition until smooth and of spreading consistency. Blend in vanilla. Add additional milk, if needed.

Try to have your cake ingredients at room temperature whenever possible; this will result in the greatest volume in your cakes.

Deep Dark Chocolate Cake

Chocolate Sock-It-To-Me Cake

STREUSEL FILLING
 1 package DUNCAN HINES® Moist Deluxe
   Butter Recipe Fudge Cake Mix, divided
 1 cup finely chopped pecans
 2 tablespoons brown sugar

CAKE
 4 eggs
 1 cup dairy sour cream
 ⅓ cup CRISCO® Oil or CRISCO®
   PURITAN® Canola Oil
 ¼ cup water
 ¼ cup granulated sugar

GLAZE
 1 cup confectioners sugar
 1 or 2 tablespoons milk

1. Preheat oven to 375°F. Grease and flour 10-inch tube pan.

2. For streusel filling, combine 2 tablespoons cake mix, pecans and brown sugar in medium bowl. Set aside.

3. For cake, combine remaining cake mix, eggs, sour cream, oil, water and granulated sugar in large bowl. Beat at low speed with electric mixer until moistened. Beat at medium speed for 2 minutes. Pour two-thirds of batter into pan. Sprinkle with streusel filling. Spoon remaining batter evenly over filling. Bake at 375°F for 45 to 55 minutes or until toothpick inserted in center comes out clean. Cool in pan 25 minutes. Invert onto cooling rack. Cool completely.

4. For glaze, combine confectioners sugar and milk in small bowl. Stir until smooth. Drizzle over cake.

Makes 12 to 16 servings

Note: *To decorate cake as shown in photo, prepare glaze with 4 to 5 teaspoons milk. Place in decorator bag fitted with writing tip. Pipe glaze onto cake.*

Tip: *For a quick glaze, heat ½ cup DUNCAN HINES® Creamy Homestyle Vanilla Frosting in small saucepan over medium heat, stirring constantly, until thin. Drizzle over cake.*

It's easiest to glaze or frost a cake on a serving plate to avoid moving it around. Place several strips of waxed paper around the edges of the plate, then place the cake on top of the waxed paper. Once the cake has been glazed or frosted, carefully pull out the waxed paper; you are then left with a clean serving plate!

Chocolate Sock-It-To-Me Cake

Chocolate Toffee Crunch Fantasy

1 package DUNCAN HINES® Moist Deluxe
 Devil's Food Cake Mix
12 bars (1.4 ounces each) chocolate-covered
 toffee bars, divided
3 cups whipping cream, chilled

1. Preheat oven to 350°F. Grease and flour 10-inch tube pan.

2. Prepare, bake and cool cake following package directions for Basic Recipe. Split cake horizontally into three layers; set aside. Chop 11 candy bars into pea-size pieces (see Tip). Whip cream until stiff peaks form. Fold candy pieces into whipped cream.

3. To assemble, place one split cake layer on serving plate. Spread 1½ cups whipped cream mixture on top. Repeat with remaining layers and whipped cream mixture. Frost sides and top with remaining filling. Chop remaining candy bar coarsely. Sprinkle over top. Refrigerate until ready to serve.

Makes 12 servings

Tip: *To quickly chop toffee candy bars, place a few bars in food processor fitted with steel blade. Pulse several times until pea-size pieces form. Repeat with remaining candy bars.*

Mississippi Nilla® Mud Cake

1½ cups margarine
 4 eggs
 1 cup unsweetened cocoa
1½ cups all-purpose flour
 2 cups granulated sugar
 ¼ teaspoon salt
1¼ cups PLANTER'S® Pecans, chopped
 3 cups miniature marshmallows
 35 NILLA® Wafers
 1 (1-pound) box powdered sugar
 ½ cup milk
 ½ teaspoon vanilla extract

Preheat oven to 350°F. In large bowl, with electric mixer at medium speed, beat 1 cup margarine, eggs and ½ cup cocoa until well combined. Blend in flour, granulated sugar, salt and pecans. Spread batter in greased 13×9×2-inch baking pan. Bake at 350°F for 30 to 35 minutes or until cake pulls away from sides of pan.

Sprinkle marshmallows over hot cake; return to oven for 2 minutes or until marshmallows are slightly puffed. Arrange wafers over marshmallow layer.

In medium bowl, with electric mixer at medium speed, beat remaining ½ cup margarine, powdered sugar, remaining ½ cup cocoa, milk and vanilla until smooth; spread immediately over wafer layer. Cool cake completely on wire rack. Cut into squares to serve.

Makes 24 servings

Chocolate Toffee Crunch Fantasy

Fudgy Banana Oat Cake

TOPPING:
  1 cup QUAKER® Oats (quick or old fashioned, uncooked)
  ½ cup firmly packed brown sugar
  ¼ cup (½ stick) margarine or butter, chilled

FILLING:
  1 cup (6 ounces) semisweet chocolate pieces
  ⅔ cup sweetened condensed milk (not evaporated milk)
  1 tablespoon margarine or butter

CAKE:
  1 (18.25-ounce) package devil's food cake mix
  1¼ cups mashed ripe bananas (about 3 large)
  ⅓ cup vegetable oil
  3 eggs
  Banana slices (optional)
  Whipped cream (optional)

Heat oven to 350°F. Lightly grease bottom only of 13×9-inch baking pan. For topping, combine oats and brown sugar. Cut in margarine until mixture is crumbly; set aside.

For filling, in small saucepan, heat chocolate pieces, sweetened condensed milk and margarine over low heat until chocolate is melted, stirring occasionally. Remove from heat; set aside.

For cake, in large mixing bowl, combine cake mix, bananas, oil and eggs. Blend at low speed of electric mixer until dry ingredients are moistened. Beat at medium speed 2 minutes. Spread batter evenly into prepared pan. Drop chocolate mixture by teaspoonfuls evenly over batter. Sprinkle with reserved oat mixture. Bake 40 to 45 minutes or until cake pulls away from sides of pan and topping is golden brown. Cool cake in pan on wire rack. Garnish with banana slices and sweetened whipped cream, if desired. *Makes 15 servings*

Marbled Chocolate Sour Cream Cake

  1 cup (6 ounces) NESTLÉ® TOLL HOUSE® Semi-Sweet Chocolate Morsels
  1 package (18.5 ounces) yellow cake mix
  4 eggs
  ¾ cup sour cream
  ½ cup vegetable oil
  ¼ cup water
  ¼ cup granulated sugar
  Powdered sugar (optional)

MICROWAVE morsels in medium, microwave-safe bowl on HIGH (100%) power for 1 minute; stir. Microwave at additional 10- to 20-second intervals, stirring until smooth. **COMBINE** cake mix, eggs, sour cream, oil, water and granulated sugar in large mixer bowl. Beat on low speed until moistened. Beat on high speed for 2 minutes. **STIR** 2 cups batter into melted chocolate. Alternately spoon batters into greased 10-cup bundt or round tube pan. **BAKE** in preheated 375°F. oven for 35 to 45 minutes or until wooden pick inserted near center comes out clean. Cool in pan for 20 minutes; invert onto wire rack to cool completely. Sprinkle with powdered sugar before serving. *Makes 24 servings*

Fudgy Banana Oat Cake

Fudgy Pistachio Cake

CAKE

1 package DUNCAN HINES® Moist Deluxe White Cake Mix

1 package (4-serving size) pistachio instant pudding and pie filling mix

4 eggs

1 cup water

⅓ cup CRISCO® Oil or CRISCO® PURITAN® Canola Oil

1 can (16 ounces) chocolate syrup
Confectioners sugar, for garnish

FUDGE SAUCE

1 can (12 ounces) evaporated milk

1¾ cups granulated sugar

4 squares (1 ounce each) unsweetened chocolate

¼ cup butter or margarine

1½ teaspoons vanilla extract

¼ teaspoon salt
Chopped pistachio nuts, for garnish

1. Preheat oven to 350°F. Grease and flour 10-inch Bundt pan.

2. For cake, combine cake mix, pudding mix, eggs, water and oil in large bowl. Beat at medium speed with electric mixer for 2 minutes. Pour half the batter into prepared pan. Combine remaining batter and chocolate syrup until blended. Pour over batter in pan. Bake at 350°F for 65 to 70 minutes or until toothpick inserted in center comes out clean. Cool in pan 25 minutes. Invert onto serving plate. Cool completely. Dust with confectioners sugar.

3. For fudge sauce, combine evaporated milk and granulated sugar in medium saucepan. Stir constantly on medium heat until mixture comes to a rolling boil. Boil and stir for 1 minute. Add unsweetened chocolate; stir until melted. Beat until smooth. Remove from heat. Stir in butter, vanilla extract and salt.

4. To serve, pour several tablespoons warm fudge sauce on each serving plate. Place cake slices on fudge sauce. Garnish with chopped pistachio nuts. Dust with confectioners sugar.

Makes 12 to 16 servings

Tip: *To keep pistachio nuts fresh, store in freezer.*

If it is difficult to test your deep cakes (such as bundt or tube cakes) for doneness with a toothpick, try using a wooden skewer or an uncooked spaghetti noodle.

Fudgy Pistachio Cake

Classic Hershey® Bar Cake

1 cup (2 sticks) butter or margarine, softened
1¼ cups granulated sugar
4 eggs
6 HERSHEY'S Milk Chocolate Bars
    (1.55 ounces each), melted
2½ cups all-purpose flour
¼ teaspoon baking soda
    Dash salt
1 cup buttermilk or sour milk*
½ cup HERSHEY'S Syrup
2 teaspoons vanilla extract
1 cup chopped pecans
    Powdered sugar (optional)

*To sour milk: Combine 1 tablespoon white vinegar plus enough milk to equal 1 cup. Stir. Wait 5 minutes before using.

Heat oven to 350°F. Grease and flour 10-inch tube pan or 12-cup fluted tube pan. In large bowl, beat butter until creamy; gradually add granulated sugar, beating on medium speed of electric mixer until well blended. Add eggs, one at a time, beating well after each addition. Add chocolate; beat until blended. Stir together flour, baking soda and salt in small bowl; add to chocolate mixture alternately with buttermilk, beating until blended. Add syrup and vanilla; beat until blended. Stir in pecans. Pour batter into prepared pan. Bake 1 hour and 15 minutes or until wooden pick inserted in center of cake comes out clean. Cool 10 minutes; remove from pan to wire rack. Cool completely. Sift powdered sugar over top, if desired.

Makes 12 to 16 servings

Kahlúa® Chocolate Decadence

½ cup butter
6 ounces (6 squares) semi-sweet baking
    chocolate
3 extra-large eggs
¾ cup granulated sugar
1¼ cups finely ground walnuts or pecans
2 tablespoons all-purpose flour
5 tablespoons KAHLÚA®, divided
1 teaspoon vanilla extract
    Sifted powdered sugar
2 ounces (2 squares) semi-sweet baking
    chocolate, melted
    Chocolate nonpareils or coffee beans
    (optional)

Preheat oven to 325°F. Melt butter and 6 ounces chocolate; cool. In large bowl, beat eggs and granulated sugar with electric mixer on high speed 3 minutes or until light and lemon colored. Stir together ground walnuts and flour in small bowl; gradually beat into egg mixture.

Stir 3 tablespoons Kahlúa® and vanilla into cooled chocolate mixture; gradually beat into egg mixture until well combined. Pour batter into 9-inch springform pan. Bake 35 to 45 minutes until top is set. Cool completely in pan.

Remove side of pan; place cake on serving plate. Sprinkle top with powdered sugar. Stir together 2 ounces melted chocolate and remaining 2 tablespoons Kahlúa® in small bowl; drizzle over cake. Decorate with nonpareils, if desired.

Makes one 9-inch cake.

Fudge Walnut Ripple Layer Cake

1⅔ cups unsifted all-purpose flour
1½ cups sugar
⅔ cup unsweetened cocoa
1½ teaspoons baking soda
½ teaspoon salt
1½ cups buttermilk
½ cup shortening
3 eggs
3 teaspoons vanilla extract, divided
1 (8-ounce) package cream cheese, softened
2 tablespoons margarine or butter, softened
1 tablespoon cornstarch
1 (14-ounce) can sweetened condensed milk
    (NOT evaporated milk)
Fudgy Frosting (recipe follows)
¾ cup chopped California walnuts

Preheat oven to 350°F. In large bowl, combine flour, sugar, cocoa, baking soda, salt, buttermilk, shortening, 2 eggs and 2 teaspoons vanilla. Beat with electric mixer on low speed until blended, scraping bowl frequently. Beat 3 minutes on high speed, scraping bowl occasionally. Pour into 2 waxed paper-lined greased and floured 9-inch cake pans. In small bowl, beat cream cheese, margarine and cornstarch until fluffy. Gradually beat in sweetened condensed milk. Beat in remaining egg and 1 teaspoon vanilla until smooth. Spoon equal portions of cream cheese mixture evenly over batter. Bake 40 to 45 minutes or until toothpick inserted in center comes out clean. Cool 10 minutes; remove from pans. Cool completely. Frost with Fudgy Frosting. Sprinkle with walnuts.

Makes 10 to 12 servings

Fudgy Frosting: In medium saucepan, over medium heat, melt ⅔ cup margarine or butter; stir in 1⅓ cups unsweetened cocoa. Cook and stir over medium heat until mixture thickens. Remove from heat. Pour into large bowl; cool completely. Add 5⅓ cups confectioners' sugar alternately with ⅔ cup milk, beating until frosting is of spreading consistency. Stir in 1 teaspoon vanilla. Makes about 3½ cups.

Favorite recipe from **Walnut Marketing Board**

If your frosting becomes too thick upon standing, simply stir in liquid, ½ teaspoon at a time, until it reaches the desired consistency. (A frosting that is too thick can tear a cake.)

Chocolate Royale

1 package **DUNCAN HINES®** Moist Deluxe
    Devil's Food Cake Mix
1 package (3 ounces) cream cheese, softened
½ cup confectioners sugar
1 teaspoon vanilla extract
1 cup whipping cream, whipped
2 large bananas, peeled and sliced
    Lemon juice
    Chocolate sprinkles

1. Preheat oven to 350°F. Grease and flour two
8-inch round cake pans.

2. Prepare, bake and cool cake following package
directions for Basic Recipe.

3. For frosting, combine cream cheese,
confectioners sugar and vanilla extract in small
bowl. Beat at low speed with electric mixer until
blended. Fold whipped cream into cheese mixture.

4. To assemble, place one cake layer on serving
plate. Spread with thin layer of frosting. Reserve
12 banana slices for garnish; dip in lemon juice.
Cover frosting with remaining banana slices.
Spread another thin layer of frosting over bananas.
Place second cake layer on top. Frost sides and top
of cake with remaining frosting. Blot reserved
banana slices dry on paper towel. Roll banana slices
in chocolate sprinkles. Garnish top of cake with
banana slices. Refrigerate until ready to serve.

Makes 12 to 16 servings

Chocolate Applesauce Cake

2½ cups all-purpose flour
⅓ cup unsweetened cocoa
2 teaspoons baking soda
¾ teaspoon salt
¾ cup shortening
1¾ cups sugar
2 eggs
1½ teaspoons vanilla
1½ cups sweetened applesauce
½ cup buttermilk

Preheat oven to 350°F. In small bowl, combine
flour, cocoa, baking soda and salt. Using electric
mixer, beat shortening and sugar in large bowl until
creamy. Beat in eggs and vanilla. In small bowl,
combine applesauce and buttermilk; mix well. Add
flour mixture to sugar mixture alternately with
applesauce mixture; mix until well blended. Pour
batter into greased 13×9-inch pan.

Bake 35 to 40 minutes or until toothpick inserted
into center comes out clean. Cool completely in
pan on wire rack. Serve plain or top with favorite
frosting. *Makes about 12 servings*

Favorite recipe from **Western New York Apple Growers
Association, Inc.**

Chocolate Royale

Berry Bundt Cake

2 cups all-purpose flour
1 tablespoon baking powder
1 teaspoon baking soda
¼ teaspoon salt
1 cup sugar
¼ cup vegetable oil
¾ cup buttermilk
½ cup cholesterol-free egg substitute
2 cups frozen unsweetened raspberries
2 cups frozen unsweetened blueberries

1. Preheat oven to 350°F. Spray 6-cup Bundt pan with nonstick cooking spray.

2. Combine flour, baking powder, baking soda and salt in large bowl. Combine sugar, oil, buttermilk and egg substitute in medium bowl. Add sugar mixture to flour mixture; stir just until moistened.

3. Fold in raspberries and blueberries. Pour batter into prepared pan. Bake 1 hour or until toothpick inserted in center comes out clean. Cool in pan on wire rack. Serve with fresh berries, if desired.

Makes 12 servings

Colonial Apple Cake

2¾ cups unsifted all-purpose flour
1 teaspoon baking powder
1 teaspoon ground cinnamon
¾ teaspoon salt
½ teaspoon baking soda
1¾ cups granulated sugar
1¼ cups CRISCO® Vegetable Oil
2 eggs
¼ cup milk
1 teaspoon vanilla
2 cups chopped, peeled apples
½ cup chopped dates
1 teaspoon grated lemon peel
1 to 2 tablespoons confectioners sugar

1. Preheat oven to 350°F. Grease and flour 12-cup fluted tube pan. Set aside.

2. Mix flour, baking powder, cinnamon, salt and baking soda in medium mixing bowl. Set aside.

3. Combine granulated sugar, oil, eggs, milk and vanilla in large mixing bowl. Beat with electric mixer at medium speed until blended, scraping bowl frequently. Add flour mixture. Beat at medium speed 2 minutes longer, scraping bowl frequently. Stir in apples, dates and lemon peel. Pour batter into pan.

4. Bake at 350°F for 1 hour to 1 hour 15 minutes, or until wooden toothpick inserted in center comes out clean. Let stand 10 minutes. Invert onto serving plate. Cool slightly. Sift confectioners sugar onto cake. Serve warm. Top with whipped cream, if desired. *Makes about 16 servings*

Berry Bundt Cake

Mom's Favorite White Cake

2¼ cups cake flour
1 tablespoon baking powder
½ teaspoon salt
½ cup margarine or butter, softened
1½ cups sugar
4 egg whites
2 teaspoons vanilla
1 cup milk
Strawberry Frosting (recipe follows)
Fruit Filling (recipe follows)
Fresh strawberries (optional)

Preheat oven to 350°F. Line bottom of two 9-inch round cake pans with waxed paper; lightly grease paper. Combine flour, baking powder and salt in medium bowl; set aside.

Beat margarine and sugar in large bowl with electric mixer at medium speed until light and fluffy. Add egg whites, two at a time, beating well after each addition. Add vanilla; beat until blended. With electric mixer at low speed, add flour mixture alternately with milk, beating well after each addition. Pour batter evenly into prepared pans.

Bake 25 minutes or until toothpick inserted into center comes out clean. Cool layers in pans on wire rack 10 minutes. Loosen edges and invert layers onto rack to cool completely.

Prepare Strawberry Frosting and Fruit Filling. To fill and frost cake, place one layer on cake plate; spread top with Fruit Filling. Place second layer over filling. Frost top and sides with Strawberry Frosting. Place strawberries on top of cake, if desired. Refrigerate; allow cake to stand at room temperature 15 minutes before serving.

Makes 12 servings

Strawberry Frosting

2 envelopes (1.3 ounces each) whipped topping mix
⅔ cup milk
1 cup (6 ounces) white chocolate chips, melted
¼ cup strawberry jam

Beat whipped topping mix and milk in medium bowl with electric mixer on low speed until blended. Beat on high speed 4 minutes until topping thickens and forms peaks. With mixer at low speed, beat melted chocolate into topping. Add jam; beat until blended. Chill 15 minutes or until spreading consistency.

Fruit Filling

1 cup Strawberry Frosting (recipe above)
1 can (8 ounces) crushed pineapple, drained
1 cup sliced strawberries

Combine Strawberry Frosting, pineapple and strawberries in medium bowl; mix well.

Banana Streusel Surprise

1 package DUNCAN HINES® Moist Deluxe
    Banana Supreme Cake Mix
1 package (4-serving size) vanilla or banana
    cream instant pudding and pie filling mix
4 eggs
1 cup dairy sour cream
⅓ cup CRISCO® Oil or CRISCO®
    PURITAN® Canola Oil
½ cup chopped pecans or walnuts
1 cup crushed chocolate-covered graham
    crackers
    Confectioners sugar, for garnish

1. Preheat oven to 350°F. Grease and flour 10-inch
Bundt pan.

2. Combine cake mix, pudding mix, eggs, sour
cream and oil in large bowl. Beat at low speed with
electric mixer until moistened. Beat at high speed
for 2 minutes. Stir in pecans. Pour one-third of
batter into pan. Sprinkle with half the crushed
graham crackers. Repeat layers, ending with batter.
Bake at 350°F for 50 to 55 minutes or until
toothpick inserted in center comes out clean. Cool
in pan 25 minutes. Invert onto serving plate. Dust
with confectioners sugar. Serve warm or cool
completely. *Makes 12 to 16 servings*

Tip: *For best results, bake cake immediately after*
mixing the batter.

Pumpkin Crunch Cake

1 package (18.25 ounces) yellow cake mix,
    divided
2 eggs
1⅔ cups LIBBY'S® Pumpkin Pie Mix
2 teaspoons pumpkin pie spice
⅓ cup flaked coconut
¼ cup chopped nuts
3 tablespoons butter or margarine, softened

COMBINE *3 cups* cake mix, eggs, pumpkin pie
mix and pumpkin pie spice in large mixer bowl.
Beat on low speed until moistened. Beat on
medium speed for 2 minutes. Pour into greased
13×9-inch baking pan.

COMBINE *remaining* cake mix, coconut and nuts
in small bowl; cut in butter with pastry blender or
two knives until mixture is crumbly. Sprinkle over
batter.

BAKE in preheated 350°F. oven for 30 to 35
minutes or until wooden pick inserted in center
comes out clean. Cool in pan on wire rack.

Makes 20 servings

Banana Streusel Surprise

Mini Morsel Pound Cake

3 cups all-purpose flour
1 teaspoon baking powder
½ teaspoon salt
2 cups granulated sugar
1 cup (2 sticks) butter or margarine, softened
1 tablespoon vanilla extract
4 eggs
¾ cup milk
2 cups (12-ounce package) NESTLÉ® TOLL HOUSE® Semi-Sweet Chocolate Mini Morsels
Powdered sugar

COMBINE flour, baking powder and salt in small bowl. Beat sugar, butter and vanilla in large mixer bowl until well blended. Beat in eggs one at a time, beating well after each addition. Gradually beat in flour mixture alternately with milk. Stir in morsels. Pour into greased and floured 10-inch bundt pan or two greased and floured 9×5-inch loaf pans.

BAKE in preheated 325°F. oven for 1 hour 5 minutes to 1 hour 15 minutes or until wooden pick inserted near center comes out clean. Cool in pan on wire rack for 15 minutes. Remove from pan; serve warm or cool completely on wire rack. Sprinkle with powdered sugar before serving.

Makes 16 servings

Lemonade Torte for a Long Hot Summer

¾ cup blanched almonds
1½ cups sugar, divided
1½ cups whole-wheat bread crumbs
1 tablespoon grated lemon peel
¼ teaspoon baking powder
¼ teaspoon ground cinnamon
6 large egg whites
1 cup NEWMAN'S OWN® Old-Fashioned Roadside Lemonade
2 tablespoons confectioners' sugar

Preheat oven to 350°F. Butter and flour 9-inch springform pan.

In food processor, process almonds with 1 cup sugar. In medium bowl, mix ground almond mixture with bread crumbs, lemon peel, baking powder and cinnamon. Set aside.

In large mixing bowl, with mixer at high speed, beat egg whites with remaining ½ cup sugar until stiff peaks form. Gently fold crumb mixture into beaten egg whites. Pour mixture into springform pan and bake on lower oven rack for 1 hour.

In small saucepan over medium-high heat, cook Newman's Own® Old-Fashioned Roadside Lemonade 10 minutes or until reduced by half.

Remove torte from oven. Pour reduced lemonade gradually over top of hot torte. Let torte stand in pan on wire rack until cool. Remove side of springform pan and dust top of torte with confectioners' sugar.

Makes 8 servings

Mini Morsel Pound Cake

Carrot Cake

4 eggs
1½ cups vegetable oil
2 cups all-purpose flour
2 cups sugar
2 teaspoons baking powder
2 teaspoons baking soda
2 teaspoons ground cinnamon
¼ teaspoon salt
3 cups shredded carrots (about 11 medium)
1½ cups coarsely chopped pecans or walnuts
Cream Cheese Icing (recipe follows)

Preheat oven to 350°F. Grease and flour bottom and sides of 13×9-inch baking pan.

Beat eggs and oil in small bowl. Combine flour, sugar, baking powder, baking soda, cinnamon and salt in large bowl. Add egg mixture; mix well. Stir in carrots and pecans. Pour into prepared pan.

Bake 30 to 35 minutes or until toothpick inserted into center comes out clean. Cool cake completely in pan on wire rack. Loosen edges and invert cake onto cake plate.

Prepare Cream Cheese Icing. Spread over cooled cake. Garnish, if desired.   *Makes 8 servings*

Cream Cheese Icing

1 package (8 ounces) cream cheese, softened
½ cup margarine or butter, softened
1 teaspoon vanilla
4 cups powdered sugar

Beat cream cheese, margarine and vanilla in large bowl with electric mixer at medium speed until smooth. Gradually add powdered sugar. Beat at low speed until well blended.   *Makes about 1½ cups*

Sour Cream Pound Cake

3 cups sugar
1 cup (2 sticks) butter, softened
1 teaspoon vanilla
1 teaspoon lemon extract
6 eggs
3 cups cake flour
¼ teaspoon baking soda
1 cup dairy sour cream

Heat oven to 325°F. Butter and flour 10-inch tube pan. In large bowl, beat sugar and butter until light and fluffy. Add vanilla and lemon extract; mix well. Add eggs, one at a time, beating well after each addition. In medium bowl, combine flour and baking soda. Add to butter mixture alternately with sour cream, beating well after each addition. Pour batter into pan. Bake 1 hour and 20 minutes or until toothpick inserted in center comes out clean. Cool in pan 15 minutes; invert onto wire rack and cool completely. Store tightly covered.

Makes 16 to 20 servings

Favorite recipe from **Southeast United Dairy Industry Association, Inc.**

Carrot Cake

Banana-Coconut Crunch Cake

CAKE

  1 package DUNCAN HINES® Moist Deluxe
    Banana Supreme Cake Mix
  1 package (4-serving size) banana instant
    pudding and pie filling mix
  1 can (16 ounces) fruit cocktail, in juices,
    undrained
  4 eggs
  ¼ cup CRISCO® Oil or CRISCO®
    PURITAN® Canola Oil
  1 cup flaked coconut
  ½ cup chopped pecans
  ½ cup firmly packed brown sugar

GLAZE

  ¾ cup granulated sugar
  ½ cup butter or margarine
  ½ cup evaporated milk
  1⅓ cups flaked coconut

1. Preheat oven to 350°F. Grease and flour
13×9×2-inch pan.

2. For cake, combine cake mix, pudding mix, fruit
cocktail with juice, eggs and oil in large bowl. Beat
at medium speed with electric mixer for 4 minutes.
Stir in 1 cup coconut. Pour into pan. Combine
pecans and brown sugar in small bowl. Stir until
well mixed. Sprinkle over batter. Bake at 350°F for
45 to 50 minutes or until toothpick inserted in
center comes out clean.

3. For glaze, combine granulated sugar, butter and
evaporated milk in medium saucepan. Bring to a
boil. Cook for 2 minutes, stirring occasionally.

Remove from heat. Stir in 1⅓ cups coconut. Pour
over warm cake. Serve warm or at room
temperature. *Makes 12 to 16 servings*

Tip: *Assemble all ingredients and utensils together
before beginning the recipe.*

Easy Carrot Cake

  1¼ cups MIRACLE WHIP® Salad Dressing
  1 two-layer yellow cake mix
  4 eggs
  ¼ cup cold water
  2 teaspoons ground cinnamon
  2 cups finely shredded carrots
  ½ cup chopped walnuts
  1 (16-ounce) container ready-to-spread cream
    cheese frosting

• Preheat oven to 350°F.

• Beat salad dressing, cake mix, eggs, water and
cinnamon in large bowl with electric mixer at
medium speed until well blended. Stir in carrots
and walnuts. Pour batter into greased 13×9-inch
baking pan.

• Bake 30 to 35 minutes or until wooden toothpick
inserted in center comes out clean. Cool
completely. Spread cake with frosting. Garnish as
desired. *Makes 12 servings*

Prep time: 15 minutes
Bake time: 35 minutes

Butterscotch Pudding Cake

CAKE
   1 package DUNCAN HINES® Moist Deluxe
      Yellow Cake Mix
   1 package (4-serving size) instant butterscotch
      pudding and pie filling mix
   3 eggs
   1⅓ cups water
   ⅓ cup CRISCO® Oil or CRISCO®
      PURITAN® Canola Oil

FROSTING
   1 package (3 ounces) cream cheese, softened
   ½ cup firmly packed brown sugar
   ½ teaspoon vanilla extract
   1 container (8 ounces) frozen whipped
      topping, thawed
   ½ cup butterscotch flavored chips, for garnish

1. Preheat oven to 350°F. Grease and flour
13×9×2-inch pan.

2. For cake, combine cake mix, pudding mix, eggs,
water and oil in large bowl. Beat at medium speed
with electric mixer for 2 minutes. Pour into pan.
Bake at 350°F for 35 to 40 minutes or until
toothpick inserted in center comes out clean. Cool
completely.

3. For frosting, combine cream cheese, brown sugar
and vanilla extract in small bowl. Beat at medium
speed with electric mixer until smooth. Fold in
whipped topping. Spread over cake. Sprinkle
butterscotch chips over frosting. Refrigerate until
ready to serve.   *Makes 12 to 16 servings*

Tip: *For best flavor, be sure to use pure vanilla extract.*

Fresh Pear Cake

   4 cups chopped peeled pears
   2 cups granulated sugar
   1 cup chopped nuts
   3 cups all-purpose flour
   2 teaspoons baking soda
   ½ teaspoon salt
   ½ teaspoon ground cinnamon
   ½ teaspoon ground nutmeg
   2 eggs
   1 cup vegetable oil
   1 teaspoon vanilla
      Powdered sugar for garnish

1. Preheat oven to 375°F. Grease and flour 10-inch
fluted tube pan.

2. Combine pears, granulated sugar and nuts in
medium bowl; mix lightly. Let stand 1 hour,
stirring frequently. Combine flour, baking soda, salt
and spices in medium bowl; set aside.

3. Beat eggs in large bowl. Blend in oil and vanilla.
Add flour mixture; mix well. Add pear mixture; mix
well. Pour evenly into prepared pan.

4. Bake 1 hour and 15 minutes or until toothpick
inserted in center comes out clean. Cool in pan on
wire rack 10 minutes. Loosen edges and remove to
rack to cool completely. Dust lightly with powdered
sugar before serving.

Makes one 10-inch tube cake

Fresh Pear Cake

Kansas Kids' Cake

½ cup (1 stick) butter, softened
¼ cup peanut butter
¾ cup honey
 2 eggs
 1 teaspoon vanilla
 1 cup all-purpose flour
 1 cup whole-wheat flour
1½ teaspoons baking powder
 ¾ teaspoon baking soda
 ½ teaspoon salt
 ¾ cup buttermilk
   Topping (recipe follows)

1. Preheat oven to 350°F. Grease and lightly flour 13×9-inch baking pan.

2. Beat together butter, peanut butter and honey in large bowl until well blended. Blend in eggs and vanilla. Sift together dry ingredients. Add to butter mixture alternately with buttermilk, beating well after each addition. Pour into prepared pan.

3. Prepare Topping; crumble over batter.

4. Bake 25 to 30 minutes or until toothpick inserted in center comes out clean. Serve warm or at room temperature.

Makes one 13×9-inch cake

Topping

½ cup peanut butter
¾ cup sugar
 2 tablespoons all-purpose flour
 1 cup semisweet chocolate chips

Combine peanut butter, sugar and flour in medium bowl, mixing until well blended. Stir in chocolate chips.

Seedy Lemon Cake

1½ cups sugar
   Grated peel of 2 lemons
 1 cup sunflower oil
 6 eggs
1⅔ cups plus 1 tablespoon all-purpose flour, divided
 2 teaspoons baking powder
 ¼ teaspoon salt
 ½ cup sunflower kernels
   Whipped cream (optional)
   Additional grated lemon peel (optional)

1. Preheat oven to 300°F. Grease and flour two (9×5-inch) loaf pans.

2. Beat together sugar, lemon peel and oil in large bowl. Add eggs, one at a time, beating well after each addition. Add 1⅔ cups flour, baking powder and salt; mix well.

3. Combine remaining 1 tablespoon flour and sunflower kernels in small bowl; toss lightly. Stir into batter. Pour batter evenly into prepared pans.

4. Bake 1 hour or until toothpick inserted in center comes out clean. Cool in pans on wire racks 10 minutes. Loosen edges; remove to racks to cool completely. Garnish with whipped cream and grated lemon peel, if desired.

Makes two 9×5-inch loaves

Kansas Kids' Cake

Chocolate Almond Pound Cake

1¼ cups chopped natural almonds, divided
1 package DUNCAN HINES® Moist Deluxe Devil's Food Cake Mix
1 package (4-serving size) chocolate instant pudding and pie filling mix
4 eggs
1 cup dairy sour cream
½ cup CRISCO® Oil or CRISCO® PURITAN® Canola Oil
2 teaspoons vanilla extract
1 cup semi-sweet mini chocolate chips
½ cup DUNCAN HINES® Creamy Homestyle Vanilla or Milk Chocolate Frosting

1. Preheat oven to 350°F. Grease and flour 10-inch Bundt pan.

2. Spread almonds on baking sheet. Toast in 350°F oven for 8 to 10 minutes or until fragrant. Cool completely. Arrange ¼ cup almonds evenly in pan.

3. Combine cake mix, pudding mix, eggs, sour cream, oil and vanilla extract in large bowl. Beat at medium speed with electric mixer for 4 minutes. Stir in chocolate chips and remaining 1 cup toasted almonds. Pour into pan. Bake at 350°F for 45 to 50 minutes or until toothpick inserted in center comes out clean. Cool in pan 25 minutes. Invert onto serving plate. Cool completely.

4. Place Vanilla frosting in microwave-safe bowl. Microwave at HIGH (100% power) for 15 to 20 seconds. Stir until smooth. Drizzle over cake.

Makes 12 to 16 servings

Tip: This recipe may also be baked in two greased and floured 9×5×3-inch loaf pans. Toast almonds as directed but do not sprinkle ¼ cup almonds in bottom of pans. Prepare batter as directed; pour into pans. Sprinkle 2 tablespoons almonds on top of batter in each pan. Bake at 350°F for 45 to 50 minutes or until toothpick inserted in center comes out clean. Cool 25 minutes before removing from pans.

Cinnamon Ripple Cake

1 package DUNCAN HINES® Angel Food Cake Mix
2¼ teaspoons ground cinnamon, divided
1½ cups frozen whipped topping, thawed

1. Preheat oven to 350°F.

2. Prepare cake following package directions. **Spoon** one-third of batter into ungreased 10-inch tube pan. **Spread** evenly. **Sprinkle** 1 teaspoon cinnamon over batter with small fine sieve. **Repeat. Top** with remaining cake batter. **Bake** and **cool** following package directions.

3. Combine whipped topping and ¼ teaspoon cinnamon in small bowl. **Serve** with cake slices.

Makes 12 to 16 servings

Tip: To slice cake, use a serrated knife and cut in a sawing motion.

Chocolate Almond Pound Cake

Apple Cinnamon Streusel Cake

Topping (recipe follows)
4 eggs
2 cups granulated sugar
2 cups sour cream
3 cups all-purpose flour
1 teaspoon baking powder
1 teaspoon baking soda
¼ teaspoon salt
1½ cups chopped peeled apples
½ cup sunflower kernels, toasted
Whipped cream and additional toasted
sunflower kernels (optional)

1. Preheat oven to 350°F. Grease 13×9-inch baking pan. Prepare Topping; set aside.

2. Beat together eggs, sugar and sour cream in large bowl until well blended. Combine dry ingredients in medium bowl. Add to sugar mixture; mix well. Stir in apples and sunflower kernels. Pour batter into prepared pan; sprinkle with Topping.

3. Bake 25 to 30 minutes or until toothpick inserted in center comes out clean. Serve warm or at room temperature. Garnish, if desired.

Makes one 13×9-inch cake

Topping

¼ cup margarine, softened
⅔ cup packed brown sugar
⅔ cup all-purpose flour
½ teaspoon ground cinnamon
½ cup sunflower kernels

Combine margarine and brown sugar in medium bowl; mix until well blended. Add flour and cinnamon; mix well. Stir in sunflower kernels.

All-purpose apples are good for both cooking and eating raw. Some of the all-purpose varieties include Cortland, Fuji, Granny Smith, Jonathan, McIntosh and Winesap. Choose firm, well-colored apples with skins that are smooth and free from blemishes and bruises.

Apple Cinnamon Streusel Cake

Orange Almond Cake

½ cup vegetable shortening
1 cup honey
1 tablespoon grated orange peel
3 eggs
1¾ cups all-purpose flour
2 teaspoons baking powder
½ teaspoon salt
¼ cup ground blanched almonds
   Honey Whipped Cream (recipe follows)
¼ cup toasted almond slices (optional)
   Orange slices, quartered (optional)

Cream shortening in large bowl with electric mixer. Gradually add honey, beating until light and fluffy. Add orange peel. Add eggs, one at a time, beating thoroughly after each addition. (Mixture may appear curdled.) Combine flour, baking powder and salt in small bowl; fold dry ingredients into creamed mixture. Mix until blended. Add ground almonds; mix well. Grease bottoms only of two 8-inch round cake pans; pour in cake batter. Bake in preheated 325°F oven 30 minutes or until wooden toothpick inserted in centers comes out clean. Cool in cake pans on wire racks 10 minutes. Remove from pans and cool on wire racks. Frost with Honey Whipped Cream; garnish with toasted almond slices and orange slices, if desired.

Makes 10 to 12 servings

Honey Whipped Cream: Beat 1 cup heavy cream in medium bowl with electric mixer until soft peaks form. Gradually add 3 tablespoons honey; beat until stiff peaks form. Fold in 1 teaspoon vanilla.

Favorite recipe from **National Honey Board**

Double Berry Layer Cake

1 package DUNCAN HINES® Moist Deluxe
   Strawberry Supreme Cake Mix
⅔ cup strawberry jam, divided
2½ cups fresh blueberries, rinsed, drained and
   divided
1 container (8 ounces) frozen whipped
   topping, thawed and divided
   Fresh strawberry slices, for garnish

1. Preheat oven to 350°F. Grease and flour two 9-inch round cake pans.

2. Prepare, bake and cool cake following package directions for Basic Recipe.

3. Place one cake layer on serving plate. Spread with ⅓ cup strawberry jam. Arrange 1 cup blueberries on jam. Spread half the whipped topping to within ½ inch of cake edge. Place second cake layer on top. Repeat with remaining ⅓ cup strawberry jam, 1 cup blueberries and remaining whipped topping. Garnish with strawberry slices and remaining ½ cup blueberries. Refrigerate until ready to serve.

Makes 12 servings

Tip: *For best results, cut cake with serrated knife; clean knife after each slice.*

Orange Almond Cake

Apple Upside-Down Cake

¼ cup (½ stick) plus 3 tablespoons butter, divided
½ cup packed brown sugar
½ teaspoon ground cinnamon
¼ teaspoon ground nutmeg
¼ teaspoon ground mace
3 McIntosh apples,* peeled, cored and cut into rings
2 teaspoons lemon juice
1⅓ cups cake flour
¾ cup granulated sugar
1¾ teaspoons baking powder
¼ teaspoon salt
½ cup milk
1 teaspoon vanilla
1 egg, separated

*Substitute any large cooking apples for McIntosh apples.

1. Preheat oven to 375°F. Melt ¼ cup butter in 8-inch square baking pan. Add brown sugar and spices; mix well. Arrange apples over brown sugar mixture in bottom of pan; sprinkle with lemon juice. Set aside.

2. Combine dry ingredients in large bowl. Cut in remaining 3 tablespoons butter with pastry blender or 2 knives until mixture resembles coarse crumbs.

3. Add milk and vanilla; beat at low speed with electric mixer until dry ingredients are moistened. Continue beating 2 minutes at medium speed. Blend in egg yolk.

4. Beat egg white in small bowl at high speed with electric mixer until stiff peaks form; gently fold into batter. Pour over apples in pan.

5. Bake 35 minutes or until toothpick inserted in center comes out clean. Cool in pan on wire rack 5 minutes. Loosen edges and invert onto serving plate. Let stand 1 minute before removing pan. Serve warm. *Makes one 8-inch square cake*

Buttermilk Pound Cake

3 cups sifted all-purpose flour
½ teaspoon baking powder
½ teaspoon baking soda
½ teaspoon salt
1 cup (2 sticks) butter or margarine, softened
2 cups superfine sugar
2 eggs
1 teaspoon vanilla
1 teaspoon lemon extract
1 cup buttermilk

Preheat oven to 350°F. Grease and flour two (9×5-inch) loaf pans. Combine flour, baking powder, baking soda and salt in medium bowl; set aside. Beat together butter and sugar in large bowl until light and fluffy. Add eggs, 1 at a time, beating well after each addition. Blend in vanilla and lemon extract.

Add flour mixture alternately with buttermilk, beating well after each addition. Pour evenly into prepared pans.

Bake 35 to 40 minutes or until wooden pick inserted in centers comes out clean. Cool loaves in pans on wire racks 10 minutes. Remove from pans; cool completely on wire racks.

Makes two 9×5-inch loaves

Apple Upside-Down Cake

White Buttermilk Cake

3 cups sifted cake flour
1 teaspoon baking soda
½ teaspoon salt
1 cup shortening
2 cups granulated sugar, divided
1 cup buttermilk
2 teaspoons clear vanilla
½ teaspoon almond extract
6 egg whites, at room temperature
1 teaspoon cream of tartar
Creamy Frosting (recipe follows)

1. Preheat oven to 350°F. Grease and flour two (9-inch) or three (8-inch) round cake pans.

2. Combine flour, baking soda and salt in medium bowl. Beat shortening and 1⅓ cups granulated sugar in large bowl until light and fluffy. Add flour mixture alternately with buttermilk, beating well after each addition. Blend in vanilla and almond extract.

3. Beat egg whites in separate bowl at medium speed with electric mixer until foamy. Add cream of tartar; beat at high speed until soft peaks form.

4. Gradually add remaining ⅔ cup granulated sugar, beating until stiff peaks form; fold into batter. Pour batter evenly into prepared pans.

5. Bake 30 to 35 minutes or until toothpick inserted in center comes out clean. Cool layers in pans on wire racks 10 minutes. Loosen edges and remove to racks to cool completely. Fill and frost cake with Creamy Frosting.

Makes one 2- or 3-layer cake

Creamy Frosting

3 tablespoons all-purpose flour
1 cup milk
1 cup (2 sticks) butter, softened
1 cup powdered sugar
1 teaspoon vanilla

Combine flour and milk in medium saucepan; stir over low heat until thickened. Cool. Beat butter in large bowl until creamy. Add powdered sugar; beat until fluffy. Blend in vanilla. Add flour mixture; beat until thick and smooth.

For best results when baking cakes, oven heat must circulate evenly between and around the pans. Arrange cake pans so there is at least 2 inches between each pan and the sides of the oven; if using two shelves, avoid placing the cake pans directly over one another.

White Buttermilk Cake

Butter Pecan Banana Cake

CAKE

- 1 package DUNCAN HINES® Moist Deluxe Butter Recipe Golden Cake Mix
- 4 eggs
- 1 cup mashed ripe bananas (about 3 medium)
- ¾ cup CRISCO® Oil or CRISCO® PURITAN® Canola Oil
- ½ cup sugar
- ¼ cup milk
- 1 teaspoon vanilla extract
- 1 cup chopped pecans

FROSTING

- 1 cup coarsely chopped pecans
- ¼ cup butter or margarine
- 1 container (16 ounces) DUNCAN HINES® Creamy Homestyle Vanilla Frosting

1. Preheat oven to 325°F. Grease and flour 10-inch Bundt or tube pan.

2. For cake, combine cake mix, eggs, bananas, oil, sugar, milk and vanilla extract in large bowl. Beat at low speed with electric mixer until moistened. Beat at medium speed for 2 minutes. Stir in 1 cup chopped pecans. Pour into pan. Bake at 325°F for 50 to 60 minutes or until toothpick inserted in center comes out clean. Cool in pan 25 minutes. Invert onto cooling rack. Cool completely.

3. For frosting, place 1 cup coarsely chopped pecans and butter in skillet. Cook on medium heat, stirring until pecans are toasted. Stir into frosting. Cool until spreading consistency. Frost cake.

Makes 12 to 16 servings

Tip: *In place of greasing and flouring pans, try using our easy pan grease recipe. Combine 2 cups Crisco Shortening and 1 cup all-purpose flour in medium bowl. Mix by hand or on low speed with electric mixer until blended. Store in airtight container at room temperature for up to 6 months. Use a pastry brush or waxed paper to coat baking pans evenly.*

Applesauce Walnut Cake

- 1 package DUNCAN HINES® Moist Deluxe Butter Recipe Golden Cake Mix
- 3 eggs
- 1⅓ cups applesauce
- ½ cup butter or margarine, melted
- 1 teaspoon ground cinnamon
- ½ cup chopped walnuts
- Confectioners sugar, for garnish

1. Preheat oven to 375°F. Grease and flour 10-inch Bundt or tube pan.

2. Combine cake mix, eggs, applesauce, melted butter and cinnamon in large bowl. Beat at low speed with electric mixer until moistened. Beat at medium speed for 4 minutes. Stir in walnuts. Pour into pan. Bake at 375°F for 45 to 55 minutes or until toothpick inserted in center comes out clean. Cool in pan 25 minutes. Invert cake onto serving plate. Cool completely. Dust with confectioners sugar. *Makes 12 to 16 servings*

Tip: *Also delicious using chopped pecans instead of walnuts.*

Butter Pecan Banana Cake

Crisco® "Americana" Cake

CAKE

    5 eggs, separated
    ½ BUTTER FLAVOR* CRISCO® Stick or
        ½ cup BUTTER FLAVOR* CRISCO
        all-vegetable shortening
    ½ CRISCO Stick or ½ cup CRISCO
        all-vegetable shortening
    1½ cups granulated sugar
    2 cups sifted all-purpose flour
    1 teaspoon baking powder
    ½ teaspoon baking soda
    ½ teaspoon salt
    1 can (8 ounces) crushed pineapple in
        unsweetened juice
    2 tablespoons sour cream
    1¼ teaspoons almond extract
    1 red apple, peeled, grated (about ½ cup)
    1 cup chopped pecans

GLAZE

    1 cup confectioners sugar
    2 tablespoons milk
    1 tablespoon fresh lemon juice
        Additional chopped pecans (optional)

*Butter Flavor Crisco is artificially flavored.

1. Preheat oven to 325°F. Grease 10-inch tube pan with shortening. Flour lightly.

2. For cake, beat egg whites in large bowl at high speed of electric mixer until stiff peaks form.

3. Combine shortenings in another large bowl. Beat at medium speed until creamy. Add granulated sugar and egg yolks. Beat at medium speed until well blended.

4. Combine flour, baking powder, baking soda and salt in small bowl. Add to creamed mixture. Beat at low speed until mixed. Beat at medium speed until well blended. Reduce speed to low. Add pineapple with juice, sour cream and almond extract. Beat until blended. Stir in egg whites, apple and nuts with spoon. Spoon into prepared pan.

5. Bake at 325°F for 40 to 50 minutes, or until cake springs back when touched lightly in center. Cool 5 to 7 minutes. Refrigerate 5 minutes before removing from pan. Place cake, top side up, on wire rack. Cool completely. Place cake on serving plate.

6. For glaze, combine confectioners sugar, milk and lemon juice in small bowl. Mix with spoon. Drizzle over top of cake, letting excess glaze run down side. Sprinkle with additional nuts, if desired, before glaze hardens.

*Makes one 10-inch tube cake
(12 to 16 servings)*

Crisco® "Americana" Cake

Kids' Confetti Cake

CAKE
- 1 package DUNCAN HINES® Moist Deluxe Yellow Cake Mix
- 1 package (4-serving size) vanilla instant pudding and pie filling mix
- 4 eggs
- 1 cup water
- ½ cup CRISCO® Oil or CRISCO® PURITAN® Canola Oil
- 1 cup semi-sweet mini chocolate chips

TOPPING
- 1 cup colored miniature marshmallows
- ⅔ cup DUNCAN HINES® Creamy Homestyle Chocolate Frosting
- 2 tablespoons semi-sweet mini chocolate chips

1. Preheat oven to 350°F. Grease and flour 13×9×2-inch baking pan.

2. For cake, combine cake mix, pudding mix, eggs, water and oil in large bowl. Beat at medium speed with electric mixer 2 minutes. Stir in 1 cup chocolate chips. Pour into pan. Bake 40 to 45 minutes or until toothpick inserted in center comes out clean.

3. For topping, immediately arrange marshmallows evenly over hot cake. Place frosting in microwave-safe bowl. Microwave at HIGH (100% power) 25 to 30 seconds. Stir until smooth. Drizzle evenly over marshmallows and cake. Sprinkle with 2 tablespoons chocolate chips. Cool completely.

Makes 12 to 16 servings

Almond Coconut Butter Cake

- ¾ cup cake flour
- 1 teaspoon baking powder
- ¼ teaspoon salt
- ⅔ cup BLUE DIAMOND® Blanched Almond Paste
- ¾ cup granulated sugar
- 2 eggs
- 1 teaspoon vanilla
- ½ cup milk
- ¼ cup plus 2 tablespoons butter, divided
- ¾ cup brown sugar
- 1 cup flaked, sweetened coconut
- ¼ cup heavy cream

Sift cake flour, baking powder and salt; reserve. Beat almond paste and granulated sugar with electric mixer until mixture resembles coarse cornmeal. Gradually beat in eggs and vanilla on medium speed, scraping sides of bowl occasionally. Stir in flour mixture. Bring milk and 2 tablespoons butter to a boil; stir into cake batter. Pour into greased 8-inch square pan. Bake at 350°F for 30 minutes or until toothpick inserted in center comes out clean. Meanwhile, combine brown sugar, remaining ¼ cup butter, melted, coconut and cream. Spread over warm cake; place about 5 inches from broiler heat source. Broil about 3 minutes or until top is golden brown. *Makes 9 servings*

Citrus Poppy Seed Cake

CAKE
WESSON® Butter Flavored No-Stick
    Cooking Spray
1⅓ cups orange juice
½ cup WESSON® Vegetable Oil
3 eggs
1 (18.25-ounce) box lemon cake mix
2 tablespoons poppy seeds
    Grated peel from 1 orange and 1 lemon

ICING
2 cups powdered sugar, sifted
2 to 3 tablespoons orange juice
    Dash salt
½ tablespoon poppy seeds (optional)
    Grated peel from 1 orange and 1 lemon

For cake, preheat oven to 350°F. Lightly spray Bundt pan with Wesson Cooking Spray. Using electric mixer, beat orange juice, oil and eggs; mix well. Slowly add cake mix to batter; mix on low speed until just moistened. Beat on medium speed for 2 minutes. Fold in poppy seeds and orange and lemon peel. Pour batter into Bundt pan; bake for 40 to 45 minutes or until toothpick inserted into cake comes out clean. Cool on wire rack for 10 minutes. Invert cake onto cake plate; let cool completely. Spoon icing over cake and top with additional orange and lemon peel, if desired.

For icing, combine all icing ingredients; mix well. Icing should be moderately thick but not thin enough to run off cake. Add more sugar or juice to achieve desired consistency.   *Makes 12 servings*

New England Streusel Cake

1½ cups 100% bran cereal
1 cup applesauce
1 cup skim milk
1 cup maple-flavored syrup
½ cup FLEISCHMANN'S® Margarine,
    melted
½ cup EGG BEATERS® Healthy Real Egg
    Product
2½ cups all-purpose flour
1 tablespoon DAVIS® Baking Powder
1 teaspoon baking soda
1 teaspoon ground cinnamon
    Streusel Topping (recipe follows)
    Powdered sugar glaze, optional

Mix bran, applesauce, milk, syrup, margarine and egg product; let stand 5 minutes.

In large bowl, blend flour, baking powder, baking soda and cinnamon; stir in bran mixture. Spread batter into greased 13×9×2-inch baking pan. Sprinkle with Streusel Topping. Bake at 350°F for 45 to 50 minutes or until toothpick inserted in center comes out clean. Cool completely in pan on wire rack. Drizzle with powdered sugar glaze if desired. Cut into 16 pieces.   *Makes 16 servings*

Streusel Topping: With mixer, beat ¼ cup FLEISCHMAN'S® Margarine and ¼ cup sugar until creamy. Stir in 1 cup 100% bran cereal, ½ cup PLANTERS® Gold Measure Walnuts, chopped, ¼ cup all-purpose flour and ½ teaspoon ground cinnamon.

Banana Cake

2½ cups all-purpose flour
1 teaspoon salt
¾ teaspoon baking powder
¾ teaspoon baking soda
1⅔ cups sugar
⅔ cup shortening
2 eggs
1¼ cups mashed ripe bananas (2 to 3 medium)
⅔ cup buttermilk
⅔ cup chopped walnuts
Frosting (recipe follows)
Banana slices and fresh mint leaves
(optional)

1. Preheat oven to 375°F. Grease and flour two
(9-inch) round cake pans.

2. Combine flour, salt, baking powder and baking
soda in medium bowl; set aside. Beat together sugar
and shortening in large bowl until light and fluffy.
Add eggs, one at a time, beating well after each
addition. Blend in bananas.

3. Add flour mixture alternately with buttermilk,
beating well after each addition. Stir in walnuts.
Pour evenly into prepared pans.

4. Bake 30 to 35 minutes or until toothpick
inserted in center comes out clean. Cool in pans on
wire racks 10 minutes. Loosen edges; remove to
racks to cool completely.

5. Fill and frost with Frosting. Run pastry comb
across top and around side of cake for ridged effect,
if desired. Garnish, if desired.

Makes one 2-layer cake

Frosting

⅓ cup plus 2 tablespoons all-purpose flour
Dash salt
1 cup milk
½ cup shortening
½ cup (1 stick) margarine, softened
1¼ cups granulated sugar
1 teaspoon vanilla

Combine flour and salt in medium saucepan.
Gradually stir in milk until well blended. Cook
over medium heat until thickened, stirring
constantly; cool. Beat together shortening and
margarine in large bowl until creamy. Add sugar;
beat until light and fluffy. Blend in vanilla. Add
flour mixture; beat until smooth.

If your bananas become overripe before you
have time to bake with them, simply freeze
them to defrost and use whenever you're
ready. Either mash the bananas and freeze
them in an airtight container, or freeze them
whole and unpeeled in a sealed plastic freezer
bag for up to 6 months.

Banana Cake

Walnut Brownie Cheesecake

CRUST

1¼ cups fine chocolate wafer crumbs (about
   25 cookies, processed in blender or food
   processor)
3 tablespoons melted margarine

FILLING

4 cups (30 ounces) SARGENTO® Light
   Ricotta Cheese
1¼ cups packed light brown sugar
⅓ cup unsweetened cocoa
½ cup half-and-half
¼ cup all-purpose flour
1 teaspoon vanilla
¼ teaspoon salt
3 eggs
½ cup (2 ounces) coarsely chopped walnuts
   Confectioners sugar (optional)

Lightly grease side of 8- or 9-inch springform pan. Combine crust ingredients; mix well. Press evenly over bottom of pan. Chill while preparing filling. In bowl of electric mixer, combine Ricotta cheese, brown sugar, cocoa, half-and-half, flour, vanilla and salt; beat until smooth. Add eggs, one at a time; beat until smooth. Stir in walnuts. Pour batter over crust. Bake at 350°F 1 hour and 10 minutes or until center is just set. Turn off oven; cool in oven with door propped open 30 minutes. Remove to wire cooling rack; loosen cake from rim of pan with metal spatula. Cool completely; chill at least 4 hours. If desired, sift confectioners sugar over cheesecake *immediately* before serving.

Makes 8 servings

Philly 3-Step™ Caramel Pecan Cheesecake

2 packages (8 ounces each) PHILADELPHIA
   BRAND® Cream Cheese, softened
½ cup sugar
½ teaspoon vanilla
2 eggs
20 caramels
2 tablespoons milk
½ cup chopped pecans
1 ready to use graham cracker pie crust
   (6 ounces or 9 inches)

1. MIX cream cheese, sugar and vanilla with electric mixer on medium speed until well blended. Add eggs; mix until blended. Melt caramels with milk in small saucepan on low heat, stirring frequently until smooth. Stir in pecans.

2. POUR caramel mixture into crust. Pour cream cheese batter over caramel mixture.

3. BAKE at 350°F for 40 minutes or until center is almost set. Cool. Refrigerate 3 hours or overnight. Garnish, if desired.   *Makes 8 servings*

Prep time: 10 minutes
Baking time: 40 minutes

Chocolate Caramel Pecan Cheesecake: *Blend 4 squares* BAKER'S® *Semi-Sweet Chocolate, melted and slightly cooled, into batter. Continue as directed.*

*Philly 3-Step™ Caramel
Pecan Cheesecake*

New York Cheesecake

1 cup graham cracker crumbs
3 tablespoons sugar
3 tablespoons butter or margarine, melted
5 packages (8 ounces each) PHILADELPHIA BRAND® Cream Cheese, softened
1 cup sugar
3 tablespoons flour
1 tablespoon vanilla
3 eggs
1 cup BREAKSTONE'S® or KNUDSEN® Sour Cream

1. *MIX* crumbs, 3 tablespoons sugar and butter; press onto bottom of 9-inch springform pan. Bake at 350°F for 10 minutes.

2. *MIX* cream cheese, 1 cup sugar, flour and vanilla with electric mixer on medium speed until well blended. Add eggs, 1 at a time, mixing on low speed after each addition, just until blended. Blend in sour cream. Pour over crust.

3. *BAKE* 1 hour and 5 minutes to 1 hour and 10 minutes or until center is almost set. Run knife or metal spatula around rim of pan to loosen cake; cool before removing rim of pan. Refrigerate 4 hours or overnight. Top with cherry pie filling and garnish, if desired. *Makes 12 servings*

Prep time: 15 minutes plus refrigerating
Baking time: 1 hour 10 minutes

Chocolate New York Cheesecake: *Substitute 1 cup chocolate wafer cookie crumbs for graham cracker crumbs. Blend 8 squares BAKER'S® Semi-Sweet Chocolate, melted and slightly cooled, into batter. Continue as directed.*

Cupid's Cherry Cheesecakes

12 NILLA® Wafers
2 (8-ounce) packages cream cheese, softened
¾ cup sugar
2 eggs
Cherry pie filling

Place 1 wafer in bottom of each of 12 (2½-inch) paper-lined muffin-pan cups; set aside.

In large bowl, with electric mixer at medium speed, beat cream cheese, sugar and eggs until light and fluffy. Spoon filling into each cup, filling about ⅔ full.

Bake at 350°F for 30 minutes. Turn off oven; open door slightly. Let cool in oven for 30 minutes. Remove from oven; cool completely. Top with pie filling. Chill at least 1 hour.

Makes 12 cheesecakes

New York Cheesecake

Raspberry-Swirled Cheesecake

14 chocolate sandwich cream cookies
3 tablespoons margarine or butter, melted
1 package (8 ounces) cream cheese, softened
1 cup powdered sugar
1 tablespoon lemon juice
1 teaspoon vanilla
2½ cups thawed nondairy whipped topping
¼ cup seedless raspberry jam
Mint leaves, raspberries and chocolate drizzle (optional)

Place cookies in food processor or blender; process with on/off pulses until finely crushed. Add margarine; process with pulses until blended. Press crumb mixture onto bottom of 8-inch square or round baking dish; refrigerate.

Beat cream cheese in large bowl with electric mixer at medium speed until creamy. Add sugar; beat well. Add lemon juice and vanilla; beat until smooth. Add whipped topping; stir with mixing spoon until blended. Pour into prepared crust.

Make 20 to 25 holes in cheesecake with teaspoon. Stir jam until smooth.* Place jam in holes. Gently swirl jam with tip of knife. Refrigerate cheesecake 2 hours. Garnish with mint leaves, raspberries and chocolate drizzle, if desired. *Makes 9 servings*

*If raspberry jam remains lumpy, place in small microwavable bowl. Microwave at HIGH 30 to 45 seconds; stir.

Philly 3-Step™ Chocolate Swirl Cheesecake

2 packages (8 ounces each) PHILADELPHIA BRAND® Cream Cheese, softened
½ cup sugar
½ teaspoon vanilla
2 eggs
1 square BAKER'S® Unsweetened Chocolate, melted, slightly cooled
1 ready to use chocolate flavor pie crust (6 ounces or 9 inches)

1. *MIX* cream cheese, sugar and vanilla with electric mixer on medium speed until well blended. Add eggs; mix until blended. Blend melted chocolate into ½ cup of the cream cheese batter.

2. *POUR* remaining cream cheese batter into crust. Spoon chocolate batter over cream cheese batter. Cut through batters with knife several times for marble effect.

3. *BAKE* at 350°F for 40 minutes or until center is almost set. Cool. Refrigerate 3 hours or overnight.
Makes 8 servings

Prep time: 10 minutes
Baking time: 40 minutes

Raspberry-Swirled Cheesecake

Philly 3-Step™ Caramel Apple Cheesecake

2 packages (8 ounces each) PHILADELPHIA BRAND® Cream Cheese, softened
½ cup sugar
½ teaspoon vanilla
2 eggs
⅓ cup frozen apple juice concentrate, thawed
1 ready to use graham cracker pie crust (6 ounce or 9 inches)
¼ cup caramel ice cream topping
¼ cup chopped peanuts

1. *MIX* cream cheese, sugar and vanilla at medium speed with electric mixer until well blended. Add eggs; mix until blended. Blend in juice concentrate.

2. *POUR* into crust.

3. *BAKE* at 350°F for 40 minutes or until center is almost set. Cool. Refrigerate 3 hours or overnight. Drizzle with topping and sprinkle with peanuts before serving. Garnish with apple slices.

Makes 8 servings

Prep time: 10 minutes
Baking time: 40 minutes

Chocolate Marble Cheesecake

1 (9-ounce) package NABISCO® Famous Chocolate Wafers, finely rolled
6 tablespoons FLEISCHMANN'S® Margarine, melted
3 (8-ounce) packages cream cheese, softened
1 cup sugar
1½ teaspoons vanilla extract
5 eggs
2 ounces semisweet chocolate, melted
2 teaspoons grated orange peel

Mix crumbs and margarine; set aside ½ cup mixture. Press remaining crumbs on bottom and 1½ inches up side of 9-inch springform pan. Chill.

With mixer, beat cream cheese, sugar and vanilla until light. Beat in eggs, one at a time. Remove 1 cup batter and blend with chocolate and reserved crumb mixture; set aside. Stir orange peel into remaining batter. Pour orange batter into prepared crust; top with spoonfuls of chocolate batter. Using knife, swirl batters to marble. Bake at 300°F for 50 to 60 minutes or until set. Chill 4 hours or overnight.

Makes 12 servings

Philly 3-Step™ Caramel Apple Cheesecake

Jeweled Brownie Cheesecake

¾ cup (1½ sticks) butter or margarine
4 squares (1 ounce each) unsweetened baking
    chocolate
1½ cups granulated sugar
4 large eggs, divided
1 cup all-purpose flour
1¾ cups "M&M's"® Chocolate Mini Baking
    Bits, divided
½ cup chopped walnuts, optional
1 (8-ounce) package cream cheese, softened
1 teaspoon vanilla extract

Preheat oven to 350°F. Lightly grease 9-inch
springform pan; set aside. Place butter and
chocolate in large microwave-safe bowl. Microwave
on HIGH 1 minute; stir. Microwave on HIGH an
additional 30 seconds; stir until chocolate is
completely melted. Add sugar and *3 eggs,* one at a
time, beating well after each addition; blend in
flour. Stir in *1¼ cups "M&M's"® Chocolate Mini
Baking Bits* and nuts, if using; set aside. In large
bowl beat cream cheese, remaining *1 egg* and
vanilla. Spread half of the chocolate mixture in
prepared pan. Carefully spread cream cheese
mixture evenly over chocolate mixture, leaving
1-inch border. Spread remaining chocolate mixture
evenly over top, all the way to the edges. Sprinkle
with remaining *½ cup "M&M's"® Chocolate Mini
Baking Bits.* Bake 40 to 45 minutes or until firm to
the touch. Cool completely. Store in refrigerator in
tightly covered container.   *Makes 12 slices*

Philly 3-Step™ Double Layer Pumpkin Cheesecake

2 packages (8 ounces each) PHILADELPHIA
    BRAND® Cream Cheese, softened
½ cup sugar
½ teaspoon vanilla
2 eggs
½ cup canned pumpkin
½ teaspoon ground cinnamon
    Dash *each* ground cloves and nutmeg
1 ready to use graham cracker pie crust
    (6 ounces or 9 inches)

1. *MIX* cream cheese, sugar and vanilla with electric
mixer on medium speed until well blended. Add
eggs; mix until blended. In separate bowl, mix
pumpkin and spices. Stir 1 cup of the cream cheese
batter into pumpkin mixture.

2. *POUR* remaining cream cheese batter into crust.
Top with pumpkin batter.

3. *BAKE* at 350°F for 40 minutes or until center is
almost set. Cool. Refrigerate 3 hours or overnight.
Garnish, if desired.   *Makes 8 servings*

Prep time: 10 minutes
Baking time: 40 minutes

Jeweled Brownie Cheesecake

Apricot Carrot Bread

1¾ cups all-purpose flour
1 teaspoon baking powder
¼ teaspoon baking soda
¼ teaspoon salt
½ cup granulated sugar
½ cup finely shredded carrots
½ cup MOTT'S® Natural Apple Sauce
1 egg, beaten lightly
2 tablespoons vegetable oil
⅓ cup dried apricots, snipped into small bits
½ cup powdered sugar
2 teaspoons MOTT'S® Apple Juice

1. Preheat oven to 350°F. Spray 8×4-inch loaf pan with nonstick cooking spray.

2. In large bowl, combine flour, baking powder, baking soda and salt.

3. In small bowl, combine granulated sugar, carrots, apple sauce, egg and oil.

4. Stir apple sauce mixture into flour mixture just until moistened. (Batter will be thick.) Fold in apricots. Spread batter into prepared pan.

5. Bake 45 to 50 minutes or until toothpick inserted in center comes out clean. Cool loaf in pan 10 minutes. Invert onto wire rack; turn right side up. Cool completely. For best flavor, wrap loaf in plastic wrap or foil; store at room temperature overnight.

6. Just before serving, in small bowl, combine powdered sugar and apple juice until smooth. Drizzle over top of loaf. Cut into 12 slices.

Makes 12 servings

Apricot Carrot Bread

Orange Fruit Bread

2 cups all-purpose flour
¼ cup sugar
1½ teaspoons baking powder
½ teaspoon baking soda
½ teaspoon salt
¼ cup Prune Purée (recipe follows) or prepared prune butter
¾ cup orange juice
½ cup orange marmalade
Grated peel of 1 orange
1 package (6 ounces) mixed dried fruit bits
¼ cup chopped toasted pecans

Preheat oven to 350°F. Coat 8½×4½×2¾-inch loaf pan with vegetable cooking spray. In mixer bowl, combine flour, sugar, baking powder, baking soda and salt. Add prune purée; beat at low speed until blended. Add juice, marmalade and orange peel. Beat at low speed just until blended. Stir in fruit bits and pecans. Spoon batter into prepared pan. Bake in center of oven about 1 hour until pick inserted into center comes out clean. Cool in pan 5 minutes; remove from pan to wire rack. Cool completely. For best flavor, wrap securely and store overnight before slicing. Serve with orange marmalade, if desired.   *Makes 1 loaf (12 slices)*

Prune Purée: Combine 1⅓ cups (8 ounces) pitted prunes and 6 tablespoons hot water in container of food processor or blender. Pulse on and off until prunes are finely chopped and smooth. Store leftovers in covered container in refrigerator up to two months. Makes 1 cup.

Cranberry Tea Loaf

1¼ cups water
¼ cup cranberry juice cocktail
4 LIPTON® Flo-Thru® Tea Bags
3 cups all-purpose flour
1 teaspoon baking soda
½ teaspoon salt
1 cup sugar
4 tablespoons butter, softened
2 eggs
1 cup chopped cranberries
1 cup chopped walnuts or pecans

Preheat oven to 350°F.

In small saucepan, bring water and cranberry juice to a boil. Add tea bags; cover and brew 5 minutes. Remove tea bags and squeeze; cool.

In small bowl, combine flour, baking soda and salt. In large mixer bowl, beat sugar and butter with electric mixer until well blended. Beat in eggs, one at a time. Beat in cooled tea mixture. Gradually beat in flour mixture at low speed until blended. Stir in cranberries and walnuts until just blended.

Turn into greased 9×5×3-inch loaf pan. Bake 1 hour 15 minutes or until toothpick inserted in center comes out clean. On wire rack, cool 10 minutes; remove from pan and cool completely before slicing.   *Makes about 8 servings*

Orange Fruit Bread

Aloha Bread

1 jar (10 ounces) maraschino cherries
1¾ cups all-purpose flour
2 teaspoons baking powder
½ teaspoon salt
⅔ cup firmly packed brown sugar
⅓ cup butter or margarine, softened
2 eggs
1 cup mashed ripe bananas
½ cup chopped macadamia nuts or walnuts

Drain maraschino cherries, reserving 2 tablespoons juice. Cut cherries into quarters; set aside.

Combine flour, baking powder and salt in small bowl; set aside.

In medium bowl, combine brown sugar, butter, eggs and reserved cherry juice; mix on medium speed of electric mixer until ingredients are thoroughly combined. Add flour mixture alternately with mashed bananas, beginning and ending with flour mixture. Stir in cherries and nuts. Lightly spray 9×5×3-inch loaf pan with nonstick cooking spray. Spread batter evenly in pan.

Bake in preheated 350°F oven 1 hour or until loaf is golden brown and wooden pick inserted near center comes out clean.

Makes 1 loaf (about 16 slices)

Favorite recipe from **Cherry Marketing Institute, Inc.**

Double Pineapple Bread

¾ cup sugar
½ cup margarine
2 eggs
2 cans (8 ounces each) DOLE® Crushed Pineapple, well drained
1 teaspoon vanilla extract
2 cups all-purpose flour
1 teaspoon baking soda
1 teaspoon baking powder
1 teaspoon ground cinnamon
½ teaspoon salt
½ teaspoon ground nutmeg
½ cup chopped walnuts, toasted

• Beat sugar and margarine until light and fluffy. Beat in eggs. Add drained pineapple and vanilla; mix well.

• Combine dry ingredients. Stir in walnuts. Add to pineapple mixture. Stir until moistened.

• Pour batter into 3 mini loaf pans (5½×3 inches) coated with cooking spray. Bake in 350°F oven 35 to 40 minutes.

Makes 3 mini loaves (10 slices per loaf)

Prep time: 20 minutes
Bake time: 40 minutes

Aloha Bread

Pumpkin Harvest Bread

1½ cups all-purpose flour
½ cup ALBERS® Yellow Corn Meal
2 teaspoons ground cinnamon
1½ teaspoons baking powder
1 teaspoon baking soda
½ teaspoon ground nutmeg
¼ teaspoon salt
1 cup LIBBY'S® Solid Pack Pumpkin
2 eggs
½ cup granulated sugar
½ cup packed brown sugar
¼ cup vegetable oil
¼ cup applesauce
½ cup raisins

COMBINE flour, cornmeal, cinnamon, baking powder, baking soda, nutmeg and salt in medium bowl. Beat pumpkin, eggs, granulated sugar, brown sugar, oil and applesauce in large mixer bowl until combined. Beat in flour mixture just until blended. Stir in raisins. Spoon into greased, floured 9×5-inch loaf pan.

BAKE in preheated 350°F. oven for 50 to 55 minutes or until wooden pick inserted in center comes out clean. Cool in pan on wire rack for 5 to 10 minutes. Remove to wire rack to cool completely.

Makes 18 servings

Carrot-Zucchini Nut Bread

1¾ cups all-purpose flour
1 cup whole wheat flour
1 cup chopped walnuts or pecans
2 teaspoons cinnamon
1½ teaspoons nutmeg
1 teaspoon salt
1 teaspoon baking soda
½ teaspoon baking powder
1 cup sugar
1 cup WESSON® Vegetable or Canola Oil
½ cup honey
3 eggs
2 cups shredded zucchini
1 cup shredded carrots

In a medium bowl, combine *first 8* ingredients, ending with baking powder; set aside. In large bowl with electric mixer at medium speed, beat sugar, oil, honey and eggs until fluffy. With spoon, stir in zucchini and carrots. Stir in dry ingredients just until moistened. Pour into 2 greased and floured 8½×4½×2½-inch loaf pans. Bake at 325°F for 50 to 60 minutes or until wooden pick inserted into center comes out clean. Cool in pans for 10 minutes. Turn out onto racks and cool completely.

Makes 2 loaves

Pumpkin Harvest Bread

Banana Nut Bread

½ cup granulated sugar
2 tablespoons brown sugar
5 tablespoons margarine
1⅓ cups mashed ripe bananas (2 medium)
1 egg
2 egg whites
2½ cups all-purpose flour
1 teaspoon baking soda
½ teaspoon salt
⅓ cup walnuts

Preheat oven to 375°F. Spray large loaf pan with nonstick cooking spray; set aside.

Beat sugars and margarine in large bowl with electric mixer until light and fluffy. Add bananas, egg and egg whites. Sift flour, baking soda and salt into medium bowl; add to banana mixture. Stir in walnuts. Pour into prepared pan.

Bake 1 hour or until toothpick inserted into center comes out clean. Remove from pan; cool on wire rack 10 minutes. Serve warm or cool completely.

Makes 1 loaf (16 servings)

Favorite recipe from **The Sugar Association, Inc.**

Cinnamon Raisin Coffee Bread

1 cup sugar, divided
¼ cup butter or margarine, melted
2 teaspoons cinnamon
2½ cups sifted all-purpose flour
1¼ teaspoons ARM & HAMMER® Pure Baking Soda
1 teaspoon salt
2 eggs
5 tablespoons white (distilled) vinegar plus enough milk to make 1 cup liquid
½ cup raisins
¼ cup melted shortening
¼ cup chopped nuts

Combine ½ cup sugar, butter and cinnamon until well blended; set aside. Sift flour, baking soda, salt and remaining ½ cup sugar into large bowl. Beat eggs in medium bowl; add vinegar mixture and mix well. Blend in raisins and shortening. Pour egg mixture all at once into flour mixture; stir just until moistened. Spread half of batter in greased 8×8×2-inch baking pan; sprinkle with half of cinnamon mixture. Top with remaining batter; draw knife through batter several times to distribute filling slightly. Sprinkle with remaining cinnamon mixture and nuts. Bake 45 minutes at 350°F. Cut into squares and serve warm.

Makes 16 servings

Banana Nut Bread

Chocolate Chunk Banana Bread

2 eggs, lightly beaten
1 cup mashed ripe bananas (about 3 medium bananas)
⅓ cup vegetable oil
¼ cup milk
2 cups all-purpose flour
1 cup sugar
2 teaspoons CALUMET® Baking Powder
¼ teaspoon salt
1 package (4 ounces) BAKER'S® GERMAN'S® Sweet Chocolate, coarsely chopped
½ cup chopped nuts

HEAT oven to 350°F.

STIR eggs, bananas, oil and milk until well blended. Add flour, sugar, baking powder and salt; stir until just moistened. Stir in chocolate and nuts. Pour into greased 9×5-inch loaf pan.

BAKE for 55 minutes or until toothpick inserted into center comes out clean. Cool in pan 10 minutes. Remove from pan to cool on wire rack.

Makes 1 loaf

Prep time: 20 minutes
Baking time: 55 minutes

Apricot Date Mini-Loaves

1 package DUNCAN HINES® Cinnamon Muffin Mix
½ teaspoon baking powder
2 egg whites
⅔ cup water
½ cup chopped dried apricots
½ cup chopped dates

1. Preheat oven to 350°F. Grease four 5⅜×2⅝×1⅞-inch mini-loaf pans.

2. Combine muffin mix and baking powder in large bowl. Break up any lumps. Add egg whites, water, apricots and dates. Stir until well blended, about 50 strokes.

3. Knead swirl packet from Mix for 10 seconds before opening. Cut off one end of swirl packet. Squeeze contents onto batter. Swirl into batter with knife or spatula, folding from bottom of bowl to get an even swirl. Do not completely mix into batter. Divide batter evenly into pans. Sprinkle with topping packet from Mix.

4. Bake at 350°F for 30 to 35 minutes or until toothpick inserted in center comes out clean. Cool 15 minutes. Loosen loaves from pans. Lift out with knife. Cool completely. *Makes 4 mini-loaves*

Tip: This recipe may also be baked in greased 8½×4½×2½-inch loaf pan at 350°F for 55 to 60 minutes or until toothpick inserted in center comes out clean. Cool 10 minutes before removing loaf from pan.

Apricot Date Mini-Loaves

Good-for-You Zucchini Bread

⅔ cup pitted prunes
3 tablespoons water
1 cup sugar
½ cup orange juice
1 teaspoon grated orange peel
2 cups grated zucchini
1½ cups all-purpose flour
1½ cups whole wheat flour
2 teaspoons pumpkin pie spice
1 teaspoon baking powder
1 teaspoon baking soda
¼ teaspoon salt
¼ cup plain low-fat yogurt, divided

Preheat oven to 350°F. Coat 9×5-inch loaf pan with nonstick cooking spray; set aside. Combine prunes and water in food processor or blender; process until smooth. Combine prune mixture, sugar, orange juice and orange peel in large bowl; mix well. Stir in zucchini.

Combine flours, pumpkin pie spice, baking powder, baking soda and salt in medium bowl. Stir half of flour mixture into zucchini mixture, then stir in half of yogurt. Repeat with remaining flour mixture and yogurt; stir just until blended. Pour batter into prepared pan.

Bake 1 hour and 15 minutes or until toothpick inserted into center of loaf comes out clean. Cool in pan 10 minutes. Remove from pan; cool completely on wire rack.

Makes 1 loaf

Orange Apricot Tea Bread

¾ cup water
6 LIPTON® Soothing Moments® Orange & Spice Flavored Tea Bags*
½ cup chopped dried apricots
2½ cups all-purpose flour
1 cup sugar
1½ teaspoons baking powder
1 teaspoon salt
⅓ cup butter or margarine, softened
2 eggs
1 container (8 ounces) vanilla yogurt

*Also terrific with Lipton® Soothing Moments® Gentle Orange Herbal Tea Bags.

Preheat oven to 350°F. Spray 9×5-inch loaf pan with nonstick cooking spray; set aside.

In 1-quart saucepan, bring water to a boil. Remove from heat and add orange & spice flavored tea bags and apricots; cover and brew 5 minutes. Remove tea bags and squeeze; cool.

In large bowl, mix flour, sugar, baking powder and salt. With electric mixer, cut in butter until mixture is size of small peas. Add eggs beaten with cool tea and yogurt; stir just until flour is moistened. Turn into prepared pan. Bake 1 hour 5 minutes or until toothpick inserted into center comes out clean. Cool 10 minutes on wire rack; remove from pan and cool completely.

Makes 1 loaf

Good-for-You Zucchini Bread

Peanut Butter Mini Chip Loaves

3 cups all-purpose flour
1½ teaspoons baking powder
1 teaspoon baking soda
1 teaspoon salt
1 cup creamy peanut butter
½ cup butter or margarine, softened
½ cup granulated sugar
½ cup light brown sugar
2 eggs
1½ cups buttermilk*
2 teaspoons vanilla
1 cup mini semisweet chocolate chips

*Or, substitute soured fresh milk. To sour milk, place 1½ tablespoons lemon juice *plus* enough milk to equal 1½ cups in 2-cup measure. Stir; let stand 5 minutes before using.

Preheat oven to 350°F. Grease 2 (8½×4½-inch) loaf pans. Sift flour, baking powder, baking soda and salt into large bowl; set aside.

Beat peanut butter, butter, granulated sugar and brown sugar in large bowl with electric mixer at medium speed until light and fluffy. Beat in eggs, one at a time. Beat in buttermilk and vanilla. Gradually add flour mixture; beat at low speed. Stir chips into batter; spoon into prepared pans.

Bake 45 minutes or until toothpick inserted into center comes out clean. Cool in pans on wire rack 10 minutes. Remove from pans; cool completely on rack. *Makes 2 loaves*

Grandma's® Molasses Banana Bread

½ cup softened butter or margarine
3 large bananas, mashed
1 cup GRANDMA'S® Gold Molasses
1 egg
1 cup whole wheat flour
¾ cup all-purpose flour
½ cup chopped walnuts
2 teaspoons baking soda
½ teaspoon salt
½ teaspoon finely grated orange peel (optional)
½ teaspoon ground nutmeg (optional)

1. Heat oven to 350°F. Beat butter in large bowl until smooth. Beat in bananas, Grandma's® Molasses and egg.

2. Mix in remaining ingredients just until blended.

3. Pour batter into greased and floured 9×5-inch loaf pan.

4. Bake in 350°F oven for 50 to 60 minutes. Cool on wire rack. *Makes 1 loaf*

Peanut Butter Mini Chip Loaf

Orange Zucchini Loaves

LOAVES
  1 package DUNCAN HINES® Orange
    Supreme Cake Mix
  3 egg whites
  ¾ cup water
  ⅓ cup CRISCO® Oil or CRISCO®
    PURITAN® Canola Oil
  1 teaspoon ground cinnamon
  1 cup grated zucchini
  2 teaspoons grated orange peel (see Tip)

SYRUP
  ¼ cup granulated sugar
  2 tablespoons orange juice
    Confectioners sugar, for garnish
    Orange slices, for garnish (optional)

1. Preheat oven to 350°F. Grease and flour two 8½×4½×2½-inch loaf pans.

2. For loaves, combine cake mix, egg whites, water, oil and cinnamon in large bowl. Beat at low speed with electric mixer until moistened. Beat at medium speed for 2 minutes. Fold in zucchini and orange peel. Divide evenly into pans. Bake at 350°F for 50 to 55 minutes or until toothpick inserted in center comes out clean. Cool in pans 15 minutes. Loosen loaves from pans. Invert onto cooling racks. Turn right-side up. Poke holes in tops of warm loaves with toothpick or long-tined fork.

3. For syrup, combine granulated sugar and orange juice in small saucepan. Cook on medium heat, stirring constantly, until sugar dissolves. Spoon hot syrup evenly over each loaf. Cool completely. Garnish with confectioners sugar and orange slices, if desired. *Makes 2 loaves (24 slices)*

Note: This recipe contains no cholesterol.

Tip: When grating orange peel, avoid bitter white portion known as the pith.

Plantation Peanut Bread

  2 cups all-purpose flour
  1 cup sugar
  2 teaspoons baking powder
  1 teaspoon salt
  1 cup PETER PAN® Chunky Peanut Butter
  1 egg
  1 cup milk

In large bowl, combine flour, sugar, baking powder and salt. Add peanut butter; mix until crumbly. In small bowl, combine egg and milk; mix well. Add to peanut butter mixture, mix until moistened. Pour batter into greased 9×5×3-inch loaf pan. Bake in 325°F oven for 50 minutes or until toothpick inserted into center comes out clean. Cool on wire rack for 10 minutes; remove from pan and let cool completely. *Makes 1 loaf*

Smucker's® Orange Marmalade Bread

2½ cups all-purpose flour
1 tablespoon baking powder
1 teaspoon salt
½ cup honey
2 tablespoons butter, softened
3 eggs, beaten
1 (12-ounce) jar SMUCKER'S® Orange Marmalade
1 tablespoon grated orange peel
1 cup finely chopped pecans (optional)

Preheat oven to 350°F.

Combine flour, baking powder and salt in bowl.

Beat honey, butter and eggs in separate bowl until smooth. Stir in Smucker's® Orange Marmalade and orange peel, mixing well.

Add flour mixture, stirring until well blended. Add nuts. Bake in greased loaf pan for 1 hour. Cool for 10 minutes. Let loaf cool completely for easier slicing. *Makes 10 servings*

Prep time: 10 minutes
Cook time: 1 hour

Orange Cinnamon Tea Cake

CAKE
1 package DUNCAN HINES® Moist Deluxe Orange Supreme Cake Mix
3 eggs
1⅓ cups orange juice
⅓ cup CRISCO® Oil or CRISCO® PURITAN® Canola Oil
1 teaspoon ground cinnamon
½ cup chopped walnuts

GLAZE
½ cup DUNCAN HINES® Creamy Homestyle Vanilla Frosting
1 tablespoon orange juice
¼ cup chopped walnuts

1. Preheat oven to 350°F. Grease and flour 10-inch Bundt or tube pan.

2. For cake, combine cake mix, eggs, 1⅓ cups orange juice, oil and cinnamon in large bowl. Beat at medium speed with electric mixer for 2 minutes. Stir in ½ cup walnuts. Pour into pan. Bake at 350°F for 40 to 50 minutes or until toothpick inserted in center comes out clean. Cool in pan 25 minutes. Invert onto serving plate. Cool completely.

3. For glaze, combine Vanilla frosting and 1 tablespoon orange juice in small bowl. Stir until smooth. Drizzle over cake. Sprinkle with ¼ cup walnuts. *Makes 12 to 16 servings*

Tip: Cake may be baked, wrapped and frozen for up to 6 weeks before using. Thaw unwrapped at room temperature.

Sour Cream Coffee Cake with Brandy-Soaked Cherries

Streusel Topping (recipe follows)
3¼ **cups all-purpose flour, divided**
1 **cup dried sweet or sour cherries**
½ **cup brandy**
1½ **cups sugar**
¾ **cup butter or margarine**
3 **eggs**
1 **container (16 ounces) sour cream**
1 **tablespoon vanilla**
2 **teaspoons baking powder**
2 **teaspoons baking soda**
¼ **teaspoon salt**

1. Prepare Streusel Topping; set aside.

2. Preheat oven to 350°F. Grease 10-inch tube pan with removable bottom. Sprinkle ¼ cup flour into pan, rotating pan to evenly coat bottom and sides of pan. Discard any remaining flour.

3. Bring cherries and brandy to a boil in small saucepan over high heat. When mixture comes to a boil, cover and remove from heat. Let stand 20 to 30 minutes or until cherries are tender. Drain; discard any remaining brandy.

4. Beat sugar and butter in large bowl with electric mixer at medium speed until light and fluffy. Add eggs, one at a time, beating until thoroughly incorporated. Beat in sour cream and vanilla.

5. Add remaining 3 cups flour, baking powder, baking soda and salt. Beat at low speed just until blended. Stir in cherries.

6. Spoon ½ of batter into prepared pan. Sprinkle with half of Streusel Topping. Repeat with remaining batter and topping. Bake 1 hour or until wooden skewer inserted into center comes out clean.

7. Cool in pan on wire rack 10 minutes. Remove from pan. Serve warm or at room temperature.

Makes 16 servings

Streusel Topping

1 **cup chopped walnuts or pecans**
½ **cup packed brown sugar**
1 **teaspoon ground cinnamon**
½ **teaspoon ground nutmeg**
2 **tablespoons melted butter or margarine**

Combine nuts, brown sugar, cinnamon and nutmeg in small bowl. Stir in butter until well blended.

Makes about 1 cup

*Sour Cream Coffee Cake with
Brandy-Soaked Cherries*

Spring Break Blueberry Coffeecake

TOPPING
- ½ cup flaked coconut
- ¼ cup firmly packed brown sugar
- 2 tablespoons butter or margarine, softened
- 1 tablespoon all-purpose flour

CAKE
- 1 package DUNCAN HINES® Blueberry Muffin Mix
- 1 can (8 ounces) crushed pineapple with juice, undrained
- 1 egg
- ¼ cup water

1. **Preheat** oven to 350°F. Grease 9-inch square pan.

2. **For topping,** combine coconut, brown sugar, butter and flour in small bowl. Mix with fork until well blended. Set aside.

3. **Rinse** blueberries from Mix with cold water and drain.

4. **For cake,** place muffin mix in medium bowl. Break up any lumps. Add pineapple with juice, egg and water. Stir until moistened, about 50 strokes. Fold in blueberries. Spread in pan. Sprinkle reserved topping over batter. Bake at 350°F for 30 to 35 minutes or until toothpick inserted in center comes out clean. Serve warm or cool completely.

Makes 9 servings

Tip: *To keep blueberries from discoloring batter, drain on paper towels after rinsing.*

Quick Crumb Coffee Cake

- 2 cups all-purpose flour
- 1½ cups sugar
- 2 teaspoons baking powder
- ¼ teaspoon salt
- ¾ CRISCO® Stick or ¾ cup CRISCO all-vegetable shortening
- 2 eggs
- ½ cup milk
- 1 teaspoon vanilla
- ½ cup chopped pecans

1. **Preheat** oven to 350°F. **Grease** two 8×1½-inch round cake pans; set aside.

2. **Combine** flour, sugar, baking powder and salt in medium mixing bowl. **Cut in** shortening until crumbly. **Reserve** *1 cup* crumb mixture for topping.

3. **Stir** together eggs, milk and vanilla. **Add** to remaining crumb mixture. **Stir** *just until moistened.* **Spread** batter evenly in prepared pans.

4. **Combine** reserved crumbs and chopped nuts. **Sprinkle** evenly over batter. **Bake** at 350°F about 25 minutes or until edges are lightly browned and toothpick inserted in center comes out clean. **Cool** on wire rack. **Serve** warm or cool.

Makes 16 servings

Spring Break Blueberry Coffeecake

Cherry Coconut Cheese Coffee Cake

2½ cups all-purpose flour, divided
¾ cup sugar
½ teaspoon baking powder
½ teaspoon baking soda
2 packages (3 ounces each) cream cheese,
  softened, divided
¾ cup milk
2 tablespoons vegetable oil
2 eggs
1 teaspoon vanilla
½ cup flaked coconut
¾ cup cherry preserves
2 tablespoons butter or margarine

1. Preheat oven to 350°F. Grease and flour 9-inch springform pan; dust with 2 teaspoons flour. Combine remaining flour and sugar in large bowl. Place ½ cup flour mixture in small bowl; set aside.

2. Stir baking powder and baking soda into flour mixture in large bowl. Cut in 1 package cream cheese with pastry blender or 2 knives until mixture resembles coarse crumbs.

3. Combine milk, oil and 1 egg in medium bowl. Add to flour-cream cheese mixture; stir just until moistened. Spread batter on bottom and 1 inch up side of prepared pan. (Batter should be about ¼ inch thick on side.)

4. Combine remaining package cream cheese, remaining egg and vanilla in small bowl; stir until smooth. Pour over batter, spreading to within 1 inch of edge. Sprinkle coconut over cream cheese mixture. Spoon preserves evenly over coconut.

5. Cut butter into reserved flour mixture with pastry blender or 2 knives until mixture resembles coarse crumbs. Sprinkle over preserves.

6. Bake 55 to 60 minutes or until browned and toothpick inserted in coffee cake crust comes out clean. Cool in pan on wire rack 15 minutes. Remove side of pan. Serve warm or cool completely. *Makes 10 servings*

To help keep cakes moist, cut an apple in half and place it in the storage container with the cake. The more airtight the container is, the longer the cake will stay fresh and moist.

Cherry Coconut Cheese Coffee Cake

Mocha Walnut Crunch Coffeecake

COFFEECAKE

- 1 (16-ounce) package hot roll mix
- 1 cup QUAKER® Oats (quick or old fashioned, uncooked)
- ¼ teaspoon salt (optional)
- ¾ cup milk
- ½ cup (1 stick) margarine or butter
- ½ cup sugar
- 3 eggs, room temperature
- ½ cup semi-sweet chocolate pieces

TOPPING

- ½ cup all-purpose flour
- ½ cup sugar
- ¼ cup QUAKER® Oats (quick or old fashioned, uncooked)
- 1 tablespoon instant coffee granules or expresso powder
- ½ cup (1 stick) margarine or butter, chilled
- ½ cup semi-sweet chocolate pieces
- ½ cup chopped walnuts

Grease 12-cup bundt pan or 10-inch tube pan. For coffeecake, in large mixing bowl, combine hot roll mix (including yeast packet), oats and salt; mix well. In small saucepan, heat milk and margarine over low heat until margarine is melted; remove from heat. Stir in sugar; cool mixture to 120°F to 130°F. Add to oat mixture; add eggs. Beat at low speed of electric mixer until well blended. Stir in chocolate pieces. Spoon into prepared pan.

For topping, combine flour, sugar, oats and coffee granules; cut in margarine until mixture is crumbly. Stir in chocolate pieces and nuts. Sprinkle evenly over top of dough. Cover loosely with plastic wrap. Let rise in warm place 30 to 40 minutes or until nearly double in size.

Heat oven to 350°F. Bake, uncovered, 45 to 50 minutes or until wooden pick inserted in center comes out clean. Cool in pan 10 minutes. Remove from pan, topping side up, onto wire rack. Cool completely. Store tightly covered.

Makes 16 servings

Note: If hot roll mix is not available, combine 3 cups all-purpose flour, two ¼-ounce packages quick-rising yeast and 1½ teaspoons salt; mix well. Continue as recipe directs.

Mocha Walnut Crunch Coffeecake

Orange Pecan Brunch Cake

**1 package DUNCAN HINES® Moist Deluxe
   Orange Supreme Cake Mix**
3 eggs
⅔ cup dairy sour cream
½ cup water
⅓ cup chopped pecans
**⅓ cup CRISCO® Oil or CRISCO®
   PURITAN® Canola Oil**
2 tablespoons lemon juice
1 teaspoon ground cinnamon
   Mandarin orange segments
   Strawberry slices
   Kiwifruit slices
½ cup apricot preserves, heated and strained
   Mint leaves, for garnish (optional)

1. Preheat oven to 350°F. Grease and flour 10-inch bundt or tube pan.

2. Combine cake mix, eggs, sour cream, water, pecans, oil, lemon juice and cinnamon in large bowl. Beat at low speed with electric mixer until moistened. Beat at medium speed for 2 minutes. Pour into pan. Bake at 350°F for 48 to 53 minutes or until toothpick inserted in center comes out clean. Cool in pan 25 minutes. Invert onto serving plate.

3. Dry fruit thoroughly between layers of paper towels. Arrange fruit pieces on top of cake. Brush with warmed preserves. Drizzle remaining preserves over top and sides of cake. Garnish with mint leaves, if desired. Serve warm or cool completely and refrigerate until ready to serve.

Makes 12 to 16 servings

Tip: For a different presentation, brush the cake with warmed preserves and serve your favorite fruit assortment on the side.

Sour Cream Streusel Cake

**1 cup BLUE DIAMOND® Blanched Almond
   Paste**
2¼ cups sugar, divided
2¼ cups cake flour, sifted and divided
½ teaspoon ground cinnamon
**1 cup BLUE DIAMOND® Chopped Natural
   Almonds**
1 cup plus 2 tablespoons butter, divided
1½ teaspoons baking powder
¼ teaspoon salt
2 eggs
1 teaspoon vanilla extract
½ teaspoon almond extract
1 cup sour cream, room temperature

With pastry blender or fork, mix almond paste, ¼ cup sugar, ¼ cup cake flour and cinnamon until mixture resembles coarse cornmeal. Mix in almonds; reserve 1 cup of mixture. Sprinkle remaining almond mixture evenly over bottom of greased 10-inch tube pan with removable bottom. Cut 2 tablespoons cold butter into 1 cup reserved almond mixture until mixture resembles coarse cornmeal; chill.

Sift together remaining 2 cups cake flour, baking powder and salt; reserve. Cream remaining 1 cup softened butter and 2 cups sugar. Add eggs, one at a time. Stir in extracts and sour cream. Fold in reserved flour mixture. Pour batter into tube pan. Bake at 350°F for 50 minutes. Gently sprinkle reserved almond mixture over top of cake. Continue baking 15 minutes or until toothpick inserted in center comes out clean and streusel mixture is browned.   *Makes 10 to 12 servings*

Blueberry Coffee Cake

2⅓ cups all-purpose flour
1⅓ cups plus 2 tablespoons granulated sugar,
   divided
½ teaspoon salt
¾ CRISCO® Stick or ¾ cup CRISCO
   all-vegetable shortening
¾ cup milk
3 eggs, divided
2 teaspoons baking powder
1 teaspoon vanilla
1 cup ricotta cheese
1 tablespoon finely grated fresh lemon peel
1 cup fresh or frozen blueberries
½ cup chopped walnuts
⅓ cup packed brown sugar
1 teaspoon cinnamon
   Confectioners Sugar Icing (recipe follows)

1. **Preheat** oven to 350°F. **Grease** 13×9×2-inch baking pan; set aside.

2. **Combine** flour, *1⅓ cups* granulated sugar and salt in bowl. **Cut in** shortening until crumbly. **Reserve** *1 cup* mixture for topping. **Add** milk, *2 eggs*, baking powder and vanilla to remaining mixture. **Beat** at medium speed 2 minutes, scraping bowl. **Spread** in prepared pan.

3. **Combine** remaining 2 tablespoons sugar, remaining egg, ricotta cheese and lemon peel in bowl. **Mix** well. **Sprinkle** blueberries over batter in the pan. **Spoon** cheese mixture over berries. **Spread** cheese mixture gently and evenly.

4. **Mix** reserved crumb mixture, nuts, brown sugar and cinnamon. **Sprinkle** over cake. **Bake** at 350°F about 45 minutes or until toothpick inserted in center comes out clean. **Cool** slightly. **Drizzle** with Confectioners Sugar Icing.   *Makes 12 servings*

Confectioners Sugar Icing: Combine 1 cup confectioners sugar, 1 tablespoon milk, orange juice or liqueur and ¼ teaspoon vanilla in small bowl. Stir in additional milk, 1 teaspoon at a time, until icing is of desired drizzling consistency. Makes about ½ cup.

Red Ribbon Cranberry Coffeecake

TOPPING
- ¼ cup all-purpose flour
- 2 tablespoons sugar
- 1 tablespoon butter

BATTER
- 2 cups all-purpose flour
- ¾ cup sugar
- 1½ teaspoons baking powder
- ½ cup butter
- ¾ cup milk
- 1 egg, beaten
- 1 teaspoon vanilla
- 1 (16-ounce) can OCEAN SPRAY® Jellied Cranberry Sauce

Preheat oven to 350°F. Grease 9¼-inch quiche pan. Place topping ingredients in small bowl. Using pastry blender or fork, work butter into dry ingredients until butter is the size of small peas.

Combine dry ingredients for batter in medium bowl. Using pastry blender or fork, work butter into dry ingredients (see topping). Combine milk, egg and vanilla in separate bowl. Add to flour mixture, mixing just until dry ingredients are moist.

Spread half of batter into pan. Place cranberry sauce in small bowl and beat with fork until smooth. Spread over batter. Dollop remaining batter over top. Gently spread with rubber scraper. Sprinkle topping over coffeecake. Bake for 20 minutes or until toothpick inserted into center comes out clean.

Makes 1 coffeecake

Blueberry Buckle

- ¾ cup granulated sugar
- ¼ cup butter
- 2 eggs
- 1 teaspoon vanilla
- 2 cups all-purpose flour
- 2 teaspoons baking powder
- ½ teaspoon salt
- ¼ teaspoon ground cinnamon
- ½ cup buttermilk
- 2½ cups fresh or frozen blueberries
- Streusel Topping (recipe follows)

Preheat oven to 375°F. Grease 9-inch square baking pan; set aside. Beat sugar and butter in large bowl with electric mixer at medium speed until well blended. Beat in eggs and vanilla. Combine flour, baking powder, salt and cinnamon. Stir flour mixture and buttermilk alternately into sugar mixture until well blended. Stir in blueberries. Spoon batter into prepared pan.

Prepare Streusel Topping; sprinkle evenly over batter. Bake 25 to 30 minutes or until toothpick inserted in center comes out clean.

Makes 9 servings

Streusel Topping: Combine ¼ cup all-purpose flour, ¼ cup granulated sugar, ¼ cup packed brown sugar and ½ teaspoon ground cinnamon until well blended. Cut in ¼ cup butter or margarine with pastry blender or 2 knives until mixture resembles coarse crumbs.

Favorite recipe from **North American Blueberry Council**

Blueberry Buckle

Sour Cream Graham Streusel Cake

8 squares graham crackers
¼ cup chopped pecans
2 tablespoons packed brown sugar
½ teaspoon ground cinnamon
3 tablespoons butter or margarine, melted
1 cup all-purpose flour
½ teaspoon baking powder
½ teaspoon baking soda
½ cup butter or margarine, softened
¼ cup granulated sugar
½ teaspoon vanilla
½ teaspoon grated lemon peel
½ cup sour cream

1. Preheat oven to 350°F. Grease 8-inch round cake pan; set aside.

2. Place graham crackers in resealable plastic food storage bag. Crush crackers with rolling pin until crackers resemble fine crumbs. Crush enough crackers to measure ¾ cup.

3. Combine graham cracker crumbs, pecans, brown sugar and cinnamon in small bowl. Add melted butter; stir until well blended. Sift together flour, baking powder and baking soda into medium bowl.

4. Beat softened butter and granulated sugar in large bowl with electric mixer at medium speed until light and fluffy. Beat in vanilla and lemon peel. Reduce speed to low. Add flour mixture alternately with sour cream, beating well after each addition.

5. Spoon half of batter into prepared pan, spreading evenly. Sprinkle ⅔ crumb mixture evenly over batter. Spoon remaining batter over crumbs, spreading carefully with back of spoon. Sprinkle remaining crumb mixture over batter; press crumbs lightly into batter.

6. Bake 30 to 35 minutes or until toothpick inserted into center comes out clean. Cool cake in pan on wire rack 10 minutes. Remove from pan; cool completely on wire rack.   *Makes 8 servings*

To lighten up this cake, substitute light sour cream for regular sour cream. The light version is made from half-and-half instead of heavy cream, so it contains about 40% less fat than regular sour cream.

Sour Cream Graham Streusel Cake

Cherry Coffeecake

TOPPING
¾ cup firmly packed brown sugar
½ cup all-purpose flour
½ cup old-fashioned or quick-cooking oats, uncooked
1 teaspoon ground cinnamon
¼ teaspoon ground nutmeg
⅓ cup butter or margarine, softened

BATTER
1½ cups all-purpose flour
½ cup granulated sugar
2 teaspoons baking powder
½ teaspoon salt
3 tablespoons butter or margarine
2 eggs
¾ cup milk
1 can (21 ounces) cherry filling and topping

For topping, combine sugar, flour, oats, cinnamon and nutmeg in medium mixing bowl; mix well. Cut in butter to make crumbly mixture. Set aside.

For batter, combine flour, sugar, baking powder and salt in large mixing bowl. Cut in butter until mixture resembles coarse crumbs. Add eggs and milk; mix just until dry ingredients are moistened. *Do not overmix.* (Batter will be lumpy.) Spread half the batter into lightly greased 13×9×2-inch baking pan. Spoon cherry filling evenly over batter; top with remaining batter. Sprinkle reserved topping over batter. Bake in preheated 350°F oven 30 to 35 minutes or until golden brown. Serve warm.   *Makes 12 servings*

Favorite recipe from **Cherry Marketing Institute, Inc.**

Orange Streusel Coffeecake

Cocoa Streusel (recipe follows)
¾ cup (1½ sticks) butter or margarine, softened
1 cup sugar
3 eggs
1 teaspoon vanilla extract
½ cup dairy sour cream
3 cups all-purpose flour
2 teaspoons baking powder
1 teaspoon baking soda
1 cup orange juice
2 teaspoons freshly grated orange peel
½ cup orange marmalade or apple jelly

Prepare Cocoa Streusel. Heat oven to 350°F. Generously grease 12-cup fluted tube pan. In large bowl, beat butter and sugar until well blended. Add eggs and vanilla; beat well. Add sour cream; beat until blended. Stir together flour, baking powder and baking soda; add alternately with orange juice to butter mixture, beating until well blended. Stir in orange peel. Spread marmalade in bottom of prepared pan; sprinkle with half of streusel. Pour half of batter into pan, spreading evenly. Sprinkle with remaining streusel; spread remaining batter evenly over streusel. Bake about 1 hour or until toothpick inserted in center of cake comes out clean. Loosen cake from side of pan; immediately invert onto serving plate.   *Makes 12 servings*

Cocoa Streusel: Stir together ⅔ cup packed light brown sugar, ½ cup chopped walnuts, ¼ cup HERSHEY'S Cocoa and ½ cup MOUNDS® Sweetened Coconut Flakes, if desired.

Orange Streusel Coffeecake

Raspberry-Applesauce Coffee Cake

1½ cups fresh or frozen raspberries
¼ cup water
7 tablespoons sugar, divided
2 tablespoons cornstarch
½ teaspoon ground nutmeg, divided
1¾ cups all-purpose flour, divided
3 tablespoons margarine
1 tablespoon finely chopped walnuts
1½ teaspoons baking powder
½ teaspoon baking soda
⅛ teaspoon ground cloves
2 egg whites
1 cup unsweetened applesauce

Preheat oven to 350°F. Spray 8-inch square baking pan with nonstick cooking spray.

Combine raspberries and water in small saucepan; bring to a boil over high heat. Reduce heat to medium. Combine 2 tablespoons sugar, cornstarch and ¼ teaspoon nutmeg in small bowl. Stir into raspberry mixture. Cook and stir until mixture boils and thickens. Cook and stir 2 minutes more.

Combine ¾ cup flour and remaining 5 tablespoons sugar in medium bowl. Cut in margarine with pastry blender until mixture resembles coarse meal. Set aside ½ cup mixture for topping; stir walnuts into remaining crumb mixture.

Add remaining 1 cup flour, baking powder, baking soda, remaining ¼ teaspoon nutmeg and cloves to walnut mixture; mix well. Stir in egg whites and applesauce; beat until well combined. Spread half of batter into prepared pan. Spread raspberry mixture over batter. Drop remaining batter in small mounds on top. Sprinkle with reserved topping.

Bake 40 to 45 minutes or until edges start to pull away from sides of pan. Serve warm or cool.

Makes 9 servings

Roman Meal Coffee Cake

2 cups whole wheat flour
1 cup ROMAN MEAL® Figs & Filberts Granola
1 tablespoon baking powder
½ cup nonfat milk
½ cup orange juice
½ cup honey
⅓ cup vegetable oil
2 egg whites, beaten
1 tablespoon molasses
1 teaspoon grated lemon peel
½ teaspoon salt
½ teaspoon ground allspice
1 cup blueberries

Heat oven to 350°F. Grease 8×8-inch baking pan. Combine flour, granola and baking powder. In separate bowl, combine all remaining ingredients except blueberries and mix well. Stir in dry ingredients. Fold in blueberries. Pour into prepared pan and bake at 350°F for 30 minutes.

Makes one 8-inch coffee cake

Raspberry-Applesauce Coffee Cake

Apple Ring Coffee Cake

3 cups all-purpose flour
1 teaspoon baking soda
1 teaspoon salt
1 teaspoon ground cinnamon
1 cup chopped walnuts
1½ cups granulated sugar
1 cup vegetable oil
2 eggs
2 teaspoons vanilla
2 cups peeled, chopped tart apples
Powdered sugar for garnish

Preheat oven to 325°F. Grease 10-inch tube pan; set aside.

Sift together flour, baking soda, salt and cinnamon into large bowl. Stir in walnuts. Combine granulated sugar, oil, eggs and vanilla in medium bowl. Stir in apples. Stir into flour mixture just until moistened. Spoon batter into prepared pan, spreading evenly.

Bake 1 hour or until toothpick inserted into center of cake comes out clean. Cool cake in pan on wire rack 10 minutes. Remove from pan; cool completely on wire rack. Sprinkle powdered sugar over cake.

Makes 12 servings

Fresh Plum Coffee Cake

2¼ cups all-purpose flour, divided
¼ cup packed brown sugar
½ teaspoon ground cinnamon
1 tablespoon margarine, softened
1½ teaspoons baking powder
½ teaspoon baking soda
¼ teaspoon salt
1 cup lemon low-fat yogurt
⅔ cup granulated sugar
2 egg whites
1 egg
1 teaspoon grated lemon peel
4 medium plums, cut into ¼-inch-thick slices

Preheat oven to 350°F. Coat 9-inch square pan with nonstick cooking spray. For topping, combine ¼ cup flour, brown sugar, cinnamon and margarine in small bowl with fork until crumbs form; set aside.

Combine remaining 2 cups flour, baking powder, baking soda and salt in large bowl. Beat yogurt, granulated sugar, egg whites, egg and lemon peel in medium bowl with electric mixer until well blended. Stir yogurt mixture into flour mixture just until ingredients are combined.

Pour batter into prepared pan. Arrange plums over batter; sprinkle evenly with reserved topping. Bake 30 to 35 minutes or until toothpick inserted in center of cake comes out clean. Cool in pan on wire rack. Serve warm or at room temperature.

Makes 9 servings

Apple Ring Coffee Cake

Blueberry Sour Cream Tea Ring

STREUSEL
¼ cup firmly packed brown sugar
¼ cup chopped pecans
½ teaspoon ground cinnamon

CAKE
1 package DUNCAN HINES® Blueberry
   Muffin Mix
¾ cup dairy sour cream
1 egg
2 tablespoons water

GLAZE
½ cup confectioners sugar
1 tablespoon milk

1. Preheat oven to 350°F. Grease 7-cup tube pan.

2. For streusel, combine brown sugar, pecans and cinnamon in small bowl. Set aside.

3. Rinse blueberries from Mix and drain.

4. For cake, empty muffin mix into bowl. Break up any lumps. Add sour cream, egg and water. Stir until blended. Spread one-third of batter in pan. Sprinkle half the streusel over batter. Place one half of blueberries over streusel. Repeat layers ending with batter on top. Bake at 350°F for 33 to 37 minutes or until toothpick inserted in center comes out clean. Cool in pan 10 minutes. Invert onto cooling rack. Turn right side up.

5. For glaze, combine confectioners sugar and milk in small bowl. Stir until smooth. Drizzle over warm cake.   *Makes 12 servings*

Tip: This recipe may be baked in one 9×5-inch loaf pan at 350°F for 50 to 55 minutes or until toothpick inserted in center comes out clean.

Cherry Crisp Coffee Cake

2 cups all-purpose flour
1 cup 100% bran cereal
2 teaspoons DAVIS® Baking Powder
1 teaspoon ground cinnamon
½ cup FLEISCHMANN'S® Margarine,
   softened
1 cup granulated sugar
½ cup EGG BEATERS® Healthy Real Egg
   Product
½ cup skim milk
1 (21-ounce) can cherry filling and topping
   Peanut Bran Topping, recipe follows
   Powdered sugar glaze, optional

In medium bowl, mix flour, bran, baking powder and cinnamon; set aside. In large bowl, with electric mixer at medium speed, beat margarine and sugar until creamy. Blend in egg product and milk. Stir in flour mixture until smooth (batter will be thick). Spread batter in a greased 9-inch springform pan.

Bake at 350°F for 40 minutes. Spoon cherry filling over batter; sprinkle with Peanut Bran Topping. Bake for 10 to 15 minutes more or until toothpick inserted in center tests done (filling will stick to toothpick).

Cool in pan on wire rack for 25 minutes. Remove side and bottom of pan; cool completely on wire rack. Drizzle with powdered sugar glaze, if desired.*   *Makes 12 servings*

*Unglazed coffee cake can be frozen for up to 1 month.

Peanut Bran Topping: Mix ½ cup coarsely chopped PLANTERS® Dry Roasted Unsalted Peanuts, ¼ cup 100% bran cereal, 2 tablespoons sugar and 1 tablespoon softened FLEISCHMANN'S® Margarine until crumbly.

Banana Coffeecake

STREUSEL
½ cup chopped pecans
⅓ cup firmly packed brown sugar
1 teaspoon ground cinnamon
1 teaspoon ground nutmeg

CAKE
1 package DUNCAN HINES® Moist Deluxe Banana Supreme Cake Mix
1 package (4-serving size) vanilla instant pudding and pie filling mix
4 eggs
1 cup ripe mashed bananas
⅓ cup CRISCO® Oil or CRISCO® PURITAN® Canola Oil
¼ cup water
Confectioners sugar

1. Preheat oven to 350°F. Grease and flour 10-inch bundt pan or tube pan.

2. For streusel, combine pecans, brown sugar, cinnamon and nutmeg in small bowl. Stir until blended. Set aside.

3. For cake, combine cake mix, pudding mix, eggs, bananas, oil and water in large bowl. Beat at medium speed with electric mixer for 2 minutes. Pour half of batter into pan. Sprinkle streusel over batter. Spread remaining batter over streusel. Swirl with knife in figure-eight pattern. Bake at 350°F for 55 to 60 minutes or until toothpick inserted in center comes out clean. Cool in pan 25 minutes. Invert onto cooling rack. Cool completely. Dust with confectioners sugar.

Makes 12 to 16 servings

Tip: Coffeecake can be made using two greased and floured 8½×4½-inch loaf pans. Pour batter into pans. Sprinkle streusel on top and press mixture lightly with fork. Bake at 350°F for 45 to 50 minutes or until toothpick inserted in center comes out clean.

A quick powdered sugar glaze can be used to dress up any coffeecake or quick bread and give it a professional look. Be sure to wait until the bread has cooled slightly before adding the glaze, or it will be absorbed into the bread.

Raspberry Tea Cake

⅓ cup whole almonds
2 cups all-purpose flour
¾ cup sugar
½ teaspoon salt
½ cup butter or margarine
¾ teaspoon baking powder
½ cup milk
1 egg
½ teaspoon vanilla
¾ cup seedless raspberry jam

1. Preheat oven to 350°F. To toast almonds, spread in single layer on baking sheet. Bake 8 to 10 minutes or until golden brown, stirring frequently. Remove almonds from pan and cool. *Increase oven temperature to 425°F.*

2. Place almonds in food processor. Process using on/off pulsing action until almonds are ground, but not pasty. Grind enough almonds to measure ⅓ cup.

3. Grease 9-inch round cake pan; set aside. Combine flour, sugar and salt in large bowl. Cut in butter with pastry blender or 2 knives until mixture resembles coarse crumbs. Reserve ½ cup mixture in small bowl.

4. Stir almonds and baking powder into remaining flour mixture. Combine milk, egg and vanilla in medium bowl with wire whisk until well blended.

5. Make well in center of flour mixture. Add milk mixture; stir until mixture forms soft dough. Spread half of dough evenly over bottom of prepared pan. Bake 10 minutes.

6. Remove crust from oven. Spread evenly with jam. Drop remaining dough by teaspoonfuls over jam. Sprinkle with reserved flour mixture.

7. Bake 20 to 25 minutes or until golden brown and toothpick inserted into center comes out clean. Cool cake in pan on wire rack 20 minutes. Cut into wedges. Store covered at room temperature.

Makes 10 servings

Toasting nuts before using them in recipes intensifies their flavor and adds crunch. Toasted nuts are also less likely to sink to the bottom of cakes and breads. Nuts can be toasted in the oven or in an ungreased skillet over medium heat. (Stir frequently when toasting nuts in a skillet.)

Raspberry Tea Cake

Sumptuous Strawberry Rhubarb Pie

CRUST
9-inch Classic Crisco® Double Crust
(page 342)

FILLING
4 cups fresh cut rhubarb (½-inch pieces)
3 cups sliced strawberries
1⅓ cups sugar
⅓ cup plus ¼ cup all-purpose flour
2 tablespoons plus 1½ teaspoons quick-cooking tapioca
½ teaspoon grated orange peel
½ teaspoon ground cinnamon
¼ teaspoon ground nutmeg
2 tablespoons butter or margarine

GLAZE
1 egg, beaten
1 tablespoon sugar

1. Prepare 9-inch Classic Crisco® Double Crust; roll and press bottom crust into 9-inch pie plate. *Do not bake.* Heat oven to 425°F.

2. For Filling, combine rhubarb and strawberries in large bowl. Combine 1⅓ cups sugar, flour, tapioca, orange peel, cinnamon and nutmeg in medium bowl; stir well. Add to fruit. Toss to coat. Spoon filling into unbaked pie crust. Dot with butter. Moisten pastry edge with water.

3. Roll out top crust. Lift onto filled pie. Trim ½ inch beyond edge of pie plate. Fold top edge under bottom crust; flute. Cut desired shapes into top crust to allow steam to escape.

4. For Glaze, brush top crust with egg. Sprinkle with 1 tablespoon sugar.

5. Bake at 425°F for 40 to 50 minutes or until filling in center is bubbly and crust is golden brown. Cover edge with foil, if necessary, to prevent overbrowning. Cool until barely warm or at room temperature before serving.

Makes 1 (9-inch) pie

Sumptuous Strawberry Rhubarb Pie

Carameled Apple Pie

CRUST
9-inch Classic Crisco® Double Crust
(page 342)
1 teaspoon cornstarch

FILLING
6 cups sliced, peeled apples (about 2 pounds)
¼ cup apple juice
2 teaspoons lemon juice
½ cup packed brown sugar
1 tablespoon quick-cooking tapioca
1 tablespoon cornstarch
1 tablespoon all-purpose flour
½ teaspoon ground cinnamon
¼ teaspoon salt
½ cup caramel ice cream topping
2 tablespoons butter or margarine

GLAZE
1 egg white, slightly beaten
1 tablespoon cold water
2 tablespoons granulated sugar
1 teaspoon brown sugar

DECORATIONS
Reserved dough scraps
Reserved egg white mixture
Red and green food color
Granulated sugar
Caramel ice cream topping

1. Prepare crust. Roll and press bottom crust into 9-inch pie plate, leaving overhang. *Do not bake.* Reserve dough scraps for Decorations. Sprinkle 1 teaspoon cornstarch in pie crust.

2. For Filling, toss apples with juices in large microwave-safe bowl. Combine ½ cup brown sugar, tapioca, 1 tablespoon cornstarch, flour, cinnamon and salt. Add to apples. Stir. Let stand 20 minutes, stirring several times.

3. Cover bowl with plastic wrap; vent. Microwave at 100% (HIGH) 7 to 15 minutes or until apples are partially cooked and mixture starts to thicken, stirring every 4 minutes. Stir in ½ cup caramel topping. Refrigerate until cold, or place bowl in ice water.

4. Heat oven to 425°F. Spoon filling into crust. Dot with butter. Moisten pastry edge with water. Cover pie with woven lattice top.

5. For Glaze, combine egg white and water; brush over lattice. Reserve extra egg white mixture. Combine 2 tablespoons granulated sugar and 1 teaspoon brown sugar. Sprinkle over lattice.

6. Bake at 425°F for 10 minutes. *Reduce oven temperature to 375°F.* Cover with foil, if necessary, to prevent overbrowning. Bake 40 minutes or until apples are tender and filling in center is bubbly.

7. For Decorations, roll out reserved dough scraps. Cut out 6 to 8 apple and leaf shapes. Divide reserved egg white mixture. Add red food color to one half and green to other half. Brush apples with red mixture and leaves with green mixture; allow to dry. Brush again. Sprinkle with additional granulated sugar. Place on greased baking sheet. Bake at 375°F for 6 to 8 minutes; cool. Spread backs with caramel topping. Arrange on pie. Cool to room temperature before serving.

Makes 1 (9-inch) pie

Carameled Apple Pie

Jubilee Pie

3 eggs
1 cup milk
½ cup buttermilk baking mix
½ cup KARO® Light or Dark Corn Syrup
¼ cup (½ stick) MAZOLA® Margarine, softened
1 cup (6 ounces) semisweet chocolate chips, melted
1 can (21 ounces) cherry pie filling
¼ teaspoon almond extract
1 cup heavy cream, whipped
Chocolate curls (optional)

1. Preheat oven to 350°F. Grease 9-inch pie plate.

2. In food processor or blender, process eggs, milk, baking mix, corn syrup, margarine and melted chocolate 1 minute. Pour into prepared pie plate; let stand 5 minutes.

3. Bake 35 to 40 minutes or until filling is puffed and set. Cool on wire rack 1 hour; center will fall, forming a well.

4. While pie bakes, mix cherry pie filling and almond extract; refrigerate. Fill center of cooled pie with cherry mixture. Refrigerate at least 1 hour.

5. Before serving, pipe or swirl whipped cream around edge. Garnish with chocolate curls.

Makes 1 (9-inch) pie

Prep time: 20 minutes
Bake time: 40 minutes, plus cooling and chilling

Cranberry-Orange Crumble Pie

1 NILLA® Pie Crust
1 egg white, lightly beaten
1 (12-ounce) package cranberries
1½ cups granulated sugar
½ cup orange juice
1 teaspoon grated orange peel
½ cup all-purpose flour
½ cup firmly packed light brown sugar
1½ teaspoons ground cinnamon
⅓ cup FLEISCHMANN'S® Margarine
½ cup quick-cooking oats
½ cup PLANTERS® Gold Measure Walnuts, chopped

Brush crust with egg white. Bake at 375°F for 5 minutes; set aside.

In saucepan, over high heat, heat cranberries, granulated sugar, orange juice and orange peel to a boil. Reduce heat; simmer 10 minutes. Pour filling into prepared crust.

In small bowl, mix flour, brown sugar and cinnamon; cut in margarine until mixture is crumbly. Stir in oats and walnuts. Sprinkle crumb mixture over pie filling. Bake at 375°F for 25 minutes or until lightly browned. Cool completely on wire rack.

Makes 8 servings

Jubilee Pie

Linzer Torte

½ cup whole almonds
1½ cups all-purpose flour
1 teaspoon ground cinnamon
¼ teaspoon salt
¾ cup granulated sugar
½ cup butter or margarine
½ teaspoon grated lemon peel
1 egg
¾ cup raspberry or apricot jam
Powdered sugar

1. To toast almonds, preheat oven to 350°F. Spread almonds in single layer on baking sheet. Bake 8 to 10 minutes or until golden brown, stirring frequently. Remove from baking sheet and let cool. *Increase oven temperature to 375°F.*

2. Place almonds in food processor. Process using on/off pulsing action until almonds are ground, but not pasty. Measure out ½ cup ground almonds.

3. Combine flour, almonds, cinnamon and salt in medium bowl; set aside.

4. Beat granulated sugar, butter and lemon peel in large bowl with electric mixer at medium speed about 5 minutes or until light and fluffy. Beat in egg until well blended.

5. Beat in flour mixture at low speed until well blended. Spoon ⅔ of dough onto bottom of 10-inch tart pan with removable bottom. Pat dough evenly over bottom and up side of pan. Spread jam over bottom of dough.

6. Roll remaining ⅓ of dough on lightly floured surface with lightly floured rolling pin into 10×6-inch rectangle. Cut dough into 10×½-inch strips using pizza wheel or sharp knife.

7. Arrange 4 to 5 strips of dough lengthwise across jam. Arrange another 4 to 5 strips of dough crosswise over jam. Press ends of dough strips into edge of crust.

8. Bake 25 to 35 minutes or until crust is golden brown. Cool completely in pan on wire rack. Remove torte from pan. Store at room temperature, tightly covered, 1 to 2 days. Sprinkle with powdered sugar before serving.

Makes 12 servings

A sprinkle of powdered sugar doesn't travel very well on most desserts because the moisture on top of baked goods liquefies the sugar. If you need to dust pies, cakes or cookies with powdered sugar at the last minute, fill up a small salt shaker to take along to the bake sale—it's quick, convenient and easy to carry.

Linzer Torte

Mixed Berry Pie

CRUST

9-inch Classic Crisco® Double Crust
(recipe follows)

FILLING

2 cups canned or frozen blackberries, thawed
and well drained

1½ cups canned or frozen blueberries, thawed
and well drained

½ cup canned or frozen gooseberries, thawed
and well drained

⅛ teaspoon almond extract

¼ cup sugar

3 tablespoons cornstarch

1. Prepare 9-inch Classic Crisco® Double Crust;
press bottom crust into 9-inch pie plate. *Do not
bake.* Heat oven to 425°F.

2. For Filling, combine blackberries, blueberries,
gooseberries and almond extract in large bowl.
Combine sugar and cornstarch. Add to berries.
Toss well to mix. Spoon into unbaked pie crust.

3. Cut top crust into leaf shapes and arrange on top
of pie, or cover pie with top crust. Flute edge. Cut
slits into top crust, if using, to allow steam to
escape.

4. Bake at 425°F for 40 minutes or until filling in
center is bubbly and crust is golden brown. Cool
until barely warm or at room temperature before
serving. *Makes 1 (9-inch) pie*

9-inch Classic Crisco® Double Crust

2 cups all-purpose flour
1 teaspoon salt
¾ CRISCO® Stick or ¾ cup CRISCO
all-vegetable shortening
5 tablespoons cold water

1. Spoon flour into measuring cup and level.
Combine flour and salt in medium bowl.

2. Cut in shortening using pastry blender or
2 knives until flour is blended to form pea-size
chunks.

3. Sprinkle with water, 1 tablespoon at a time.
Toss lightly with fork until dough forms a ball.

4. Divide dough in half. Press half of dough
between hands to form a 5- to 6-inch "pancake."
Flour rolling surface and rolling pin lightly. Roll
dough into circle. Trim circle 1 inch larger than
upside-down pie plate. Carefully remove trimmed
dough. Set aside to reroll and use for pastry cutout
garnish, if desired. Repeat with remaining half of
dough. *Makes 2 (9-inch) crusts*

Mixed Berry Pie

Apple Cranberry Pie

1 package (8 ounces) PHILADELPHIA
   BRAND® Cream Cheese, softened
½ cup firmly packed brown sugar, divided
1 egg
1 unbaked pastry shell (9-inch)
2 cups sliced peeled apples
½ cup halved cranberries
1 teaspoon ground cinnamon, divided
⅓ cup flour
⅓ cup old-fashioned or quick-cooking oats,
   uncooked
¼ cup (½ stick) butter or margarine
¼ cup chopped nuts

MIX cream cheese and ¼ cup of the sugar with electric mixer on medium speed until well blended. Blend in egg. Pour into pastry shell.

TOSS apples, cranberries and ½ teaspoon of the cinnamon. Spoon over cream cheese mixture.

MIX flour, oats, remaining ¼ cup sugar and ½ teaspoon cinnamon; cut in butter until mixture resembles coarse crumbs. Stir in nuts. Spoon over fruit mixture.

BAKE at 375°F for 40 to 45 minutes or until lightly browned. Cool slightly before serving.

Makes 8 to 10 servings

Prep time: 15 minutes
Baking time: 45 minutes

Berry Cheesy Tart

CRUST
1 sheet refrigerated pie crust pastry

FILLING
2 cups fresh raspberries
1 cup fresh blackberries
1 cup fresh blueberries
¾ cup sugar
¼ cup tapioca
1 tablespoon lemon juice

STREUSEL TOPPING
1 cup all-purpose flour
½ cup sugar
1 cup shredded Aged Wisconsin Cheddar
   cheese
¼ cup butter

Line 9-inch tart pan (with removable bottom) with pastry. Combine all berries, ¾ cup sugar, tapioca and lemon juice; pour into pastry-lined pan. In medium bowl, combine flour, ½ cup sugar and cheese. Cut in butter to form crumbs. Sprinkle topping over fruit. Bake in preheated 400°F oven for 50 to 60 minutes or until top is well browned. Cool on wire rack. Remove side of pan and place tart on serving plate.

Makes 10 servings

Favorite recipe from **Wisconsin Milk Marketing Board**

Apple Cranberry Pie

Peach Delight Pie

FILLING
2½ cups sliced, peeled peaches (about
　　1¼ pounds or 2 to 3 large)
¾ cup granulated sugar
¼ cup quick-cooking tapioca
1 teaspoon lemon juice
1 teaspoon peach-flavored brandy

CRUMB MIXTURE
¼ cup all-purpose flour
¼ cup packed brown sugar
¼ cup chopped almonds
3 tablespoons butter or margarine, melted

CRUST
　　9-inch Classic Crisco® Double Crust
　　(page 342)

GLAZE
　　1 egg white, slightly beaten
　　Granulated sugar

1. For Filling, combine peaches, ¾ cup granulated sugar, tapioca, lemon juice and brandy in medium bowl. Stir well. Set aside.

2. For Crumb Mixture, mix flour, brown sugar, nuts and butter until crumbly.

3. Heat oven to 425°F.

4. Prepare 9-inch Classic Crisco® Double Crust; press bottom crust into 9-inch pie plate. *Do not bake.* Sprinkle half of the crumb mixture over unbaked pie crust. Add filling. Top with remaining crumb mixture.

5. Roll out top crust. Cut out desired shapes with cookie cutter. Place on filling around edge of pie.

6. For Glaze, brush cutouts with egg white. Sprinkle with granulated sugar. Cover edge of pie with foil to prevent overbrowning.

7. Bake at 425°F for 10 minutes. *Reduce oven temperature to 350°F.* Bake 25 minutes. Remove foil. Bake 5 minutes. Cool until barely warm or at room temperature before serving.

Makes 1 (9-inch) pie

Cranberry Pecan Pie

3 eggs, slightly beaten
1 cup light or dark corn syrup
⅔ cup sugar
2 tablespoons margarine, melted
1 cup coarsely chopped fresh cranberries
1 cup coarsely chopped pecans
1 tablespoon grated orange peel
1 unbaked (9-inch) pie shell

Preheat oven to 350°F. In medium bowl, stir together eggs, corn syrup, sugar and margarine until well blended. Stir in cranberries, pecans and orange peel. Pour into pie shell. Bake 1 hour or until knife inserted halfway between center and edge comes out clean. Cool on wire rack.

Makes 1 (9-inch) pie

Favorite recipe from **Pecan Marketing Board**

Tipsy Apple Pecan Pie

½ cup seedless raisins
2 tablespoons bourbon
¼ cup FLEISCHMANN'S® Margarine, softened
1 cup PLANTERS® Gold Measure Pecan Halves
½ cup firmly packed light brown sugar
Pastry for 2-crust 9-inch pie
7 cups peeled and sliced apples
½ cup granulated sugar
1 tablespoon lemon juice
1 tablespoon all-purpose flour
½ teaspoon ground cinnamon
¼ teaspoon salt
½ cup heavy cream, whipped

Combine raisins and bourbon; set aside. Spread margarine evenly over bottom and side of 9-inch pie plate. Press pecans, top-side down, into margarine; pat brown sugar evenly over pecans. Divide pastry in half; roll out one half to 10-inch circle. Place in pie plate over brown sugar and pecans.

In bowl, toss apples, drained raisins, granulated sugar, lemon juice, flour, cinnamon and salt; spoon into pie crust. Roll out remaining pastry; place over apple mixture crimping edges together. Prick crust with fork to vent.

Bake at 450°F for 10 minutes; reduce heat to 350°F and bake 45 minutes more.* Cool on wire rack until filling stops bubbling, about 5 minutes. Place serving plate over pie; carefully invert onto plate.

Remove pie plate. Cool at least 3 hours. Serve warm topped with whipped cream.

Makes 8 servings

*Place pan or foil under pie plate in case the pie bubbles over.

Lemon Buttermilk Pie

9-inch unbaked pie crust*
1½ cups sugar
½ cup (1 stick) butter, softened
3 eggs
1 cup buttermilk
1 tablespoon cornstarch
1 tablespoon fresh lemon juice
⅛ teaspoon salt

*If using a commercial frozen pie crust, purchase a deep-dish crust and thaw before using.

Heat oven to 350°F. Prick crust all over with fork. Bake until light golden brown, about 8 minutes; cool on wire rack. *Reduce oven temperature to 325°F.* In large bowl, beat sugar and butter until creamy. Add eggs, one at a time, beating well after each addition. Add buttermilk, cornstarch, lemon juice and salt; mix well. Pour filling into crust. Bake 55 to 60 minutes or just until knife inserted near center comes out clean. Cool; cover and chill.

Makes 8 servings

Favorite recipe from **Southeast United Dairy Industry Association, Inc.**

Cream Cheese Cranberry Tart

1¼ cups all-purpose flour
3 tablespoons chopped pecans
⅛ teaspoon salt
¼ cup margarine, cut into 4 pieces and chilled
2 to 3 tablespoons ice water
Vegetable cooking spray
⅔ cup 1% low-fat cottage cheese
⅓ cup HEALTHY CHOICE® Fat Free Cream Cheese
¼ cup sugar
1 egg
3 cups fresh cranberries
⅔ cup sugar
¼ cup water
1 tablespoon cornstarch
2 tablespoons unsweetened orange juice
1 teaspoon grated orange rind

Position knife blade in food processor bowl; add flour, pecans and salt. Process, pulsing 2 or 3 times, until combined. Add margarine; pulse 6 to 8 times or until mixture resembles coarse meal. With processor running, slowly add ice water through food chute, processing just until combined. (Do not form a ball.)

Press mixture into 4-inch circle on heavy-duty plastic wrap; cover with additional plastic wrap. Roll dough, still covered, to 12-inch circle; place in freezer 5 minutes or until plastic wrap can be easily removed.

Remove bottom sheet of plastic wrap; fit dough into 11-inch round tart pan coated with cooking spray. Remove top sheet of plastic wrap. Prick bottom of pastry with a fork. Bake at 375°F for 15 minutes. Cool on wire rack.

Place cottage cheese in blender container; cover and blend until smooth. Add cream cheese, ¼ cup sugar and egg; cover and blend until smooth. Pour mixture into pastry shell. Bake at 350°F for 20 minutes. Cool on wire rack.

Combine cranberries and next 5 ingredients in saucepan; mix well. Bring to a boil; cook, stirring constantly, 1 minute. Remove from heat; let cool. Spoon mixture over cream cheese filling. Cover and chill.

Makes 12 servings

Cranberries are usually sold in 12-ounce plastic bags, which amounts to about 3 cups of whole berries or 2½ cups finely chopped berries. Choose cranberries that are an intense red color; avoid bags with soft or shriveled berries. Kept in an airtight plastic bag, cranberries can be stored in the refrigerator for up to one month or in the freezer for up to one year.

Apple-Buttermilk Pie

2 medium Granny Smith apples
3 eggs
1½ cups sugar, divided
1 cup buttermilk
⅓ cup margarine or butter, melted
2 tablespoons all-purpose flour
1 tablespoon ground cinnamon, divided
2 teaspoons vanilla extract
2 teaspoons ground nutmeg, divided
1 (9-inch) unbaked pie shell

Preheat oven to 350°F. Peel and core apples; cut into small chunks. Place apples in bowl; cover with cold water and set aside.

Beat eggs briefly at low speed of electric mixer until mixed. Add all but 1 teaspoon sugar, buttermilk, margarine, flour, 2 teaspoons cinnamon, vanilla and 1½ teaspoons nutmeg; mix at low speed until well blended. Drain apples thoroughly and place in unbaked pie shell.

Pour buttermilk mixture over apples. Combine remaining 1 teaspoon sugar, 1 teaspoon cinnamon and ½ teaspoon nutmeg; sprinkle over top. Bake 50 to 60 minutes. Serve warm or at room temperature for the best flavor. Store in refrigerator.

Makes 1 (9-inch) pie

Cranberry Raisin Tart

1 (15-ounce) package refrigerated pie crusts
1½ cups OCEAN SPRAY® Fresh or Frozen Cranberries
1 cup golden raisins
½ cup chopped walnuts
½ cup packed brown sugar
1 teaspoon ground cinnamon
¼ teaspoon *each* ground nutmeg, ginger and allspice
⅛ teaspoon ground cloves

Preheat oven to 400°F.

Lightly dust one side of bottom crust with flour. Place flour side down on jelly-roll pan. Lightly press out creases with fingers. Cut second crust into ½-inch strips using pastry trimmer or knife. Set aside.

Combine remaining ingredients. Place filling on bottom crust to within 1½ inches of pastry edge. Place pie crust strips lengthwise and crosswise over filling. Trim any strips longer than bottom crust. Seal crust by pressing top of spoon or fork into folded edges. Bake for 25 minutes or until golden brown.

Makes 1 tart

Apple-Buttermilk Pie

Delaware Blueberry Pie

CRUST
**9-inch Classic Crisco® Double Crust
(page 342)**

FILLING
**4½ cups fresh blueberries, divided
½ cup granulated sugar
½ cup firmly packed brown sugar
2 tablespoons plus 1½ teaspoons cornstarch
½ teaspoon ground cinnamon
⅛ teaspoon salt
1 tablespoon butter or margarine
1 teaspoon peach schnapps
2 tablespoons quick-cooking tapioca
4 to 5 drops red food coloring (optional)**

DECORATIONS
**Reserved dough
2 tablespoons melted vanilla frozen yogurt**

1. Preheat oven to 425°F. Prepare 9-inch Classic Crisco® Double Crust; reserve dough scraps for decorations, if desired.

2. For Filling, place ½ cup blueberries in resealable plastic sandwich bag. Crush berries. Pour juice and berries into strainer over liquid measuring cup. Press berries to extract all juice. Pour water over berries until juice measures ½ cup.

3. Combine sugars, cornstarch, cinnamon and salt in large saucepan. Add blueberry juice mixture. Cook and stir on medium heat until mixture boils. Remove from heat. Stir in butter and schnapps. Set pan in cold water about 5 minutes to cool. Stir in tapioca. Add food coloring, if desired. Carefully stir in remaining 4 cups blueberries. Spoon into unbaked pie crust. Moisten pastry edge with water.

4. Cover pie with top crust. Fold top edge under bottom crust; flute with fingers or fork.

5. For Decorations, cut stars and diamonds from reserved dough. Dip cutouts in melted yogurt. Place on top of pie and around edge. Cut slits in top crust to allow steam to escape.

6. Bake at 425°F for 15 minutes. Cover cutouts and edge of pie with foil, if necessary, to prevent overbrowning. Reduce oven temperature to 375°F. Bake 20 to 25 minutes or until filling in center is bubbly and crust is golden brown. Cool to room temperature before serving.

Makes 1 (9-inch) pie

Upside-Down Apple Pie

¼ cup butter or margarine, softened
½ cup pecan halves
½ cup packed light brown sugar
1 package refrigerated pie crusts (2 crusts)
4 large Granny Smith apples, peeled and cut
   into ¼-inch slices
4 teaspoons lemon juice
1 tablespoon all-purpose flour
½ cup granulated sugar
1 teaspoon ground cinnamon
¾ teaspoon ground nutmeg

Preheat oven to 400°F. Spread butter evenly onto bottom and up side of 9-inch pie plate. Press pecans into butter, rounded sides down. Pat brown sugar evenly over pecans. Roll out one pie crust to fit pie plate; place on top of pecans. Trim edge even with edge of pie plate.

Place apples in large bowl; toss with lemon juice. Add flour, granulated sugar, cinnamon and nutmeg; mix well.

Place apple mixture in prepared pie crust; spread evenly to make top level. Roll out remaining pie crust to fit over top of pie. Place pie crust over apple mixture; trim edge leaving ½-inch overhang. Fold overhang under so crust is even with edge of pie plate. Flute pastry, if desired. Pierce top crust with fork.

Bake 50 minutes. Remove from oven; cool 5 minutes on wire rack. Place serving plate over pie plate and invert plates so serving plate is on the bottom. Remove pie plate. Serve pie warm or at room temperature. *Makes 8 servings*

Strawberry Cream Pie

1 cup plus 1½ teaspoons all-purpose flour,
   divided
¼ cup plus 1 teaspoon sugar, divided
¼ teaspoon salt
¼ cup cold margarine, cut into pieces
¾ teaspoon white or cider vinegar
3 tablespoons ice water, divided
6 ounces nonfat cream cheese
2 ounces Neufchâtel cheese
¼ cup vanilla nonfat yogurt
2 egg whites
½ teaspoon vanilla
1½ cups fresh strawberries, halved
¼ cup strawberry jelly

Combine 1 cup flour, 1 teaspoon sugar and salt in medium bowl. Cut in margarine until small crumbs form. Add vinegar and 2 tablespoons ice water; stir until moist but slightly firm. If necessary, add remaining ice water. Gather dough into a ball. Preheat oven to 450°F. Roll out dough into 12-inch circle on lightly floured surface. Place in 9-inch glass pie dish. Bake 10 to 12 minutes or until lightly browned. Cool on wire rack. *Reduce oven temperature to 325°F.* Combine cream cheese, Neufchâtel, remaining sugar and flour in large bowl; beat until creamy. Beat in yogurt, egg whites and vanilla. Pour cheese mixture into cooled pie crust. Bake 25 minutes or until set. Cool on wire rack. Place strawberries on top of cooled pie. Melt jelly in small saucepan over low heat to form glaze. Carefully brush over strawberries. Refrigerate 3 hours or overnight. *Makes 8 servings*

Upside-Down Apple Pie

Fresh Lemon Meringue Pie

1½ cups sugar
¼ cup plus 2 tablespoons cornstarch
½ teaspoon salt
½ cup cold water
½ cup fresh squeezed lemon juice
3 egg yolks, well beaten
2 tablespoons butter or margarine
1½ cups boiling water
    Grated peel of ½ SUNKIST® Lemon
2 to 3 drops yellow food coloring (optional)
1 (9-inch) baked pie crust
    Three-Egg Meringue (recipe follows)

In large saucepan, combine sugar, cornstarch and salt. Gradually blend in cold water and lemon juice. Stir in egg yolks. Add butter and boiling water. Bring to a boil over medium-high heat, stirring constantly. Reduce heat to medium and boil 1 minute. Remove from heat; stir in lemon peel and food coloring. Pour into baked pie crust. Top with Three-Egg Meringue, sealing well at edges. Bake at 350°F 12 to 15 minutes. Cool 2 hours before serving. *Makes 6 servings*

Three-Egg Meringue

3 egg whites
¼ teaspoon cream of tartar
6 tablespoons sugar

In large bowl with electric mixer, beat egg whites with cream of tartar until foamy. Gradually add sugar and beat until stiff peaks form.

Traditional Cherry Pie

3 cups frozen tart cherries, not thawed
1 cup granulated sugar
2 tablespoons quick-cooking tapioca
½ teaspoon almond extract
    Pastry for 2-crust (double) 9-inch pie
2 tablespoons butter or margarine

Preheat oven to 400°F. Combine cherries, sugar, tapioca and almond extract in medium bowl; mix well. Let cherry mixture stand 15 minutes.

Line 9-inch pie plate with 1 pastry crust; fill with cherry mixture. Dot with butter. Cover with top pastry crust. Cut slits near center for steam to escape. Seal edges and flute.

Bake 50 to 55 minutes or until crust is golden brown and filling is bubbly.

Makes 6 to 8 servings

Favorite recipe from **Cherry Marketing Institute, Inc.**

Fresh Lemon Meringue Pie

New York Apple Maple Cream Pie

CRUST
9-inch Classic Crisco® Double Crust
(page 342)

FILLING
6 cups sliced, peeled baking apples (about
2 pounds or 6 medium)
1 cup sugar
3 tablespoons cornstarch
½ teaspoon salt
¾ cup pure maple syrup*
½ cup whipping cream

GLAZE
Milk
Sugar

*Use maple flavor pancake and waffle syrup, if desired.

1. For crust, prepare 9-inch Classic Crisco® Double Crust. Roll and press bottom crust into 9-inch pie plate. Reserve pastry scraps. *Do not bake.* Heat oven to 400°F.

2. For filling, place apples, 1 cup sugar, cornstarch and salt in large bowl. Toss to coat. Combine maple syrup and whipping cream in small bowl. Pour over apple mixture. Mix gently. Spoon into unbaked pie crust. Moisten pastry edge with water.

3. Roll top crust same as bottom. Lift onto filled pie. Trim ½ inch beyond edge of pie plate. Fold top edge under bottom crust. Flute. Decorate with pastry cutouts if desired. Cut slits in top crust to allow steam to escape.

4. For glaze, brush with milk. Sprinkle with sugar.

5. Bake at 400°F for 50 to 60 minutes or until filling in center is bubbly and crust is golden brown. Refrigerate leftover pie.

Makes 1 (9-inch) pie

Note: *Golden Delicious, Granny Smith and Jonathan apples are all suitable for pie baking.*

Chocolate Pie

½ cup reduced-fat biscuit mix
3 tablespoons cocoa powder, sifted
1½ cups sugar
2 tablespoons margarine, melted
1 egg
3 egg whites
1½ teaspoons vanilla
Powdered sugar

1. Preheat oven to 350°F. Spray 9-inch pie pan with nonstick cooking spray.

2. Combine biscuit mix, cocoa and sugar in large bowl; mix well. Add margarine, egg, egg whites and vanilla; mix well. Pour mixture into prepared pan.

3. Bake 40 minutes or until knife inserted in center comes out clean. Garnish with powdered sugar.

Makes 8 servings

New York Apple Maple Cream Pie

Classic Pecan Pie

3 eggs
1 cup sugar
1 cup KARO® Light or Dark Corn Syrup
2 tablespoons MAZOLA® Margarine or
 butter, melted
1 teaspoon vanilla
1½ cups pecans
 Easy-As-Pie Crust (recipe follows) or 1 (9-
 inch) frozen deep-dish pie crust*

*To use prepared frozen pie crust: Do not thaw. Preheat oven and cookie sheet. Pour filling into frozen crust. Bake on cookie sheet. (Insulated cookie sheets are not recommended.)

1. Preheat oven to 350°F.

2. In medium bowl with fork, beat eggs slightly. Add sugar, corn syrup, margarine and vanilla; stir until well blended. Stir in pecans. Pour into pie crust.

3. Bake 50 to 55 minutes or until knife inserted halfway between center and edge comes out clean. Cool on wire rack. *Makes 8 servings*

Prep time: 6 minutes
Bake time: 50 minutes, plus cooling

Almond Amaretto Pie: Substitute 1 cup sliced almonds for pecans. Add 2 tablespoons almond-flavored liqueur and ½ teaspoon almond extract to filling.

Butterscotch Pecan Pie: Omit margarine; add ¼ cup heavy or whipping cream to filling.

Chocolate Chip Walnut Pie: Substitute 1 cup walnuts, coarsely chopped, for pecans. Sprinkle ½ cup semisweet chocolate chips over bottom of pie crust. Carefully pour filling into pie crust.

Easy-As-Pie Crust

1¼ cups unsifted all-purpose flour
⅛ teaspoon salt
½ cup (1 stick) MAZOLA® Margarine
2 to 3 tablespoons cold water

1. In medium bowl combine flour and salt. With pastry blender or 2 knives, cut in margarine until mixture resembles fine crumbs.

2. Sprinkle water over mixture while tossing to blend well. Press dough firmly into ball.

3. On lightly floured surface, roll into 12-inch circle. Fit loosely into 9-inch pie plate. Trim and flute edge. Fill and bake according to recipe.
Makes single pie crust

Baked Pie Shell: Preheat oven to 450°F. Pierce pie crust thoroughly with fork. Bake 12 to 15 minutes or until light golden brown.

*Top to bottom: Almond Amaretto Pie
and Classic Pecan Pie*

Praline Pie

1 (9-inch) HONEY MAID® Honey Graham Pie Crust
1 egg white, slightly beaten
1 cup firmly packed light brown sugar
¼ cup margarine, melted
¾ cup all-purpose flour
1 teaspoon baking powder
1 egg
1 teaspoon vanilla extract
1 cup PLANTERS® Pecans, coarsely chopped
Prepared whipped topping, for garnish

Preheat oven to 375°F. Brush pie crust with egg white. Bake at 375°F for 5 minutes; set aside. *Reduce oven temperature to 350°F.*

In medium bowl, with electric mixer at low speed, beat brown sugar and margarine until blended. Mix in flour, baking powder, egg and vanilla until well combined. Stir in ¾ cup pecans. Spread in prepared crust; sprinkle top with remaining ¼ cup pecans. Bake at 350°F for 25 to 30 minutes or until lightly browned and filling is set. Cool completely on wire rack. Garnish with whipped topping.

Makes 6 servings

Chocolate Velvet Pie

2 cups (11.5-ounce package) NESTLÉ® TOLL HOUSE® Milk Chocolate Morsels
1 package (8 ounces) cream cheese, softened
1 teaspoon vanilla extract
1 cup heavy whipping cream, whipped
1 prepared 8-inch (6 ounces) chocolate crumb crust
Sweetened whipped cream (optional)
Chocolate curls (optional)
Chopped nuts (optional)

MICROWAVE morsels in microwave-safe bowl on MEDIUM-HIGH (70%) power for 1 minute; stir. Microwave for additional 30 seconds; stir until smooth. Cool to room temperature.

BEAT melted chocolate, cream cheese and vanilla in large mixer bowl until light in color. Fold in whipped cream. Spoon into crust. Chill until firm. Top with sweetened whipped cream, chocolate curls and nuts.

Makes 8 servings

Praline Pie

Peanut Butter Cream Pie

¾ cup powdered sugar
⅓ cup creamy peanut butter
1 baked (9-inch) pie crust
1 cup milk
1 cup sour cream
1 package (4-serving size) instant French
     vanilla pudding and pie filling mix
5 peanut butter candy cups, divided
2 cups thawed nondairy whipped topping

Combine powdered sugar and peanut butter with fork in medium bowl until blended. Place evenly in bottom of pie crust.

Place milk and sour cream in large bowl. Add pudding mix. Beat with wire whisk or electric beater 1 to 2 minutes or until thickened. Pour half of filling over peanut butter mixture. Coarsely chop 4 candy cups; sprinkle over filling. Top with remaining filling.

Spread whipped topping over filling. Cut remaining candy cup into 8 pieces; place on top of pie. Refrigerate until ready to serve.

Makes 8 servings

Oreo® Mud Pie

26 OREO® Chocolate Sandwich Cookies
 2 tablespoons margarine, melted
 1 pint chocolate ice cream, softened
 2 pints coffee ice cream, softened
 ½ cup heavy cream, whipped
 ¼ cup chopped walnuts
 ½ cup chocolate fudge topping

Finely roll 12 cookies; mix crumbs with margarine. Press crumb mixture on bottom of 9-inch pie plate; stand remaining 14 cookies around edge of plate. Place in freezer for 10 minutes. Evenly spread chocolate ice cream into prepared crust. Scoop coffee ice cream into balls; arrange over chocolate layer. Freeze 4 hours or until firm. To serve, top with whipped cream, walnuts and fudge topping.

Makes 8 servings

Peanut Butter Cream Pie

Turtle Nut Pie

3 eggs
1 cup KARO® Light Corn Syrup
⅔ cup sugar
⅓ cup (5⅓ tablespoons) MAZOLA®
   Margarine, melted
½ teaspoon salt
1 cup pecans
2 squares (1 ounce each) semisweet chocolate,
   melted
   Easy-As-Pie Crust (page 360) or 1 (9-inch)
   frozen deep-dish pie crust*
½ cup caramel-flavored ice cream topping

*To use prepared frozen pie crust: Do not thaw. Preheat oven and cookie sheet. Pour filling into frozen crust. Bake on cookie sheet. (Insulated cookie sheets are not recommended.)

1. Preheat oven to 350°F.

2. In medium bowl with fork, beat eggs slightly. Add corn syrup, sugar, margarine and salt; stir until well blended. Reserve ½ cup egg mixture; set aside.

3. Stir pecans and chocolate into remaining egg mixture; pour into pie crust. Mix caramel topping and reserved egg mixture; carefully pour over pecan filling.

4. Bake 50 to 55 minutes or until filling is set about 3 inches from edge. Cool completely on wire rack.

Makes 8 servings

Prep time: 20 minutes
Bake time: 50 minutes, plus cooling

Tinker Bell Peanut Butter Pie

1 (18-ounce) jar PETER PAN® Creamy
   Peanut Butter
2 (8-ounce) packages cream cheese, room
   temperature
1¾ cups sugar
2 tablespoons unsalted butter
2 teaspoons vanilla extract
2 cups heavy whipping cream
2 ready-to-use graham cracker pie crusts
4 squares (1 ounce each) semi-sweet baking
   chocolate
½ cup brewed coffee
   Whipped cream (optional)

In large bowl, beat together first 5 ingredients until smooth. In small bowl, beat whipping cream until stiff peaks form. Fold whipped cream into peanut butter mixture; divide mixture evenly into crusts. Refrigerate until chilled. In top of double boiler, melt chocolate with coffee. Cool mixture. Evenly drizzle chocolate mixture over pies and chill until ready to serve. Garnish with whipped cream.

Makes 2 pies (8 to 10 servings each)

Turtle Nut Pie

Amaretto Coconut Cream Pie

¼ cup flaked coconut
1 container (8 ounces) thawed nondairy whipped topping, divided
1 container (8 ounces) coconut cream-flavored or vanilla-flavored yogurt
¼ cup amaretto liqueur
1 package (4-serving size) instant coconut pudding and pie filling mix
1 prepared (9-inch) graham cracker pie crust
Fresh strawberries (optional)

Preheat oven to 350°F. To toast coconut, place coconut on baking sheet. Bake 4 to 5 minutes or until golden brown, stirring frequently. Cool completely.

Place 2 cups whipped topping, yogurt and amaretto in large bowl. Add pudding mix. Beat with wire whisk or electric beater on low speed, 1 to 2 minutes or until thickened.

Pour pudding mixture into crust; spread remaining whipped topping over filling. Sprinkle with toasted coconut. Garnish with fresh strawberries, if desired. Refrigerate. *Makes 8 servings*

Southern Peanut Pie

3 eggs
1½ cups dark corn syrup
½ cup granulated sugar
¼ cup butter, melted
½ teaspoon vanilla extract
¼ teaspoon salt
1½ cups chopped roasted peanuts
9-inch unbaked deep-dish pastry shell

Beat eggs until foamy. Add corn syrup, sugar, butter, vanilla and salt; continue to beat until thoroughly blended. Stir in peanuts. Pour into unbaked pastry shell. Bake in preheated 375°F oven 50 to 55 minutes. Serve warm or cold. Garnish with whipped cream or ice cream, if desired.

Makes 6 servings

Favorite recipe from **Texas Peanut Producers Board**

Amaretto Coconut Cream Pie

Peanut Chocolate Surprise Pie

1 cup granulated sugar
8 tablespoons (1 stick) butter, melted
2 eggs
½ cup all-purpose flour
½ cup chopped peanuts
½ cup chopped walnuts
½ cup semisweet chocolate chips
¼ cup bourbon
1 teaspoon vanilla extract
1 (9-inch) unbaked deep-dish pie shell
Whipped cream, for garnish
Chocolate shavings, for garnish

Preheat oven to 350°F. Beat sugar and butter in large bowl until creamy. Add eggs and beat until well mixed. Gradually add flour, then stir in nuts, chips, bourbon and vanilla. Spread mixture evenly in unbaked pie shell. Bake 40 minutes. Cool pie on wire rack; garnish with whipped cream and chocolate shavings.

Makes one 9-inch pie

Nestlé® Toll House® Chocolate Chip Pie

2 eggs
½ cup all-purpose flour
½ cup granulated sugar
½ cup packed brown sugar
¾ cup (1½ sticks) butter, softened
1 cup (6 ounces) NESTLÉ® TOLL HOUSE®
Semi-Sweet Chocolate Morsels
1 cup chopped nuts
1 *unbaked* 9-inch (4-cup volume) pie shell*
Sweetened whipped cream or ice cream (optional)

*If using frozen pie shell, use deep-dish style, thawed completely. Bake on baking sheet; increase baking time slightly.

BEAT eggs in large mixer bowl on high speed until foamy. Beat in flour, granulated sugar and brown sugar. Beat in butter. Stir in morsels and nuts. Spoon into pie shell.

BAKE in preheated 325°F. oven for 55 to 60 minutes or until knife inserted halfway between outside edge and center comes out clean. Cool on wire rack. Serve warm with whipped cream.

Makes 8 servings

Peanut Chocolate Surprise Pie

ACKNOWLEDGMENTS

The publisher would like to thank the companies and organizations listed below for the use of their recipes and photographs in this publication.

Arm & Hammer Division, Church & Dwight Co., Inc.

Best Foods Division, CPC International Inc.

Blue Diamond Growers

California Prune Board

California Table Grape Commission

California Strawberry Commission

Cherry Marketing Institute, Inc.

Colorado Potato Administrative Committee

Dole Food Company, Inc.

Domino Sugar Corporation

Grandma's Molasses, a division of Cadbury Beverages Inc.

Healthy Choice®

Hershey Foods Corporation

Jack Frost

Jolly Time® Pop Corn

Kahlúa® Liqueur

Kellogg Company

Kraft Foods, Inc.

Leaf®, Inc.

Lipton™

M&M/MARS

Minnesota Cultivated Wild Rice Council

MOTT'S®, Inc., a division of Cadbury Beverages Inc.

Nabisco, Inc.

National Honey Board

Nestlé USA

Newman's Own, Inc.®

North American Blueberry Council

Ocean Spray Cranberries, Inc.

Pecan Marketing Board

The Procter & Gamble Company

The Quaker® Kitchens

Roman Meal Company

Sargento® Foods Inc.

The J.M. Smucker Company

Southeast United Dairy Industry Association, Inc.

The Sugar Association, Inc.

Sunkist Growers

Texas Peanut Producers Board

Walnut Marketing Board

Wesson/Peter Pan Foods Company

Western New York Apple Growers Association, Inc.

Wisconsin Milk Marketing Board

Index

METRIC CONVERSION CHART

VOLUME MEASUREMENTS (dry)

⅛ teaspoon = 0.5 mL
¼ teaspoon = 1 mL
½ teaspoon = 2 mL
¾ teaspoon = 4 mL
1 teaspoon = 5 mL
1 tablespoon = 15 mL
2 tablespoons = 30 mL
¼ cup = 60 mL
⅓ cup = 75 mL
½ cup = 125 mL
⅔ cup = 150 mL
¾ cup = 175 mL
1 cup = 250 mL
2 cups = 1 pint = 500 mL
3 cups = 750 mL
4 cups = 1 quart = 1 L

VOLUME MEASUREMENTS (fluid)

1 fluid ounce (2 tablespoons) = 30 mL
4 fluid ounces (½ cup) = 125 mL
8 fluid ounces (1 cup) = 250 mL
12 fluid ounces (1½ cups) = 375 mL
16 fluid ounces (2 cups) = 500 mL

WEIGHTS (mass)

½ ounce = 15 g
1 ounce = 30 g
3 ounces = 90 g
4 ounces = 120 g
8 ounces = 225 g
10 ounces = 285 g
12 ounces = 360 g
16 ounces = 1 pound = 450 g

DIMENSIONS

$\frac{1}{16}$ inch = 2 mm
⅛ inch = 3 mm
¼ inch = 6 mm
½ inch = 1.5 cm
¾ inch = 2 cm
1 inch = 2.5 cm

OVEN TEMPERATURES

250°F = 120°C
275°F = 140°C
300°F = 150°C
325°F = 160°C
350°F = 180°C
375°F = 190°C
400°F = 200°C
425°F = 220°C
450°F = 230°C

BAKING PAN SIZES

Utensil	Size in Inches/Quarts	Metric Volume	Size in Centimeters
Baking or	8×8×2	2 L	20×20×5
Cake Pan	9×9×2	2.5 L	23×23×5
(square or	12×8×2	3 L	30×20×5
rectangular)	13×9×2	3.5 L	33×23×5
Loaf Pan	8×4×3	1.5 L	20×10×7
	9×5×3	2 L	23×13×7
Round Layer	8×1½	1.2 L	20×4
Cake Pan	9×1½	1.5 L	23×4
Pie Plate	8×1¼	750 mL	20×3
	9×1¼	1 L	23×3
Baking Dish	1 quart	1 L	—
or Casserole	1½ quart	1.5 L	—
	2 quart	2 L	—